China's Education, Curriculum Knowledge and Cultural Inscriptions

With a focus on the role of discourse and language in education, this book examines China's educational reform from an original perspective that avoids mapping on Westernized educational sensibilities to a Chinese environment. Zhao untangles the tradition–modernity division expressed in China's educational language about the body and teacher–student difference. Exploring the historical and cultural implications of the ways China's schooling is talked about and acted upon, Zhao argues that Chinese notion "wind" (*feng*) is a defining aspect of Chinese teaching and learning. Incorporating Western and Chinese literature, this book explores the language of education, curriculum and knowledge on a cross-cultural landscape and as cultural inscriptions.

Weili Zhao is Assistant Professor of Curriculum Studies at the Chinese University of Hong Kong, Hong Kong, China.

Routledge Cultural Studies in Knowledge, Curriculum, and Education
Series editors:
Thomas S. Popkewitz and Daniel Tröhler

Democratic Education as a Curricular Problem
Historical Consciousness and the Moralizing Limits of the Present
Daniel S. Friedrich

The Educated Subject and the German Concept of Bildung
A Comparative Cultural History
Rebekka Horlacher

Struggling for the Soul and Social Exclusion in Teaching and Teacher Education
A Critical Ethnography
Thomas S. Popkewitz

The Paradox of Making In/equality
A Cultural History of Reforming Math for All
Jennifer D. Diaz

China's Education, Curriculum Knowledge and Cultural Inscriptions
Dancing with the Wind
Weili Zhao

China's Education, Curriculum Knowledge and Cultural Inscriptions
Dancing with the Wind

Weili Zhao

NEW YORK AND LONDON

First published 2019
by Routledge
711 Third Avenue, New York, NY 10017

and by Routledge
2 Park Square, Milton Park, Abingdon, Oxon, OX14 4RN

Routledge is an imprint of the Taylor & Francis Group, an informa business

© 2019 Taylor & Francis

The right of Weili Zhao to be identified as author of this work has been asserted by her in accordance with sections 77 and 78 of the Copyright, Designs and Patents Act 1988.

All rights reserved. No part of this book may be reprinted or reproduced or utilised in any form or by any electronic, mechanical, or other means, now known or hereafter invented, including photocopying and recording, or in any information storage or retrieval system, without permission in writing from the publishers.

Trademark notice: Product or corporate names may be trademarks or registered trademarks, and are used only for identification and explanation without intent to infringe.

Library of Congress Cataloguing-in-Publication Data
A catalog record for this book has been requested

ISBN: 978-0-415-78754-3 (hbk)
ISBN: 978-1-315-22584-5 (ebk)

Typeset in Sabon
by Apex CoVantage, LLC

To my mom and my daughter, who have helped me to understand past, present, and future as being coeval at the present *moment.*

Contents

List of Figures and Tables — ix
Series Foreword — x
Foreword — xiv
THOMAS S. POPKEWITZ

Preface — xix
Acknowledgments — xxx
Permissions to Reprint — xxxi
Author Note — xxxii

Introduction: Encountering the Chinese "Wind" and "Body" Aporia as a Starting Point — 1

PART I
Overcoming "Epistemicide" in Cross-cultural Educational Studies — 23

1 "Epistemicide" as an Effect of Comparative Paradigms and Globalized Discourses — 25

2 An Archaeological-Historical Mode of Inquiry — 51

3 An Ontological Language–Discourse Perspective — 73

PART II
Paradigmatic Unpackings of China's Language, Knowledge, and Education — 97

4 Beyond Representation: Yijing Thought and Confucius' Wind-Pedagogy — 99

viii *Contents*

5 Beyond Conceptual Thinking: Chinese Body-Thinking and Educational Body 122

6 Beyond Identity vs. Difference Division: A Daoist Teacher–Student (Re)Ordering 149

PART III
Revisiting My Research-Learning Journey as a Post-foundational Case Study 169

7 Daoist Onto-un-learning Way and Post-foundational Study 171

Index 187

Figures and Tables

Figures

I.1	School-Motto Wall Inscription	3
I.2	Feng 風 (Wind) Entry in *Shuowenjiezizhu*	6
I.3	Bagua 八卦 (Eight Trigram) Concentric Diagram	7
I.4	"Right" Writing Body Posture	11
3.1	*Wen* 文 Entry in *Shuowenjiezizhu*	91
4.1	Bagua 八卦 (Eight Trigram) Concentric Diagram	113

Tables

5.1	Confucian Ritual Body Versus Current Schooling Body	144
6.1	China's Teacher Education Policy Documents on Teacher–Student Ordering	152

Series Foreword: *Routledge Cultural Studies in Knowledge, Curriculum, and Education*

This series brings interdisciplinary studies together that focus on knowledge of education, school, school reforms, curriculum, and research projects. Central to the studies are how "we" think, order, and act in schooling—its systems of reason or languages—as cultural practices about how life is to be lived and how the possibilities of the future are envisaged. The studies are referred to as "critical" in the sense that they make visible the principles governing and regulating what is known, done, and acted on in schooling and in research.

Our interest is to provide ways of re-conceptualizing approaches to the study of school change and reform in policy, curriculum, and teacher education. The series provokes thoughts about schooling as cultural practices to think about the principles that order the construction of the subjects and subjectivities of schooling in different societies. It takes what is given as natural and taken-for-granted in the everyday life of schooling, asking about the conditions that make schooling possible as objects of reflection and action.

It is within this moving against the grain of *The Routledge Cultural Studies in Knowledge, Curriculum, and Education* that Weili Zhao's makes, we believe, an important contribution. It brings into focus three major strands of contemporary scholarship and poses important challenges for the study of education.

One is the study of difference. Questions of difference dominate the landscape of policy and educational programs. Discussions of migration and immigration and school programs have become more central with the increasing diversity in what was previously considered as homogenous populations. The mobility of people within the European Union as well as an influx of non-European immigrants into northern and western European nations, for example, have raised important issues about how to think anew about differences that cannot be confined solely to the prior categorical distinctions of race, class, and gender. Multi-cultural curriculum in the United States and intercultural education in European policy has brought the question of difference into how a society considers itself and the qualities and characteristics of citizenship that are intertwined in practices of education. At a different point of entrance are the international assessments of student performance, such as the Programme for International Student Assessment by the Organisation for Economic Co-operation and Development. The international assessment creates statistical measures to compare differences among nations and creates a universal measure of a nation's "well-being" to talk about differences among people within nations.

The question of difference, as Zhao correctly assesses, embodies questions of theory and philosophy. Across different subjects and layers of research is a consistency: There is an ontological object that is given—"culture" or "the national citizen" as universal categories about people from which variations, activity, and motion constitute differences. This notion of difference is assumed in the idea of "the achievement gap" in the United States and cross-Atlantic studies of "urban" education. Neo-institutional theory in comparative education functions with a similar notion of difference. Differences are embodied in populational variation and convergences across nations and, over time, for example, in rates of going to school. Critical studies of pedagogy, as well, embrace this principle of difference expressed in a social structural language of resistance, empowerment, and voice. Zhao's study provides an important challenge to the underlying assumptions and principles that order how difference is studied in contemporary policy, research, and educational practices. Difference is the variation of some standard that performs as the given object of comparison.

If we take the above examples, difference is formed through principles drawn from the philosophy of representation and identity. There is an assumed "nature" to the child, the school curriculum, and learning whose processes and modes of communication can be standardized, codified, and compared across places. Historical studies of schools also entail this inscription of difference, although assuming that the categories of school—what is taught and the childhood of the child—have fixed identities and representation that can be compared. Difference is "seen" through systems of representation that fix standards of the subject as norms or models from which to judge the others. Differences become embedded in a hierarchy composed by the values mediated by sameness.

Zhao focuses on difference to constrain the politics of sameness. She explores cultural difference in a radical way by suspending the principle of transparency assumed in translation. The subtitle of the book expressed this interest as *Dancing with "The Wind."* For example, there is a continual cultural reference to "wind" in Chinese discourses about schooling—"school wind," "teaching wind," and "learning wind." In contemporary studies of Chinese education, "wind" becomes a concept translated as the school atmosphere, teaching style, and manner of learning. Treating "wind" as a "concept" elides the cultural principles embodied in "wind-education." To render visible the cultural difference, Zhao brackets the semantic translation and puts them into a range of cultural principles performed in the language of schooling when saying "school wind," "teaching wind," and "learning wind."

The book considers the system of reason through which the objects of Chinese education are given intelligibility. The argument draws on a range of Western philosophers ranging from Agamben, Heidegger, Derrida, and Foucault and connects them with classical Chinese modes of though, both disciplines mutually informing without reducing one to the other. The exploration entails a deep linguistic and historical understanding of Chinese characters and the analysis into being the particular cultural principles about society and the child that cannot be reduced to Western ideas of "concepts" or metaphors. The latter gives a structure to language that makes the world through the given representations and identities.

Zhao calls her study a Daoist onto-un-learning way that relates to what is called post-foundational *study*. Zhao's exploration is to think about the conditions that make possible the knowledge of schooling as cultural, historical, and political practices. It considers how the objects of education are constituted to shape and fashion boundaries in the choices that arise and that constitute the educated subject. It explores the spaces that create the potentials for experience in the contingencies of events.

Second and related to the first challenge, difference is the notion of comparison. The book enters into the question of comparative studies through two dimensions. One is how the past becomes a part of the present, not as the evolution of thought or practices, but through the continual assembly and connection of historical patterns that have no single origin. If we return to the discussion of difference, contemporary research continually inscribes particular categories of representation and identity as the origin of change, with comparison typically as difference-in-time. The most prominent exemplar is the pre-posttest talk about change. The more complex notion of comparison is the international assessments of student performance. The assessment creates higher-order statistical measures to produce a system of equivalence to measure the differences among nations. Thus, the object of analysis for schools is formed through the magnitudes of variations and differences in the qualities and characteristics assigned to children across geographical sites.

The second challenge in this book, comparison, is to historicize the practices of schooling without reducing its epistemological qualities from which to think about the self and other. The method is to explore difference as embodied on a plane that has its own style of reason and does not appear as a continuum of value and hierarchy. It brings to mind Derrida's discussion of the philosophy of Levinas, thinking of the other in relation to the self in a manner in which diminishing the other diminishes the self.

The third challenge is that the book seeks to undo the binary logic found in much of educational research. That logic is expressed in different ways. It appears in the universalizing of the West as against its others—the colonial versus colonialized, the East versus West, indigenous knowledge versus its Other, and so on. To challenge the binary logics is not to diminish their importance in the political representation. The binaries have played important sources of intervention and mobilization of social groups in the contemporary political landscape. Zhao's challenge to binary logic follows, in one sense, a long trajectory of social and cultural thought related to European continental theories as well as within Chinese classical studies.

The book concretely works against the binary logic in educational studies through two intellectual moves. First is the recognition of European "continental" philosophy as working against the analytical traditions of language as having pure identities. In this sense, she draws on philosophical traditions that enable thought about the relation of language, culture, ethics, and power, such as Agamben, Derrida, and Foucault. These readings are further integrated and related to the writing of Heidegger to think about difference as discussed above.

But the reading of continental philosophy entails thinking about the problem-at-hand, the cultural and historical conditions in which Chinese education is enacted, performed, and given intelligibility. The analysis "translates" the different intellectual trajectories in a manner that "sees" the disparate connections that are not merely the sum of its parts and reducible to "difference from sameness." What is created is a set of principles for ordering and thinking about the flows and moment of things and people that "sees" relations and not the representations of "things" and their binaries. The historicizing of reason directs attention to the social and cultural practices that produce the subjects and objects of schooling. The research asks about how the subjects of schooling are made possible as objects of reflection and action.

Zhao's book challenges the very conventions and traditions of educational studies that underlie current efforts to understand schooling. The broader implications of the theoretical concerns in the study of differences have implications for understanding issues of school knowledge in different historical spaces and national contexts. The book offers an alternative style of thought that disrupts the hierarchy of values that differentiate the self and others. The exploration of "seeing" difference as relational has implications that crosses the fields of curriculum and comparative and policy studies in education.

Thomas S. Popkewitz,
University of Wisconsin–Madison
Daniel Tröhler,
University of Vienna
February 14, 2018

Foreword

Zhao's *China's Education, Curriculum Knowledge and Cultural Inscriptions: Dancing with the Wind* provides an important and intellectually creative contribution to the fields of curriculum and comparative and educational studies. Zhao focuses on the historical system of reason that gives intelligibility to contemporary Chinese education. The book directs attention to the cultural and historical principles that order thought and practices in school for understanding differences. The question of difference in comparative studies is rarely addressed epistemologically and historically, often reduced to seeing "others" as matters of variations of the categorical imperatives inscribed as conceptual universals in social theories. Zhao's comparative strategy moves against the grain of comparative education and curriculum studies. The approach considers what constitutes "differences" and comparisons through the concrete exploration of Chinese educational events.

The intellectual elegance of this book begins with a simple observation. Throughout Zhao's education in China, posters about "wind," "wind-learning," and "wind-teaching" were hanging in schools. The reference to wind was so culturally taken for granted that it blended into the background and seemed to need no discussion. What previously felt as natural and unquestionable, however, became visible in her encounters during her graduate studies. Zhao probes "wind" as an historical-cultural artifact present in everyday life and the practices of schooling. The text explores how the encounters with different scholarship formed as a method to (re)-think about difference, drawing "wind" into the elaboration of the cultural and historical conditions that give sensibilities to this modern institution of the school. But the question of culture is not the traditional cultural question about social behaviors, norms, and institutions by which life is organized and meaning expressed. Nor is culture what Clifford Geertz (1973) called "thick descriptions." The later focused on the role of symbols in constructing public meaning. Zhao's interest in wind is how it "acts" within a system of reason that generates rules and standards that work into the conduct of schooling.

The cultural inscription of wind as an historical assemblage of rules and standards gives expression to the book's subtitle, *Dancing with the Wind*. The wind that Zhao speaks about does not "fit" the representational and identity language of the West. Wind is not a concept that is typically expressed when thinking about science; that is, it is not a representation that performs to demarcate boundaries to interpret and assess the world and its components. Wind does not have the qualities of a noun that suggests an ontological essence or nature to objects and people. And wind is not a metaphor of speech that functions as an analogy to apply for understanding schooling and culture.

As one reads, the Chinese character of wind appears and merges into a complex cultural sense of difference that needs to be accounted for in the study of schooling. The Chinese character of wind is bound to other Chinese characters to form a sensitivity to the complex movements of thought and cultural practices. Wind is a cultural and historical way of being. Embodied in the character of wind are ways of making judgments and recognizing of types of objects in schools. Wind, as Zhao explores continually, is a mode of thinking and acting, (re)visioning the Yi/jing of thought and Confucius' wind-pedagogy that places in motion what is seen, thought, felt, and acted on.

Dancing with the Wind is about sensibilities and dispositions that locate society and people in the flow of relations to form particular historical principles about collective belonging that schooling fabricates in modernity. While studying of a national controversy about the respect given to the Chinese in the teachers' or student–teacher relations, for example, the movement and flow apprehended by "wind-teaching," "wind-pedagogy," or "wind-learning," it expresses reasoning moves against the ontologies that give intelligibility to notions of representation and identity. It instantiates a priori rules and standards that form the basis of what is to be known, how it is to be known, and what counts as reasonable knowledge and reasonable people.

The book engages in the broader questions about the mode of analysis to think about constructions of difference through the particular specificity of the system of reason that orders Chinese education. While difference is a major mantra of contemporary research, it is often assumed rather than seriously thought about. The book engages philosophically and culturally, through a form of dialectical logic, to understand the flow of relations in giving intelligibility to educational phenomena.

Central in this recognition of culture, language, and difference is the issue of translation. Zhao recognizes the issues of translation as not simply writing in English about Chinese cultural principles. She appreciates that the task of translation is never making copies, but creative articulations that pose a number of challenges that are not merely about finding the right words. The challenge of communicating differences in historical, social, and cultural systems of reasoning is not to inscribe differences as a continuum of epistemological values.

Zhao locates the study within a field of post-foundational scholarship. Zhao connects traditions of hermeneutics, linguistics, philosophical, and historical discourses and assembles them as an encounter with classical Chinese thought. The registers of thought are not the sum produced by adding the Western authors to Chinese authors, events, and language. She thoughtfully plays with Western thinkers, for example Agamben, Foucault, Heidegger, and Deleuze, but in ways that are not reductive, or merely using the category of non-Western as a phrase of counter balance against the West.

The analysis combines Western linguistic, cultural, historical, and philosophical analyses that not only engage, but also disengage those prior authors for the purpose to understanding the educational events of contemporary China. The dialogue produces a distinct perspective that historicizes ontologies in a relativist epistemology. The European philosophers are connected with Chinese modes of thought related to Yijing, Confucius' windpedagogy, and Daoist thought, which is not merely the adding of one on to the other. It entails the translation into something different and original as a mode of thought about schools.

The argument is spiral. It continually expands ideas and gives nuance and depth as you travel with Zhao on a journey to see what you did not see before. The analysis intersects with Chinese cultural dispositions to animate, vitalize, and produce an original approach for thinking about the cultural practices of schooling.

Lurking in the subterranean recesses of the book is the question of comparative studies. The question of comparing and the making of difference bring into the forefront a major and continual conundrum of educational studies, whether in transnational hihstorical studies, comparative studies, and curriculum studies.

The conundrum is how to understand differences that does not reduce others to the self; that is, reducing differences to qualities of sameness. Gilles Deleuze (1968/1994) argues that Western thought has tended to take for granted differences through its emphasis on representation and identify in forming the objects of inquiry. In comparative education, this occurs in studying other cultures through the categorical imperatives of social and psychological theories that appear in particular historical circumstances, yet are applied reductively to other social/cultural spaces. The existing categories serve as concepts whose cultural principles ascribe a nature to the social order and people. The concepts "act" as the ultimate commandment of reason from which all duties and obligations derive. Bourdieu and Wacquant (1999) explore the inadequacy of this categorical imperative through the representations and conceptualization of "race" in American theories. When applied to other historical contexts, principles of reasoning are inscribed about "others" that reduce the distinctions and differentiations to standards of representations that elide the very phenomena under scrutiny (Popkewitz, Khurshid, & Zhao, 2014).

Differences become a hierarchy and continuum of value from resemblances defined in the classifications. Identities are generated about people that appear as universal, transhistorical criteria to order and classify what is seen and thought about as different. The qualities that constitute comparativeness are often erased in what Cowen (2006) calls the banalities of educational studies. The educational banalities that Cowen addresses are embodied in binary distinctions between the "self" and others, expressed in the words such as globalization and localization, and internationalization and regionalism. These distinctions historically erase, Cowen argues, the very practices associated with the changes occurring since at least the nineteenth century. The challenge of comparative study and the understanding of difference, if explored further, are in seeing events "relationally" in a manner that does not give rise to the categorical imperatives that dominate much of social and cultural research.

The conundrum rears its head further when seeking to understand differences in a manner that speaks as being outside of "the West." The paradox of this movement to be outside of the West is that it occurs through the provenance of academic cultures of science and the humanities, which maintains traces of Western epistemological principles of comparison and difference. While there are efforts to talk about indigenous knowledge and non-Eurocentric approaches, the idea of comparing and comparative research is a strategy of reflection that embodies an attitude of the enlightenment's notions of reason and rationality. To engage in comparative studies can seek to push the limits of reasoning by being sensitive to the different epistemological systems that are not merely the recouping of the West. But this pushing of the limits, as Chakrabarty's *Provincializing Europe* (2000) recognizes, is never totally outside of "the West." Chakrabarty recognizes this challenge when he argues that Western notions and categories are indispensable but inherently insufficient to narrate the processes of change in and outside of the West.

This conundrum is important to recognize when people argue for non-Western modes of studies and speak of voice and empowerment of indigenous knowledges. While these are important movements in relation to the politics of representation, the claim elides the historical epistemological questions about how the very notion of comparison in the human sciences emerges and its relation (but not reduction) to the European Enlightenment. This is not to say that other historical spaces outside of "the West" did not compare, or comparing to understand was not present prior to the Enlightenment itself. It is rather to say that a particular mode of reasoning about people and differences emerged to make possible the practices of research as a comparative style of reasoning, but also to consider how "reasoning" travels and changes over time and spaces to make possible the variations of the human sciences that today have different assemblages and connections (and disconnections) that are not merely replicating the "West."

Zhao's study recognizes and productively engages this conundrum. The challenge is to assemble and connect Western thought in a manner that maintains the integrity of Chinese culture and history. The text provides a unique, novel, and intellectually challenging approach for culturally and historically understanding the assumptions and implications of schooling. The analyses of the Chinese character of wind is combined with other Chinese characters to bring into focus a cultural and linguistic terrain of the educational body that engages yet disengages Westernized modes of thought and the construction of difference. The book makes possible a way of thinking about the theoretical difficulties of comparison and offers a style of study for understanding difference. Its style engages in the self and other without the diminishing of either.

Thomas S. Popkewitz

References

Bourdieu, P., & Wacquant, L. (1999). On the cunning of imperialist reason. *Theory Culture Society*, 16(1), 41–58.

Chakrabarty, D. (2000). *Provincializing Europe: Postcolonial through and historical difference*. Princeton, NJ: Princeton University Press.

Cowen, B. (2006). Acting comparatively upon the educational world: Puzzles and possibilities. *Oxford Review of Education*, 32(5), 561–573.

Deleuze, G. (1968/1994). *Difference and repetition*. (P. Patton, Trans.). New York: Columbia University Press.

Geertz, C. (1973). *The interpretation of cultures: Selected essays*. New York, NY: Basic Books.

Popkewitz, T. S., Khurshid, A., & Zhao, W. (2014). Comparative studies and the reasons of reason: Historicizing differences and "seeing" reforms in multiple modernities. In L. Vega (Ed.), *Empires, post-coloniality, and interculturality: New challenges for comparative education* (pp. 21–43). Rotterdam, The Netherlands: Sense Publisher.

Preface

As Michel Foucault writes in the Preface of his book, *The Order of Things* (1969/1973), it arose out of his laughter and a haunting sense of uneasiness when reading a passage, quoted in Borges, on a Chinese way of classifying animals. Laughable as this Chinese animal taxonomy is, like a utopia, it oddly yet enchantingly heaps all together, on an operating table (*tabula*), animals that are otherwise not appropriately proximate or congruous in Foucault's eyes. As Foucault uneasily realized soon afterward, such a Chinese ordering of things is more like a dangerous heterotopia, which destroys the syntax and meanwhile exposes the limitation of the Western system of thought. To Foucault, it is starkly impossible for the West to think *that* (p. xv) as the above operating table, that is, the Chinese way of *holding together* things itself is nowhere to be found in the West as an epistemic condition in the first place.

It can be said that this (my) book arose out of Foucault's "uneasy laughter." I encountered this passage when I was a Chinese doctoral student in curriculum studies at the University of Wisconsin–Madison, USA, interested in, yet not sure how to, explore current China's education and curriculum discourses at a nexus, and as a (dis)assemblage, of tradition and modernity, East and West. Foucault's reflection provides a guiding direction for my entire intellectual journey, alerting me to the boundaries of each cultural system of thought and possible gaps there-in-between. His way of incubating a research project upon some cross-cultural difference at its limit, along with his archaeological-historical thinking, re-shapes the overall question for my research as this: *How is it possible to first discern and then render intelligible cross-culturally some Chinese educational sensibilities that seem to be naturalized to Chinese and yet unthinkable to Westerners?* A rendering that unfolds in the English language yet still exhibits the Chinese epistemological sensibilities as they are. A rendering that goes with and beyond using of the Western categories and frameworks as a reference point and yet not getting entrapped within a stagnant cultural relativist stand.

To fulfill this agenda, this book adopts an intertwined archaeological-historical mode of inquiry and ontological language–discourse perspective to cut into the reasons of knowledge and schooling in modern China. It picks up and historicizes the Chinese "wind" language and "body" events as examples to problematize the ways in which the Chinese modern language/reason, educational body, and teacher–student difference are gauged through as well as caught up within a Westernized mode of signification and representation. Using the Western epistemological frameworks to eugenically gauge the non-Western educational-cultural sensibilities is a hidden form of epistemicide such that the non-Western becomes what the West is not, rather than what it is. This book, titled *China's Education, Curriculum Knowledge and Cultural Inscriptions: Dancing with the Wind*, aims to re-unpack China's knowledge, education, and curriculum beyond such an epistemicide conundrum. It is heavily methodological and builds a style of thought outside of the conventions of sorting out literature reviews, defining concepts, and applying borrowed methods. That is, a dividing line between theory, method, and practice is obscured in its pavement toward a space where they intersect and play with each other, seriously.

This being said, this Preface clarifies the main agendas the book aims to achieve, the methodological-theoretical lens it enacts, as well as the ways it will to unpack the "wind" and "body" examples as presented below. As the defining feature of this book, such a brief clarification hopes to guide the readers in understanding the overall structure and flow of argument running throughout the whole book.

Archaeological-Historical Inquiry, Comparative Studies, and Post-foundational Study

The Foucauldian questioning of "How is it possible?" defines my book to be archaeological-historical in its nature, henceforth distinguishing itself from other books on China's education and curriculum, which mostly explicate the content, features, and knowledge, as well as changes thereof along a *what-is* question or a history-of-ideas logic. In contrast, this book aims to explore on what basis knowledge and styles of reasoning about China's education and curriculum become possible, and within what space of order they are constructed. It unpacks the historical-cultural a priori, which makes it possible for teaching, learning, and the teacher–student relationship in the past and present China to be said and enacted as they were and are. In other words, this book doesn't track the historical vicissitudes of China's education and curriculum reform; rather, it gets deeper into the epistemological field, examining the positivity of knowledge, as well as the historical-cultural principles as conditions of possibility for today's educational thinking and practice in China on a cross-cultural landscape.

The mission of discerning the conditions of possibility of knowledge goes one step further than identifying the specific content or value of knowledge. Let's relate this back to Foucault's "uneasy laughter" for further clarifications. The laughter indicates Foucault's intuitive impression of the Chinese animal taxonomy as a form of knowledge far from his cognitive repertoire of the Western rules of categorizing animals. However, the uneasy feeling comes later when Foucault ponders the possibility and impossibility of such form of knowledge in the Chinese and Western epistemological fields. Moving one step further from the form of knowledge to its epistemological possibility enables Foucault to realize the very limit of the Western system of thought, the boundary of the modern syntax, and accordingly to problematize the otherwise naturalized ground on which his thinking and subjectivity stand.

In other words, an archaeological-historical mode of inquiry involves two interrelated conditions or effects. First, it suspends the rational value or objective form of knowledge toward a problematization of the positivity of knowledge itself. That is, it doesn't merely examine the truth or falsity of this knowledge proposition. Rather, it asks how it is possible for the knowledge form to become as it is. Second, it problematizes the inquirer's subjectivity or mode of being as expressed in his or her viewpoints, presumptions, and styles of reasoning. As Agamben (2009) argues, in archaeological inquiry,

> it is not possible to gain access in a new way, beyond tradition, to the sources without putting in question the very historical subject who is supposed to gain access to them. What is in question, then, is the epistemological paradigm of inquiry itself.
>
> (p. 89)

I foreground these two conditions–effects of an archaeological-historical inquiry because they correspondingly speak to the two broad intellectual fields this book situates itself in and the two missions it intends to fulfill. The two intellectual fields are comparative/international educational-cultural studies and post-foundational educational research. The former has been and continues to be confronted by a paradigmatic challenge, especially when mapping out non-Western sensibilities with and beyond Western frameworks. The latter post-foundational research is an emerging scholarship spearheaded by, say, Tyson Lewis in (re)envisioning *study* as an alternative or oppositional educational logic to push back against *learning* as the governing epistemological principle of education in neoliberal societies. Whereas learning is to draw out students' potentialities along a measurable scheme, to train students with necessary skills and competencies anticipated in the twenty-first century, *study* is a wondering and wandering journey itself, without subjecting itself to a definite goal or transferable skills.

This book intends to fulfill two parallel missions. First, it provides a paradigmatic exemplar to address a comparative methodological challenge and a possible epistemological crisis that results from it. The strategy is to historicize the events of language, education, and curriculum in modern China. Second, it provides an exemplary case of post-foundational *study* by scrutinizing and theorizing my intellectual research journey itself as a Daoist onto-un-learning *way*. I coin the term "Daoist onto-un-learning" to resonate what

Dao De Jing murmurs, "doing learning gains and doing Dao loses" 為學日益為道日損 (Chapter 48). By Daoist un-learning, it means my otherwise naturalized presuppositions of learning, teaching, and the teacher–student relationship are suspended and bracketed toward new openings of possibilities. For example, learning is no longer an accumulation of knowledge, but rather a getting rid of the imposed "norms" toward a re-turning to the Being of Dao. These two missions comply with the two conditions–effects as mentioned above of an archaeological-historical inquiry, that is, the positivity of knowledge and the inquirer's subjectivity, and their compliance can be further clarified as below.

First, with a focus on the conditions of knowledge, this book does not provide another (re)presentation of the semantic meanings as well as syntactical organizations of these distinct objects of language, education, curriculum, and knowledge in China. Nor does it laud the success, or lament the failure, of current China's education and curriculum reforms, or proffer a salvation future for it. Rather, it treats language, education, curriculum, and knowledge as theoretical constructs, as material events and happenings, and examines their conditions of possibility from a historical and cross-cultural perspective. Specifically, how is it possible for Chinese people to say, reason, and act about these issues as they do, and furthermore to rethink them in alternative ways? Alternative to some "normative" ordering principles like a West-based comparative framework, a planetary mode of signification and representation, a signature instrumental learning logic, and a binary style of reasoning. These "normative" principles as expressions of the modern Enlightenment Western thinking crisscross and structure such distinct fields as comparative studies, language philosophy, social and human sciences, and educational research paradigms. This book, cross-disciplinary and multidimensional, clears the grounding presumptions and limits of these normative principles as a (pre-)condition toward exploring new perspectives, say, drawn from the Yijing, Confucian, and Daoist wisdoms, to re-understanding China's education, curriculum, and knowledge both in the past and at present.

Second, as an exemplary case of post-foundational *study*, this book recounts and scrutinizes my intellectual research journey as an educational experience in a way to problematize, expose, and turn in my subjectivity about the objects of language, knowledge, educative body, and teacher–student ordering. The transformation of my mode of being as a researcher often happens in aporetic moments when my naturalized viewpoints, styles of reasoning, and presumptions are paralyzed. For example, encountering the etymological/analytic definition of the Chinese wind-character, *feng* 風, as "the wind blows and insects get germinated and hatched within eight days" in China's first comprehensive dictionary is one such aporetic moment. It is a point where I found myself in the hands of language, not vice versa, not knowing where to go. This aporetic moment turned over an otherwise naturalized subject–object ordering between me and language into a relational movement between two beings. This transformed (inter-)subjectivity enabled me to *see* "wind" as a signature language of China's education, and Confucius' "wind-pedagogy" as expressed in *Yijing* as another originary (re)source of the entire Confucian educational culture, originary not in the sense of being original, but in the sense that a lot has remained unsaid in it and can be untapped to shed new light on what has already been said. Neither point has so far been discerned, let alone scrutinized in scholarship on Confucius and Confucian educational culture.

This post-foundational dimension gives the book an onto-ethnographic characteristic. With it I assume a double role of researcher and learner, placing myself in a singular position to reflexively ponder what learning could mean from an immanent perspective, no longer merely as a detached researcher who looks at the ethnographic schooling practices from an "objective" viewpoint. Subsuming my being into this whole educational endeavor has enabled me to savor Plato's statement better, "Education is not an art of putting sight into the eye that can already see, but one of turning the eye towards the proper gaze of Being" (cited in Duarte, 2012, p. 1).

Epistemological Crisis, Representational vs. Ontological Language Perspectives

Epistemological crisis, or "epistemicide" (Paraskeva, 2016), often refers to the eclipse of non-Western epistemological systems by the Northern–Western counterparts, a subjugation and discrediting of the creation of alternative forms of knowledge in the Southern and developing countries. It is a hidden form of mental imperialism. Epistemicide indeed happened with the modern China's thought and culture in the name of modernization, especially since the 1920s New Cultural Movement when the radical Chinese intelligentsia collectively aligned themselves to the Western science, technology, and language as a eugenic norm, and accordingly called to eradicate the "backward" Chinese Confucian tradition and to Romanize the Chinese language. Epistemicide continues in today's China in the name of globalization.

To address this epistemicide issue and foreground its relevance to my overall research agenda of mapping out Chinese educational sensibilities with and beyond the Western frameworks and categories, this book confines the issue of epistemicide as an effect of two practices, namely, a "normative" comparative paradigm and a globalization of the Western discourses in the rest of the world. A "normative" comparative paradigm means using the Western epistemological frameworks as a reference point to gauge the non-Western knowledge and practices. A globalized Western discourse not only refers to such Western terms as "science," "democracy," and "twenty-first-century skills/competencies/literacies," but more important, it indicates an epistemological treatment of the modern language as a representational system and mode of signification that have already become planetary (Heidegger, 1977a). Henceforth, apart from the archaeological-historical mode of inquiry to constrain the "normative" comparative paradigm, this book also deploys a Heideggerian-Foucauldian ontological language–discourse perspective to confront the Westernized Chinese language terms and its concomitant conceptual mode of signification. By an ontological language perspective, it means language is not merely a linguistic tool for humans to express our ideas and thoughts, nor an enclosed system where meaning rests with the grammatical arrangements within sentences. Rather, language–discourse is a material being by itself that embodies as well as delimits our thinking and being.

The modern Chinese language since the early twentieth century has been devoured by the Western-introduced terminology and epistemology at an unparalleled pace and degree (see, e.g., Hayhoe, 2014). Specifically, when the modern Western discourses-terms enter into China, either traditional Chinese terms are re-invoked, or neologisms of mono-graphical characters are coined as their semantic glosses. Either way, the mode of translation often transfigures or overwrites the original cultural-historical senses as well as the epistemological meanings nurtured within each mono-graphical Chinese character (*hanzi* 漢字). For example, the Chinese term for education, *jiaoyu* 教育, is a cultural notion re-invoked in modern China as a gloss of the English word "education." Even though *jiaoyu* 教育 originally embraces a dual sense of teaching and nurturing, the latter sense of nurturing is mostly glossed over in its modern usage, namely, signifying the overall teaching and learning practices in China's modern schooling.

A note of clarification is needed on the contested notions of language and discourse. Language usually refers to a linguistic system and discourse specific language in use. It goes without saying that almost all research uses language–discourse as its means or object of examination. In Western philosophy and literary studies, language is closely linked with the grounding issues of metaphysics, signification, and representation. In comparative educational studies, language is treated as a cultural sign, competency, or medium that interconnects with the issues of power, identity, equity, and hegemony in colonialism, post-colonialism, multiculturalism, and diversity at both policy and curriculum levels. In post-modern or post-structural thinking, language becomes an ontological being, an embodiment of a historical-cultural style of reasoning which structures our thinking. Unpacking language–discourse in this way is to render visible the broader landscape of educational thought and practice, and the theoretical-methodological force of such a language–discourse perspective is just beginning to gain scholars' attention in comparative or cultural-educational studies. For example, Tröhler (2011/2013) specifically scrutinizes how the rooted religious languages–discourses of Protestantism and republicanism, in confrontation or negotiation, have historically and politically structured schooling in Germany, the United States, and Switzerland. This way of re-conceptualizing language–discourse as theoretical regulating systems can "give us insights that go beyond Whig and Marxist interpretations" (van Brummelen, 2013, p. x).

Historicizing the Chinese "Wind" and "Body" as Paradigmatic Examples

With the Westernization of the modern Chinese language, scholars concur that Confucius' educational thinking, albeit still viable and traceable in some "forgotten and muted sphere of common life" (Wu, 2014, p. 329) in contemporary China, is unlikely to find its expression in the modern Chinese language or discourse (ibid.). However, drawing upon Heidegger and Foucault's language perspective, this book argues that modern Chinese language, albeit primarily operationalized within a Westernized conceptual mode of reasoning, is still one forgotten, muted yet living expression of Confucian pedagogical heritage. Reparsing them in a Heideggerian-Foucauldian way can indeed become a first and fundamental step in critiquing modern China's pedagogy as well as its historical–cultural–epistemological conditions of possibility.

Heidegger argues "language first gives to every purposeful deliberation its ways and underways. Without language, there would be lacking to every doing every dimension in which it could bestir itself and be effective" (1977b, pp. 40–41). Accordingly, he masterfully plays with, reparses, and works back some manifest discourses used in daily life from their naturalized meaning toward a revelation of language in its crude being or a thought whose essential life has not yet been caught in the network of grammar. For example, in *The Question Concerning Technology* (1977a), he works back the manifest discourse of "technology" back to its Greek "techne," exposing the essence of technology not as anything technological, but as a mode of self-revealing in ancient Greece. With that, Heidegger problematizes modern technology as an already metamorphosed mode of "challenging revealing" in that it seizes upon and reframes modern man, among all other objects, as a standing reserve along a use line. In going back to the past, Heidegger cuts into the present.

Following a similar strategy, my examples are the Chinese "wind-education" discourses and the educational "body," which I grew up with and yet whose cultural uniqueness I didn't *see*, both physically and intellectually, until after I started my doctoral studies in the United States. The Chinese "wind-education" discourse refers to the literal schooling discourses of "school wind, teaching wind, and learning wind," prevalent yet silent in China's current schools. These wind-terms are commonly treated as linguistic metaphors and accordingly interpreted as "school atmosphere, teaching manners, and learning styles," as a result of which the literal-cultural "wind-education" association in China's educational thinking is glossed over. To borrow Foucault's phrasing, we are subsumed to a trap of philology, assuming the a priori existence of linguistic metaphors and primarily seeking their semantic meanings.

Heidegger and Foucault's thinking on language has *encountered* me to this aporetic Chinese "wind-education" discourse and enabled me to ask not about its semantic meaning, but how it is possible for the notions of "wind" and "education" to get culturally associated in the first place. The second mode of questioning set me off on a serendipitous journey of following the dancing Chinese "wind" toward ultimately discovering a Yijing style of thinking, not reducible to the modern representation and signification, Confucius' educational vision, and "wind-pedagogy" as expressed in Yijing so far rarely discerned. As the book will argue, the Chinese wind-notion, *feng* 風, etymologically nurturing a sense of *transforming* and even more primordial than the familiar concept of *qi* 氣, can be re-viewed as a signature language of Chinese Confucian education, in a way akin to the notion of *Bildung* for German education (Horlacher, 2016). Furthermore, Yijing can be treated as another originary (re)-source of the whole Confucian educational thinking, construing and constructing how teaching, learning, and teacher–student ordering are thought and acted upon in China over the past two millennia.

The educational Chinese "body" is my other example. In ancient China, "body" nurtures a holistic mind–heart–body and registers an ontological "body-thinking" to the extent that the English statement of "a model of self for others" is expressed in Chinese as "a model of body for others" (*yishenzuoze* 以身作則). Nevertheless, in modern China, "body" has metamorphosed into a given object and concept entangled and conflated with a mind–body dualism. While Confucius' teaching and learning have "body" as its rubric and structure, China's current educational "body" has become the site of contention, yet rarely problematized and historicized, in (dis)ordering the Chinese teacher–student inter-subjectivity along an identity politics and a power dynamic. This book suspends the given-ness of "body" as an educational "object" often in discipline and punishment and re-examines it as a theoretical construct to see how it construes and constructs the way teaching/teachers, learning/learners, and the teacher–student relationship have been ordered historically and in the present.

To sum, I treat the Chinese "wind" and "body" as ways of reasoning rather than, or more than, a conceptual designator of natural-cultural wind and physical-biological human body. Furthermore, I mobilize both "wind" and "body" as an example in Agamben's (2009) sense, with not metaphorical but analogical logic, to make intelligible "a broader problematic context that it both constitutes and makes intelligible" (p. 17). This making-intelligible endeavor entails deactivating Chinese wind and body from their commonsensical uses, suspending them as semantic, linguistic signifiers to designate different things, and presenting the rules of their analogical use as singular cases. The rules cannot be applied or stated a priori but have to be shown and made visible through presenting their singularity as expressed in the aporia events. Henceforth, methodological notes run throughout the entire book, with a guiding paradigm to be laid out in Part I, some specific notes throughout Chapters 4–6 on how I respectively problematize the issues of Chinese language, educative body, and teacher–student difference, and a revisit of it as a "Daoist-onto-un-learning" *way* to be dialogued with the Western post-foundational *study* in Part III (Chapter 7).

Assembling Western Notions with Ancient Chinese Wisdom as a Style of Thought

An apparent irony is immediately sensible to some readers. To the extent that I am arguing against an epistemological colonialism of the West on the non-West, it seems that I am nevertheless picking up some Western perspectives to help me explicate some non-Western cultural-educational sensibilities. Yes, I do draw upon some Western notions and frameworks, but please note that I deploy them as a method and placeholder (like Derrida's aporia, Agamben's paradigmatic example, Foucault's tabula) rather than a eugenic "norm" to gauge and judge the Chinese context as the Other.

This can be further understood in two ways. First, their style of reasoning as a placeholder provides me with a language or a term to describe my encountering of the Chinese language and body events. For example, Derrida describes "aporia" as a paralyzing and fascinating experience when one gets stuck in a place or at a certain border to the extent that one doesn't know where to go. My encountering of the "wind" definition as "wind moves and insects get germinated and hatched within eight days" in the ancient Chinese dictionary is such an aporetic moment in that it desiccates our naturalized understanding of wind as air in movement. Similarly, Heidegger and Foucault critiques modern Western language as an enclosed representational system where meaning is delimited to a grammatical arrangement, and we need to suspend such a treatment of language toward unpacking it as an ontological being and saying. Their perspective alerts me to the normativity of language forms and exposes me to the literal linking of "wind" and "education" as expressed in the discourse of "school wind" in current China. Inspired by their historical mode of inquiry, I ask not about the semantic meaning of "school wind," but how it is culturally possible for "wind" and "education" to get associated in the first place.

Yet, these Western notions and frameworks are not sufficient for me to unpack the ancient Chinese system of knowledge, reason, and style of reasoning. Just as Heidegger says, a thought can only be re-generated by turning to its own root. I historicize the Chinese "wind" language and "body" events to the ancient Chinese system of thought for new understandings, which in turn helps to enrich and inform the Western notions and style of reasoning. For example, historicizing the Chinese "wind" language helps to explicate a diachronic Confucian exegesis, namely, understanding the textures and tones of a Chinese character calls for a historical tracing back to the ancient scriptures. Such a diachronic interpretation enriches the Western modern mode of signification and representation. Furthermore, I envision my whole learning-and-unlearning experiences as a Daoist onto-un-learning way, which is to be further dialogued with and inform the Western post-foundational study logic.

Seen this way, I am not dialoguing Heidegger and Foucault with Confucius, Yijing, or other Chinese scholars on their viewpoints on language or body. Rather, I am arguing how Heidegger and Foucault's thinking has enabled me to constrain a conceptual mode of signification so as to encounter the Chinese "wind" and "body" prevalent yet silent in today's Chinese schooling as an entry point for the whole research project. Furthermore, I am dialoguing them as a style of reasoning with the ancient Chinese wisdom for mutual enrichment. In so doing, I am assembling the Eastern and Western notions, frameworks, and styles of reasoning in a manner that is unique for me to rethink about current China's knowledge, education, and curriculum at the nexus, and as the (dis)assemblage of East and West, past and present. In this sense, this book provides a paradigmatic example on how to unpack the cultural-historical sensibilities of China's education on a cross-cultural landscape, with and beyond a Westernized epistemological framework.

To summarize, this book is to address the paradigmatic challenge and a concomitant epistemological crisis in comparative studies and to envision itself as a post-foundational case of *study* with an archaeological-historical mode of inquiry and ontological language–discourse perspective. It aims to cut into the reasons of knowledge, education, and curriculum in modern China as expressed through its modern language, the educational body, and the teacher–student difference. The book is heavily methodological and post-foundational and builds a style of thought outside of the conventions of sorting out literature reviews, defining concepts, and applying borrowed methods. That is, a dividing line between theory, method, and practice is obscured in its pavement toward a space where they intersect and play with each other, seriously. Specifically, I work out my method with particular "wind" and "body" examples from both classical and contemporary Chinese discourses and practices as a demonstration and enactment of my *transformative* learning and un-learning way. This un-learning experience counts as an example of the post-foundational *study*, a wondering and wandering journey without subjecting itself to a definite *learning* goal.

To some, this book may seem broad in its coverage yet not profound enough in unpacking the Yijing thought, the Chinese body-thinking, and the teacher–student difference per se. While I am fully aware of this constraint, I hope this book as a case study provides readers with a new perspective and adequate arguments for re-understanding China's current educational thinking and practice, or rather, its conditions of possibility, at the nexus and also as a (dis)assemblage, of tradition and modernity, East and West. I hope readers will heed how it is possible and justified for the author, through a detour into the thinking of Heidegger, Foucault, and others, to access and juxtapose the otherwise disparate domains and historical strata of language, knowledge, Yijing thought, Confucian educational thinking, and China's current education and curriculum practices onto an operating table (tabula) in Foucault's sense.

References

Agamben, G. (2009). *The signature of all things: On method*. New York, NY: Zone Books.
Duarte, E. M. (2012). *Being and learning: A poetic phenomenology of education*. Rotterdam, The Netherlands: Sense Publishers.
Foucault, M. (1969/1973). *The order of things: An archaeology of the human sciences*. New York, NY: Vintage Books. (Original work published 1966)
Hayhoe, R. (2014). Hopes for Confucian pedagogy in China? *Journal of Curriculum Studies*, 46(3), 313–319.
Heidegger, M. (1977a). *The question concerning technology and other essays* (W. Lovitt, Trans. with an introduction). New York: Harper Torchbooks.
Heidegger, M. (1977b). The turning. In M. Heidegger, *The question concerning technology and other essays* (pp. 36–49), (W. Lovitt, Trans. with an introduction). New York: Harper Torchbooks.
Horlacher, R. (2016). *The educated subject and the German concept of Bildung: A comparative cultural history*. New York, NY and Oxon: Routledge.
Lewis, T. E. (2013). *On study: Giorgio Agamben and educational potentiality*. London, UK: Routledge.
Paraskeva, J. M. (2016). *Curriculum epistemicide: Towards an itinerant curriculum theory*. New York, NY: Routledge.
Tröhler, D. (2011/2013). *Languages of education: Protestant legacies, national identities, and global aspirations*. New York, NY: Routledge.
Van Brummelen, H. (2013). Review article on Daniel Tröhler: Languages of education: Protestant legacies, national identities, and global aspirations. *Historical Studies in Education*, 25(1), 130–132.
Wu, Z. J. (2014). "Speak in the place of the sages": Rethinking the sources of pedagogic meanings. *Journal of Curriculum Studies*, 46(3), 320–331.

Acknowledgments

Chinese people say *drink the water and remember its source*. Since this book builds upon my doctoral research with Professor Thomas S. Popkewitz at the University of Wisconsin–Madison in the United States, I would like to start by thanking him for his unfailing support and guidance on my exotic, if not eccentric, research. I am truly grateful that he gave me enough intellectual freedom, inspirational guidance, as well as encouragement to work and walk out my own *way* over the years. Now I thank him and Daniel Tröhler for including me in this book series. I would also like to thank Bernadette Baker, Zongjie Wu, Donald Blumenfeld-Jones, Tero Autio, Amy Sloane, Derek Ford, Caiping Sun, Ezequiel Gomez Caride, Jennifer DeNet Diaz, and my Wednesday Group friends at Madison for many inspiring conversations and comments that have all pushed me to develop my thinking in this book. I could not end here without thanking my parents, brother, husband, and daughter, for always being with me, no matter near or afar. Without their love, support, and tolerance, I could not have gone this far both physically and intellectually. With love, I dedicate this book to my big family!

Permissions to Reprint

Chapter 4 of this book is derived, in part, from an article "Re-invigorating the being of language in educational studies: Unpacking Confucius' 'wind-pedagogy' in Yijing as an exemplar" published in *Discourse: Studies in the Cultural Politics of Education* on July 17, 2017, available online at www.tandfonline.com/doi/full/10.1080/01596306.2017.1354286.

One section of Chapter 5 of this book was published as a chapter "Voluntary servitude as a new form of governing: reinstating kneeling-bowing rites in modern Chinese education" included in Thomas Popkewitz (ed.) (2015), *The "Reason" of Schooling: Historicizing Curriculum Studies, Pedagogy and Teacher Education*, pp. 82–96. New York: Routledge.

One section of Chapter 6 of this book was published in a co-authored article "Agamben's potentiality and Chinese Dao: On experiencing gesture and movement of pedagogical thought" published in *Educational Philosophy and Theory* on Mar 21, 2014, available online www.tandfonline.com/doi/full/10.1080/00131857.2013.775057.

Author Note

Weili Zhao obtained her Ph.D. from the University of Wisconsin–Madison, USA in June of 2015 and is currently an Assistant Professor in the Department of Curriculum and Instruction at the Chinese University of Hong Kong. With intellectual training in both discourse analysis and curriculum studies, she is interested in unpacking China's current educational thinking and practices at the nexus, and as the (dis)assemblage, of tradition and modernity, East and West. Specifically, her research explicates the historical–cultural–philosophical insights of Chinese knowledge, curriculum, and educational thinking to hopefully dialogue with, for mutual informing and clarifications, the latest intellectual *turns* (say, the linguistic/body/cultural/study/affect turns) in the Western scholarship.

Introduction
Encountering the Chinese "Wind" and "Body" Aporia as a Starting Point

This introductory chapter has three parts. First, I explore the aporetic experiences to consider the uniqueness of the Chinese "wind" and "body" system of reason and knowledge on a cross-cultural landscape. I borrow Jacques Derrida's interpretation of "aporia" as a paralyzing yet fascinating experience to describe my cross-cultural encounters with the present and historical Chinese "wind" and "body" language–discourses in relation to education and beyond as the starting points of my entire research journey. Second, I clarify how I mobilize the Chinese "wind" and "body" as "paradigm examples" in Agamben's sense to historicize China's language, the educational body, and the teacher–student difference. This historicization is to cut into the broader issues of knowledge/reason, education, and curriculum in present China. Finally, I end this chapter with a projected structure of the book.

Aporia as an Entry Point

As mentioned in Preface, this book recounts, expands, and theorizes my doctoral research journey, a journey set off serendipitously upon my encountering the "wind" and "body" discourses in China's current schooling, a journey that can't be anticipated beforehand but can only be understood and recounted backward. Unanticipated as my encountering experiences with the Chinese "wind" and "body" can be described as an "aporia," paralyzing and fascinating at the same time. According to Derrida (1993), a paralyzing and fascinating aporetic experience happens when one gets stuck in a place or at a certain border to the extent that there is no longer any problem, neither a projection ahead nor a protection behind to shield oneself. Simply put, one doesn't know where to go (pp. 12–13). Derrida says he encounters aporia as an experience and/or a word with formalizable regularity.

For example, in *Aporia* (1993), Derrida contemplates on the unstable multiplicity inherent in the statement, *Il y va d'un certain pas*, as it could designate three possible propositions, including (a) it involves a certain step, (b) it involves a certain not, and (c) he goes along at a certain pace. This unstable multiplicity renders the statement untranslatable to other non-French languages as translating it into any one of the three propositions will be essentially incomplete. Even within the French language, there exists a shibboleth effect. That is, a certain non-discursive programmatic gestural and contextual mark already "exceeds meaning and the pure discursivity of meaning" (p. 10). Put simply, this eventful mark of *pas* as a step or a crossing line contaminates the determination of the totality of the sentence, and thus makes it no longer identical to itself, no longer identifiable and determinable. Therefore, "the identity of a language can only affirm itself as identity to itself by opening itself to the hospitality of a difference from itself or of a difference with itself" (ibid.).

In other words, identity entails an institution of an indivisible line. When this line is compromised, the identity to oneself and therefore the possible identification of an intangible edge become a problem, a problem that signifies both a projection ahead and protection behind to shield oneself. However, when there is no longer a problem in these two senses, an experience of aporia occurs, getting one stuck or paralyzed in a place not knowing where to go. It could be the nonpassage of impermeability, the nonpassage of the impasse or aporia with no limit, the aporia of the impossible, like a coming *pas* or event "which has no relation to the passage of what happens or comes to pass" (p. 21).

Jean-Luc Nancy (2007) clarifies such an aporia experience to be "the question of the impossible experience or the experience of the impossible: an experience removed from the conditions of possibility of a finite knowledge, and which is nevertheless an experience" (p. 65). Raffoul and Pettigrew, who translated Nancy's book, in their introduction further interpret this impossible experience as "the experience of the excess with respect to the conditions of *anticipating possibilities*" that "takes place in the excess of the impossible as the structure of the event" (p. 9, author's emphasis).

To me, no word is more appropriate than Derrida's "aporia" to describe my encountering of (a) the "wind-education" discourses prevalent yet silent in China's current schooling, (b) the "wind" entry in the first most comprehensive Chinese dictionary, (c) the Yijing *guan*-hexagram with an image of "wind blowing over the earth," which Confucius envisions into an ideal teaching and learning movement, and (d) the Chinese educational "body" as embodied in the "right" writing posture. I use a few pictures to illustrate these aporetic moments that guide my intellectual research journey as signposts, and also adumbrate the major concerns this book aims to address.

My First "Wind" Aporia: "Wind-Education" Discourses in China's Current Schooling

The first picture (Figure I.1), which I took during my 2009 school visit, is a school-motto wall inscription, a common sight in most, if not all, schools in China.

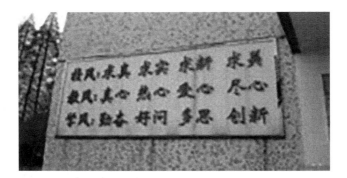

Figure I.1 School-Motto Wall Inscription

> *School wind*: seeking truth, seeking practicality, seeking newness, and seeking beauty
> *Teaching wind*: true heart, warm heart, loving heart, and full heart
> *Learning wind*: diligent, questioning, thinking, and creative

This wall inscription says, "school wind, teaching wind, and learning wind." I, like many other Chinese, grew up with these school wind-discourses but had never ever *seen* the literal, let alone the cultural, "wind-education" association therewith till 2009 when I already started my doctoral studies in the United States. One reason is that we naturally treat these wind-terms as linguistic metaphors and interpret–translate them as "school atmosphere, teaching manners, and learning styles" with semantic fillers, say, "being diligent, questioning, thinking, and creative" for "learning styles." A literal rendering of them into "school wind, teaching wind, and learning wind" rarely happens as these terms don't make good senses semantically to the English readers. To borrow Foucault's phrasing, we are subsumed to a modern grammar, a trap of philology, assuming the a priori existence of linguistic arrangements like metaphors and primarily seeking their semantic meanings. Henceforth, both the Chinese and English readers fail to *see* the literal "wind" language therein in the first place, let alone ask how and why the notions of "wind" and "education" are culturally linked to each other. Consequently, albeit prevalent in China's present schooling and, as this book will argue, significant in historically ordering the whole Confucian educational thinking, the Chinese "wind" language has not gained its due attention in the academia both nationally and internationally (Fang, 2003).

Then how could and did I *see* the Chinese "wind-education" discourses? I honestly don't know exactly how, but I guess two factors possibly account for my luck. First, I have an intellectual background in linguistics and sociolinguistics, particularly interested in critical discourse analysis (CDA) as a field and research method (Fairclough, 2001; van Dijk, 2007). This linguistic training has sharpened my overall sensitivity to language in use and developed my attitude of treating language as a mechanism that best embodies as well as most delimits our ways of reasoning and understanding about the world and ourselves. With this background, I am more intrigued by the styles of reasoning of those post-modern and post-structural thinkers, say, Martin Heidegger, Michel Foucault, Jacque Derrida, Gilles Deleuze, and Giorgio Agamben, who take up language or discourse as one, but not the only, crucial lens to problematizing, dissecting, and disrupting the issues of meaning, signification, and representation as the key configurations of the Western metaphysics and epistemology.

Second, my cross-cultural intellectual *detour* in the United States has granted me a reflexive, not just reflective, positioning as what Terri Kim calls an "inside outsider and outside insider" (2014), which as a vantage point helps me better *access* and question what are otherwise taken-for-granted in the Chinese systems of knowledge. This detour-access perspective draws upon Francois Jullien's (2004) apt book title, *Detour and Access: Strategies of Meaning in China and Greece*. With Jullien, it is the subtlety of the Chinese meaning-making mechanism that enables him to render visible his own Western tacit mode of interpretation. To me, it is Heidegger and Foucault's critique of the modern Western language and its concomitant conceptual mode of signification in its historicity that alerts me to the metamorphosis of the Chinese language and system of reason ever since the early twentieth century. Basically, their critique of the modern Western language as an enclosed representational system also applies to the modern Chinese language and discourses, and henceforth to re-understand the ordering of the Chinese language in its historicity calls for a de-normalization of our otherwise naturalized treatment of language and discourse.

This being said, one day when I was translating the above school-motto "wind-discourses" into English, the Chinese wind-character, *feng* 風, grabbed my attention and set me wondering: Why is it wind, not water? Why do I naturally read them into teaching manners, schooling atmosphere, or learning styles, but not teaching–schooling–learning wind? Then, just as Friedrich Hölderlin says: For as you began, so you will remain.

This aporetic experience is significant in that it exposes a principle of transparency presumed in translation that may end up assimilating rather than explicating cultural differences. For example, rendering the Chinese term *xuefeng* 學風 (school wind) as "school atmosphere" in English inadvertently glosses over the Chinese literal-cultural "wind-education" association. Seen this way, translation can be a hidden form of epistemicide (Paraskeva, 2016) in comparative or cultural studies, a concern to be addressed in this book. This aporetic "wind" experience also registers the whole problematic of signification and representation as another concern this book is to address, particularly the planetary signifier–signified conceptual mode of signification and representation, which has largely re-configured the epistemological structures of the human and social sciences in both Western and non-Western societies ever since the seventeenth century and from which we have not emerged (Foucault, 1973).

My Second "Wind" Aporia: "Wind" Entry in the First Chinese Dictionary

Puzzled and intrigued, I followed the dancing "wind" to China's first comprehensive etymological-analytic dictionary *shuowenjiezi* 說文解字 compiled by Xu Shen 許慎 (58–147 CE). This dictionary groups ancient Chinese characters (*hanzi* 漢字) into 540 graphic classifiers and 9,353 characters (*zi* 字). The *wen* (文) are characters consisting of only a single graphic element (single-bodied characters), and thus are not susceptible of analysis into the constituent parts smaller than the graphs themselves; the *zi* (字) are characters made up of more than one identifiable graphic component (joined-bodied characters), and thus are capable of analysis into those individual parts (Boltz, 1993). Entries for this *wen* and *zi* are often narrative segments collated from various classical source texts. *Shuowenjiezizhu* (說文解字注 *Annotations on Shuowenjiezi*) by Duan Yucai 段玉裁 (1735–1815) (see the 1981 version by Shanghai Guji Press) in Qing Dynasty, compared to the sporadic editions theretofore, is often claimed to have given more justice to Xu's version with a comprehensive collation of source texts to intertextually support Xu's original entries.

Figure I.2 is the Chinese "wind" entry in *Shuowenjiezizhu* from right top to left bottom, with Xu's original defining entry in bold interspersed with Duan's collated wind-texts from various sources in the smaller font. Reading into this short text, as to be clarified below, is indeed another aporetic experience for me.

Here is a literal rendition of the original entry text in bold, expressing the (con)textures of the Chinese "wind":

> Feng (wind): Eight winds. (Wind blowing from) East is named *Mingshifeng*; (Wind from) Southeast *Qingmingfeng*; (Wind from) South *Jingfeng*; (Wind from) Southwest *liangfeng*; (Wind from) West *Changhefeng*; (Wind from) Northwest *Buzhoufeng*; (Wind from) North *Guangmofeng*; (Wind from) Northeast *Rongfeng*. (Character) 風 constitutes two parts, a meaning-derivative image of *chong* 蟲 (insects) inside a phonetic part of *fan* 凡. Wind moves, insects get germinated and transformed within eight days.
> 八風也。東方曰明庶風，東南曰清明風，南方曰景風，西南曰涼風，西方曰閶闔風，西北曰不周風，北方曰廣莫風，東北曰融風。風動蟲生。故蟲八日而化。从虫凡聲。凡風之屬皆从風。

6 Introduction

Figure I.2 Feng 風 (Wind) Entry in *Shuowenjiezizhu*
Retrieved from www.zgzkw.com/shuowen/imgbook/index9_1.htm

Etymologically, we can see the Chinese wind-character 風 contains two components, a meaning part associated with an image of *chong* 蟲[1] (insects/snakes/animals) inside a sound part of *fan* 凡, saying "wind moves and insects get generated and transformed after eight days." What makes it an aporetic experience to me is that I recognize most of the Chinese word-characters in the wind names, but put together, it doesn't make any sense to me. For example, my best guess for the northeast wind name, *rongfeng* (融風), is that *rong* commonly denotes ice melting. However, how is this related to the wind blowing from the northeast? Why is there a correspondence between eight winds and eight spatial directions? Why would the moving wind intersect the germination and transformation of insects and why within eight, not nine, days? Here the questioning of "what does it mean" flounders as these words already paralyze our current grammar and syntax and our habit of seeking meaning synchronically from the grammatical structure of the statement itself. It seems the ancient Chinese language as a being and system of reason follows an ordering principle, distinct from that of the modern Western(ized) languages and unthinkable to us modern people.

To make such an aporetic experience even worse, the smaller intertextual texts from various historical strata don't help much. Instead, they delineate a more complicated picture in that these *eight winds* (*bafeng* 八風), besides speaking to the eight directions they blow in (*bafang* 八方), also correspond to the eight musical tones produced by different instruments (*bayin* 八音), the eight gua-trigrams (*bagua* 八卦), and the eight seasonal transitional timings (*bajie* 八節). It says "eight gua-trigrams, eight seasonal timings, and eight directions are coeval or the same in nature." To be specific, they, although situated in different epistemological domains, follow the same pattern of ordering. Picking up and following King Wen's cosmological positioning of East, South, West, and North, I transform the above narratives into the diagram presented in Figure I.3, with five layers of concentric circles denoting, in an outward direction, spatial directions, trigram musical tones, seasonal timing nodes, wind names, and their interpretations.

It is here that the Chinese "wind" brings out an aporetic "operating table" (Foucault, 1966/1973) that further implodes our modern grammar and conceptual ways of reasoning. That is, these ancient Chinese statements sound like empty murmurs to most people in current China to the extent that what is said remains what is said, sensible only at the literal level. Put differently, words are stopped in their tracks. Why so? It is not because the characters

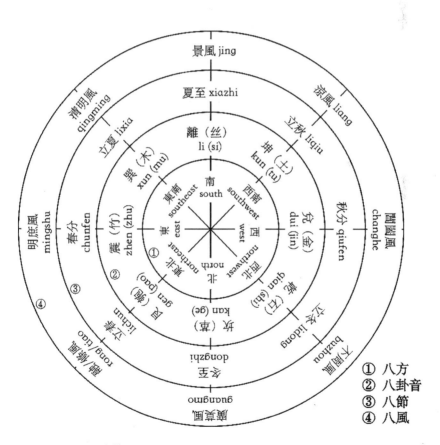

Figure I.3 Bagua 八卦 (Eight Trigram) Concentric Diagram

themselves are too esoteric to be understandable. On the contrary, they are very simple and recognizable even to elementary school students except for a few wind names. What is esoteric is the way that such disparate things as the wind, insects, spatial directions, and musical tones are held together on the same "operating table" 2000 years ago. To us modern people, the simple act of *holding together* these disparate and maybe incongruous things into a heterotopia, not a utopia, in Foucault's wording is unthinkable. This unthinkability nevertheless exposes the limits of the modern epistemology. Then, what kind of historical-cultural epistemology, worldviews, and ways of reasoning can justify and legitimize such an esoteric ordering of things in ancient China? All this needs a reading back of the ancient narratives to its logic in history, and this is why this book mainly adopts an archaeological-historical perspective.

My Third "Wind" Aporia: Confucius' Wind-Pedagogy in Yijing

Following the dancing Chinese "wind," I was finally exposed to Confucius' educational vision and wind-pedagogy as expressed in his commentary on the Yijing *guan*-hexagram, numbered 20 out of the 64 hexagrams and with an image of wind blowing over the earth. Depicting a scenario of a King performing a ritual ceremony with his subjects watching, the hexagram's eight-character theme statement zooms in on one moment when "hands washed/ yet not offering/a sincere reverent outlook" 盥而不薦有孚顒若, which to Confucius is the only scene worthy of observation in such ritual-performing scenarios (*Lunyu: Baqiao*). The hexagram itself says nothing about teaching and learning, yet Confucius adds a 54-character commentary and envisions it into one ideal teaching–learning movement between the King and his subjects by an image of wind blowing over the earth. Here is Confucius' complete commentary text and my translation with the original theme statement italicized:

> 大觀在上/順而巽/中正以觀天下/*盥而不薦*/*有孚顒若*/下觀而化也/觀天之神道而四時不忒/聖人以神道設教而天下服矣/風行地上/觀/先王以省方觀民設教
>
> Great guan-observe on the top/(the King is) situated in a center-right positioning to guan-observe the whole world under the sky/*hands washed yet not offering/ a sincere reverent outlook with head(s) up*/(the subjects) guan-observe (the King performing the ritual) from below and (get) transformed/(saintly Kings) guan-observe the magical Dao of Heaven/ the four seasonings move unchanged/saintly Kings set up teaching accordingly and the whole world under the sky become submissive and transformed /wind blows over the earth/ guan-observe/ Kings visit and observe people in different regions and set up teaching accordingly.

This is another aporetic, although more fascinating than paralyzing, encounter for me. Even though research and scholarship on Confucius and the Confucian philosophy and practice of education thrive both in China and abroad, such a wind-pedagogy, or this particular *guan*-hexagram as another originary (re)source of Confucius' educational vision, has so far rarely been discerned, let alone problematized. Since Confucius (551–479 BC) mostly "transmits/comments but not writes" (*shuerbuzuo* 述而不作) (*Lunyu: Shu'er*), it is commonly believed that his thought is scattered throughout the so-called *Four Books and Five Classics* (*sishuwujing* 四書五經). Confucian philosophy of education, as the gist of Confucius' thought (Chen, 2016), is primarily "rooted" (Ames, 2016) in *Lunyu (The Analects* 論語), *Xueji* (*On Teaching and Learning* 學記), and *Daxue* (*The Great Learning* 大學). *Lunyu* records succinct theme-based dialogues between Confucius and his disciples. *Xueji* systematically discourses on the educational philosophy and practice during the Han Dynasty. *Daxue* emphasizes a transformative character of Confucian education with personal cultivation (person-making) as the root and goal of its learning. As a "cultural script" (Tan, 2015), these texts are believed to largely define the way teaching and learning are currently re-configured in negotiation with the Western-introduced educational theories and practices in the East Asian countries with Confucian Heritage Culture (CHC).

Intrigued by this *guan*-hexagram and its image of "wind blowing over the earth," I couldn't help wondering: In which ways does the Chinese "wind" configure and order Confucius' educational vision? What epistemological theses have made it possible for Confucius to do such an envisioning in the first place? Other Confucian narratives indeed say "wind (is) teaching, wind moves and teaching transforms" (Han Preface to *Book of Odes*, around 200 AD) and "gentleman's virtue is (like) wind and petty man's virtue is (like) grass; when wind blows across it, the grass must bend" (*Analects*, around 500 BCE). But isn't it challenging here not to simply interpret "wind" as a metaphor? In which ways, can this "wind," the Yijing hexagram, and the overall Yijing thought and its "image-number" style of reasoning inform, enrich, and/or rectify the current scholarship on Confucian educational culture and its impact in current China and other Confucian societies? Part II of this book intends to answer these questions with specific examples.

Placing the Chinese "Wind" in a Global Context

Despite my above aporetic experiences, the Chinese "wind" is not totally distinct from the Western winds. For example, scholars find that wind, as a ubiquitous, natural yet transparent phenomenon of air in motion, is actually a theme central to the thinking of peoples in both contemporary and ancient cultures (Low & Hsu, 2007). As a phenomenal effect, a metaphor and/or a sign, it can be picked up as a thread to "orient oneself in a captivating labyrinth that has decisive implications for many disciplines, from history to philosophy, from art to medicine" (Nova, 2011, p. 11).

Following this invisible wind as a material example to tackle the issue of transparency, Nova (2011) maps out the historical context of the metaphorical value that the wind has assumed in Western literature and art, and "challenges the concept of mimesis favored by Western tradition" (p. 7). Collecting global winds blowing from various directions, Low and Hsu's (2007) special edition on the anthropology of wind shows a cross-cultural congruency in relating the wind to issues of life and death, sickness and healing, breath/spirit, weather, body, seasons, song, and music. These anthropological perspectives broaden our understanding of the ways in which "the experience of the wind, as natural phenomenon, has shaped social practice and become intrinsic to core cultural concepts" (ibid., p. 14) and also "critique[d] the nature-culture dichotomy that has long entrenched Western thought" (ibid., p. 2). Dallair (2011) views the Canadian wind as an "apt metaphor for Canadian soul" and proposes to "teach with the wind" in Canadian civil spirituality education. By that, he contends "when the heart and the classroom are opened up to such searching (as turning the soul to the world), there is room for the wind to blow, fluid and unencumbered" (p. 152).

In cultural China, the imagination of wind looms large in and across domains of education, politics, poetry, and Chinese medical body (Fang, 2003; Hsu, 2007; Kuriyama, 1994; Yang, 2005). Apart from its appearance in Confucian texts, the notion of wind also permeates in China's current political discourses like "party wind, social wind." The Proletarian Cultural Revolution was launched in 1966 under the claim of it as "an unparalleled-great cause of changing winds and transforming customs (*yifengyisu* 移風易俗) in the human history" (People's Daily 1966, as cited in Yang, 2005).

What is shared then between the Chinese and other cultural (Greek or Christian) winds, among others, are its connotations as a life-generating force/breath/spirit, a sign of bodily sickness and healing, or a natural-turned-cultural concept. However, as Kuriyama (1994) rightly puts it, "the fascination of the Chinese winds lay in their power to *transform*" (my italics) (p. 23), making them distinct from other cultural winds. This is because, as shown above, the Chinese wind-character, *feng* 風, etymologically nurtures a sense of transforming that is visible in the defining statement, "wind blows, and insects germinate and are hatched within eight days" (風動蟲生八日而化) in the first comprehensive Chinese dictionary. Seen this way, its "inexhaustible efficacy" (Kern, 2001) in connecting with song-poetry, governing, teaching, cosmic directions, and seasons in the Chinese culture does not sufficiently reside in the material wind that blows our face in daily life, although the qualities of the material wind could be concomitant to its other connotations. Rather, its "basic openness" (Kern, 2001, 2008) as an historical-cultural way of reasoning accounts for a wind-ish understanding of Chinese song-poetry, teaching, governance, music tones, and seasonal changes through an analogical rather than a metaphorical logic, which is to be further clarified below.

Aporetic Chinese Educational "Body": The 'Right' Writing Posture

As far as I can remember, the first thing we learned in the Chinese schooling is the *right* body posture for writing (see Figure I.4): back straight with stomach at a fist distance from the edge of desk, eyes one foot from the desktop and feet placed together and flat on the ground, the right thumb and index fingers holding onto the pencil at its two centimeters tightly pressed against the first joint of my middle finger. The ring and pinky fingers following in repetition curl under as a support against the desktop and the left palm presses the writing paper. When writing, the pencil should move at a 45-degree angle to the desktop, and the body should maintain in a beautiful bow-like shape. The handwriting should look clean and orderly too, as one's handwriting is claimed to embody a person's manner in the Chinese way of thinking (*wenruqiren* 文如其人). That is, a shabby handwriting stands for an untidy person. Whenever my body slacks down or drifts aside, my teacher or mother would immediately warn me of the risk of eyes getting near-sighted and often add some old Chinese sayings like "standing like

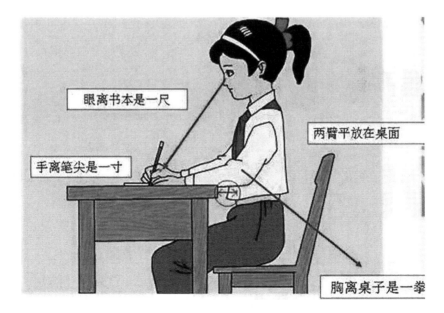

Figure I.4 "Right" Writing Body Posture
Retrieved on August 16, 2017 from www.sohu.com/a/124899445_372441

a pine tree and sitting like a bow" as a cultural, more than their personal, model of a body in shape.

However, when my daughter started her schooling in the United States, she wrote in all kinds of body postures but my model, and she even played-wrote with her left hand sometimes. My initial reaction was, of course, an immediate admonition with a rhetorical question: Didn't the teachers in the United States ever teach kids how to write with *right* pencil-holding gesture and body position? As I saw more people around write with left hands and in exaggerated manners in schooling as well as daily life, I realized that *my* normalized learning body and the Chinese body in general is indeed very Chinese characteristic and in numerous ways. In this book, I explore the ways in which the cultural sensibilities of the Chinese body, in conflation with the modern mind–body division, orders the conduct of conduct of teachers and students in China's current schooling practices.

It is commonly believed that the distinctness of the Chinese body as a language and way of reasoning lies in the fact that the Chinese body historically points toward a "psychosomatic" self (Ames, 1993) instead of a container for an individual in the Western sense, and culturally defines a Chinese individual self in relation to others (Sun, 1991). For example, in English, we say a model of self for others, while in Chinese, it becomes a model of the body for others (*yishenzuoze* 以身作則). Although running a risk of reduction, Wu Kuang-Ming (1997) describes Chinese thinking as body-thinking in contrast to the mainstream Western conceptual mind-thinking such that *body thinks and thinking is enacted through bodily engagement.* For example, Confucian learning is to beautify a learner's body partly through ritual-performing in that Xunzi, a Confucian scholar, says,

> An exemplary person's learning (is supposed to) enters into his ear, reach his heart, permeate through the limbs and embody itself fully in a person's every single movement and posture, spanning a whole body of 7 feet, while petty person's learning enters into his ear and exits from his mouth, spanning only four inches.
>
> (*Xunzi: Quanxue*)

君子之學也,入乎耳,箸乎心,布乎四體,形乎動靜;小人之學也,入乎耳, 出乎口。 口、耳之間則四寸耳,曷足以美七尺之軀哉?

（荀子：勸學）

However, this is no longer the case in current China. For example, with the revival of Confucianism in current China, some schools have re-invoked a Confucian kneeling-bowing practice where hundreds of students are called to kneel down to show their respect to teachers and parents. However, whenever students' knees fall to the ground, national debates follow with a vociferous outcry of such events as pain and shame to current Chinese education. According to these people, a physical kneel-down marks a spiritual subservience, and such educational kneeling-bowing will only train students into servile slaves rather than the expected standing-up democratic citizens. Visible in these popular debates is a Chinese mind–body conflation, turning the body into a most sensitive bone of contention about an ostensible clash between what is often characterized as Confucian hierarchical versus modern liberal egalitarian student–teacher relationships.

In Chapter 5 of this book, I juxtapose two bodily events, that is, the Confucian ritual-performing body as depicted in the Yijing *guan*-hexagram and the current schooling kneeling-bowing event, for a glimpse into the historical and cultural imprint and destruction of the Chinese body, in relation to the dynamics of teaching, learning, and teacher–student engagement.

Unpacking "Wind" and "Body" as Paradigmatic Examples

Since the Chinese "wind" and "body" connote more than a common sense of air in movement and the physical-material body in the Western sense, a note of clarification is needed here regarding how I would mobilize them in this book. Inspired by Agamben's thinking of paradigm, I treat the Chinese "wind" and "body" not as given concepts, but as theoretical constructs, as paradigmatic examples of a style of reasoning, and as strategic signposts to help me cut into, de-construct, and re-envision the ordering of, among other themes, language/reason, the educational body, and the teacher–student difference in China from a cross-cultural and historical-archaeological perspective.

Picking up Kuhn's novel understanding of paradigm as "simply a singular example," Agamben (2009) argues that paradigm can "establish a broader problematic context that it both constitutes and makes intelligible" (p. 17). As a further clarification of Aristotle's observation of paradigm as a paradoxical proceeding from the particular to the particular, unlike particular–universal induction or universal–particular deduction, Agamben states,

> Paradigms obey not the logic of the metaphorical transfer of meaning but the analogical logic of the example. Here we are not dealing with a signifier that is extended to designate heterogeneous phenomena by virtue of the same semantic structure; more akin to allegory than to metaphor, the paradigm is a singular case that is isolated from its context only insofar as, by exhibiting its own singularity, it makes intelligible a new ensemble, whose homogeneity it itself constitutes. That is to say, to give an example is a complex act which supposes that the term functioning as a paradigm is deactivated from its normal use, not in order to be moved into another context but, on the contrary, to present the canon—the rule—of that use, which cannot be shown in any other way.
>
> (p. 18)

As an illustration, Agamben says when we explain the rule of performatives using the example of "I swear," it is clear that this statement can't be understood as a performative speech act of uttering a real oath. For "I swear" to be used as an example here, its normal function as a speech act needs to be suspended. Nevertheless, it is in the suspending that the rule of speech act is stated and shown. Furthermore, the fact that the example is excluded from the rule is not because it doesn't belong to the normal case. Rather, the exclusion exhibits its belonging to the rule. Henceforth, the example works in an opposite way to the exception in that "whereas the exception is included through its exclusion, the example is excluded through the exhibition of its inclusion" (p. 24). In other words, this rule of paradigmatic use cannot be applied or stated (a priori), but can only be shown in the exhibition alone of the paradigmatic case that constitutes a rule and the paradigm is never already given but is generated and produced by showing and exposing.

I think one scene from the movie *Kongfu Panda* can help to illuminate Agamben's thinking on his paradigmatic example. Near the Sacred Tears pond where Wugui first discovered Kongfu, Shifu no accidentally catches a drop of water dripping from the overhead dragon's mouth, guides it along with his slow yin-yang *taiji* movement and elegantly slides it onto a small plant leaf before it finally drops into the lake with visible ripples spreading out. Analogically, this water drop functions as a paradigm and the ripples are the new homogeneous ensembles that it makes visible as well as constitutes. Moving along with Shifu's *taiji* movement channels the water drop from its usual course, deactivates it from its normal character, and shows its paradigmatic singularity through Shifu's whole process of catching, moving, working, and showing.

In this book, I use the Chinese "wind-風" and "body-身" as two examples to make intelligible a "grid of intelligibility" (Foucault, 1966/1973), weaving together the Chinese wind-language, educational body, teacher–student difference, teaching, and learning, whose historical mode of holistic kinship is still unrecognized in the mainstream understanding of China's education discourses and practices. As I said above, "wind-discourses" are still prevalent but largely unrecognized in contemporary Chinese educational research, although such a wind-education association can be historically traced to Confucius' vision as expressed in the Yijing book. The Chinese "body" has already become a high stake in China's current teacher–student relationship partly due to a Chinese unique mind–body separation–conflation complex. Furthermore, the Chinese teacher–student difference is still enthralled within a Confucian hierarchy vs. modern egalitarianism power ordering. In other words, the Chinese wind-風 and body-身 in these senses are singular in themselves, and its paradigmatic function of their singularity is not yet recognized and explored. My project endeavors to show and make visible their paradigmatic singularity through historically and cross-culturally presenting their singularity intersected with Chinese teaching, learning, and teacher–student engagement.

Projected Structure

This book aims to fulfill two missions. First, it is to paradigmatically unpack China's knowledge, education, and curriculum with and beyond the Western frameworks and categories and also beyond a relativist cultural stand. Using the Western frameworks and categories to describe China's educational thinking and practices, as most scholars do nowadays, can be seen as a hidden form of epistemicide. However, going to the other extreme, namely, holding a relativist cultural stand, is equally epistemologically problematic in the current globalizing and globalized world. This book is to go the middle way, examining China's current educational thinking and praxis as an (dis)assemblage of East and West, past and present. Second, it is to recount and theorize my own research-learning experience, which I call a "Daoist onto-un-learning," as an exemplary case of post-foundational *study* that is an emerging Western rationale built upon post-modern and post-structural turns. Post-foundational *study*, a concept proposed by Tyson Lewis in interpreting and relating Agamben's thought to education, is an alternative logic to confront and push back against the instrumental *learning* logic predominant in the twenty-first-century neoliberal education and curriculum reform globally. Whereas learning is to draw out students' potentialities along a measurable scheme, to train students with necessary skills and competencies anticipated in the twenty-first century, *study* is a wondering and wandering journey itself, without subjecting itself to a definite goal or transferable skills.

Toward that goal, the book is divided into three parts, plus a preface and introduction. The Preface succinctly lays out the main features of this book as guiding or pre-cautionary notes to readers. The introduction presents my aporia experiences with the Chinese "wind" and educational "body" as starting points of as well as signposts along my research journey. Part I and Part II are developed primarily to realize the first mission, while Part III the second. Part I contains three chapters that proffer the overall situating of the book, the major concerns it is to address, and the theoretical-methodological perspectives it employs. Part II also has three chapters that are concrete paradigmatic examples on how to historicize China's system of knowledge, education, and curriculum with and beyond the Western categories and frameworks.

Specifically, Chapter 1 situates the book within a broad field of comparative or cross-cultural studies, intersecting the domains of education, curriculum, and knowledge. It identifies "epistemicide" (Paraskeva, 2016), or epistemological crisis, as often a hidden effect of a "normative" comparative paradigm and a globalizing of West-Eurocentric discourses as epistemic rules in the rest of the world. Take the modern China as an example, such an epistemicide happened especially during the New Cultural Movement in the 1920s when the Chinese intelligentsia collectively and willingly aligned themselves with the Western democracy and science as their eugenic reference. This epistemological self-alignment justified the intelligentsia's collective call to review and eradicate their Confucian Chinese tradition and culture as "backward and barbaric man-eating feudal dross." China's collective and self-aligned demolition of its own culture in the face of the imperial colonialism of Western culture is a "cultural absurdity seldom accounted for so far" (Zhang X., 2013). This epistemological coloniality continued in the name of modernization and globalization, currently expressed through such globalized West-Eurocentric discourses as "the twenty-first-century skills/competencies/literacies" and an already planetary conceptual mode of signification, both of which imprisons the ways current China's system of knowledge, education, and curriculum are said and done.

Two theoretical-methodological perspectives are proposed to hopefully overcome such an epistemological crisis, namely, an "archaeological-historical mode of inquiry" borrowed from Martin Heidegger, Michel Foucault, and Giorgio Agamben (Chapter 2) and an "ontological language–discourse perspective" from Martin Heidegger and Michel Foucault (Chapter 3). The archaeological-historical perspective calls to legitimize a culture's knowledge system in its own historical and ethnographical context. In so doing, it confronts the "normative" comparative paradigm in cultural studies, namely, using the West as a eugenically advanced standard to gauge the non-West, which often results in the suppression and elimination of the existence of alternative forms of knowledge in the latter. In other words, the binary and eugenic comparative conundrum in cross-cultural studies needs to be rethought, and I propose a "difference at its limit" as a strategic entry point in explicating local-cultural sensibilities for a healthy and mutually informing cross-cultural dialogue. Methodologically, it is to be noted that my borrowing the thought of the above Western thinkers is not merely a replicating of their thought into the Chinese context. Rather, I assemble their thought as a style of reasoning in relation to China's Yijing, Confucian, and Daoist wisdom. In so doing, what is produced is not a sum of the parts but itself a mode of reasoning in close relation to the way in which the text itself is constructed.

Chapter 3 further links this archaeological-historical mode of inquiry with an ontological language perspective to bracket an otherwise naturalized conceptual mode of signification and a representational language attitude. A rigorous unpacking of Foucault's *The Order of Things* exposes the limits of treating the modern language as an enclosed representational linguistic system and the trope of a conceptual mode of signification, namely, meaning is generated only through a delay and relay of ideas. On top of that is what Foucault puts as "a trap of philology," presuming the a priori existence of grammatical arrangements for what can be expressed through and in language. As a counter strategy, Foucault suggests we need to work back our naturalized viewpoints and philosophies toward hopefully revealing a word or thought not yet subsumed to the modern grammar. With this strategy, the Chinese language, or rather, the Chinese characters (*hanzi*) are rethought as a material being itself, the (con)textures and (over)tones of which need to be re-interpreted not through the Western categories of "representation" or "ideograph" but a Confucian exegesis. By the latter, it means tracing each Chinese character back to its etymological source for its possible textures and tones to evoke its vitality in the present. In other words, a Chinese mode of signification entails a diachronic-historical dimension as compared to the modern representational signification largely delimited to the synchronic grammatical arrangement within a statement.

Part II (Chapters 4, 5, and 6) proffers three paradigmatic examples of unpacking China's knowledge, education, and curriculum around the three interrelated topics of language, the educational body, and the teacher–student difference. These three topics of language, body, and difference were interlaced and coordinated both incidentally and deliberately as an ongoing process of my three-dimensional movement: (a) following the dancing Chinese "wind" back and forth to the ancient Chinese texts, (b) exploring the (dis)ordering of identity and difference to cut into the modern issues of representation and signification, and (c) examining China's current education and curriculum reform discourses and practices at the nexus and as the (dis) assemblages of East and West, past and present. Structurally, an unpacking of the Yijing *guan*-hexagram and Confucius' wind-pedagogy in Chapter 4 is an example on language and reason, rendering visible an ontological educational body. This body dimension paves its way for a historicization of the Chinese "body" in ordering its teaching/teachers, learning/students, and the teacher–student relationship in Chapter 5, rendering visible a grounding binary division. This binary division builds into a theoretical re-envisioning of it to rethink the issue of difference in general and the Chinese teacher–student difference in particular in Chapter 6. In a word, I order these three chapters so that one builds into the next.

Chapter 4 evokes an originary Yijing style of thought as onto-epistemological principles ordering and correlating the otherwise disparate things of knowledge, cosmology, education, writing, and governance onto an operating table. The evocation is not to provide a thorough picture of the Yijing thought which, considering its unfathomable wisdom and my narrow knowledge of it, is simply impossible. Rather, my unpacking is to explicate a few epistemological themes such as *wen* (crisscrossing pattern), *guan* (onto-hermeneutic observing), *xiang* (phenomenal forms), *shu* (number), and *shi* (timing) as nodes that grid the Yijing thought. These themes are chosen partly to elicit a "correlative style of thinking" as a response to the "wind" aporia laid out in Introduction. More importantly, I approach these themes as the conditions of possibility which enabled Confucius to envision his teaching and learning movement as expressed in Yijing, which has so far rarely been discerned let alone scrutinized in the scholarship on Confucius and his educational thinking. It is my aporetic encountering of the "wind-education" discourses prevalent yet silent in China's current schooling as well as Heidegger–Foucault's ontological language perspective that enabled me to see Confucius' wind-pedagogy and educational vision in *Yijing*. Henceforth, I argue for re-invoking "wind" as a signature language of Chinese education and *Yijing* as another originary (re)source for the entire Confucian educational heritage.

Chapter 5 shows a historical imprint and destruction (Foucault, 1984) of the Chinese body by juxtaposing two body events: Confucius' ritual body as performed in the Yijing *guan*-hexagram and the current reinstated yet controversial school kneeling-bowing events. In the former, the body grounds and configures the Confucian teaching and learning that happens like wind blowing over the earth. In the latter, the body has become a conceptual symbolic sign, a bone of contention that has entangled China's current teacher–student ordering within a Confucian hierarchical versus modern democratic relationship. Putting them one alongside the other, I show an epistemic transformation from a Chinese ontological body-thinking toward a modern Westernized conceptual mind-thinking and explores the possibility of revisiting and re-enacting the Chinese body-thinking. In so doing, I suspend a taken-for-granted treatment of the body as a given object subjugated to discipline and punishment in education. Rather, I historicize the textures, tones, and structures of body itself as a theoretical construct to see how it is normalized as an object from a subject, how it configures the very nature of Confucian teaching and learning in that learning is basically to beautify one's body, and finally how a Chinese holistic body-thinking, not bodily thinking, can dialogue with and supplement the predominant Western(ized) mind-thinking. Furthermore, a re-invoked body-thinking enabled me to expose the limits of applying Michel Foucault's power-based governmentality to understand the Chinese teacher–student ordering.

Chapter 6 rethinks the issue of difference with and beyond the ordering of identity as a way to push further the problematic of the Chinese language and body with China's teacher education reform and teacher–student relationship as its example. Specifically, it aims to flatten out the modern Western "abyssal thinking" (Sousa Santos, 2007) as expressed in the binary division logic that predominantly orders the issues of identity and difference, presence and absence, mind and body, dominance and resistance, subject and object, and teaching and learning. Discerning this binary division as a presumed grounding principle that confines the Chinese teacher–student relationship to a hierarchical vs. egalitarian binary pendulum, I resort to Heidegger's rethinking of identity and difference and a Daoist bipolar movement for new insights. Specifically, I dialogue, for reciprocal informing, the ancient Chinese Daoist yin-yang bipolar reasoning with the thinking of Heidegger, especially his intellectual efforts to bracket and go beyond a metaphysical-binary mode of reasoning through re-envisioning the nature of as well as the ordering between difference and identity. Such a theoretical unpacking and dialoguing are informed by an "abnormal" kneeling event wherein a Chinese middle school principal drops his knees in front of over 1,000 students and teachers as his last pedagogical resort. Moving within this example that has incurred national outcry, I hope to explicate the Dao De Jing statement, *what is abnormal/returning to root re-activate the dao movement and what is weak sustains the dao movement*, to help us rethink the ordering of difference and identity in a way not reducible yet conducive to Heidegger's non-metaphysical gesture.

Part III (Chapter 7) revisits and theorizes my intellectual journey that I tentatively call "a Daoist onto-un-learning way" as a post-foundational *study* example in dialogue with the Western *study* scholarship spearheaded by Tyson Lewis as an alternative to the learning logic predominant in the current neoliberal society. It furthermore relates study and learning into a yin-yang movement, imploding the presupposed binary logic that conceptualizes study as an oppositional or alternative logic to learning. The term Daoist onto-un-learning way is inspired by the Dao De Jing statement *doing learning gains each day whereas doing dao loses* (Chapter 48), with *way* intersecting a journey, a method, and a Dao movement. It is not a journey that can be projected beforehand, but it can only be understood backward and recalled as a record of the wandering and wondering on the *way*. In this sense, this last chapter, to me, is not a coming to end of my whole research project with some replicable results, but rather, a continuing or furthering of my intellectual journey that has been opened up and will continue opening to unpredictable wonderlands across cultures.

Note

1. It is commonly believed that Chinese characters/words were first made by Cang Jie 倉頡 as primordial imitations of the traces and images of natural beings. However, unlike sun, moon, clouds, and rain, wind doesn't have an apparent image. This may account for the fact that the ancient Chinese oracle bone scripture doesn't have the word for wind. Instead the character for a magical-bird of phoenix, 鳳, is used for wind in divination. The character 風 may be coined by Xu Shen 許慎 himself with a sound part encasing a radical of 蟲, the latter a nomenclature then for beasts, fish, birds, shellfish, and human beings (see, Liu S., 2011). In this book, for simplicity, I use insects as a rough gloss for 蟲.

References

Agamben, G. (2009). *The signature of all things: On method*. New York, NY: Zone Books.

Ames, R. T. (1993). The meaning of body in classical Chinese thought. In T. P. Kasulis, R. Ames, & W. Dissanayake (Eds.), *Self as body in Asian theory and practice* (pp. 39–54). Albany, NY: State University of New York Press.

Ames, R. T. (2016). On teaching and learning (Xueji 學記): Setting the root in Confucian education. In X. Di & H. McEwan (Eds.), *Chinese philosophy on teaching and learning: Xueji (學記) in the twenty-first century* (pp. 21–38). Albany, NY: State University of New York Press

Boltz, W. G. (1993). Shuo wen chieh tzu. In M. Loewe (Ed.), *Early Chinese texts: A bibliographical guide* (pp. 429–442). Berkeley, CA: Society for the Study of Early China, and the Institute of East Asian Studies, University of California.

Chen, L. (2016). The ideas of "educating" and "learning" in Confucian thought. In X. Di & H. McEwan (Eds.), *Chinese philosophy on teaching and learning: Xueji (學記) in the twenty-first century* (pp. 77–96). Albany, NY: State University of New York Press.

Dallair, M. (2011). *Teaching with the wind: Spirituality in Canadian education*. Lanham, MD: University Press of America, Inc.

Derrida, J. (1993). *Aporias* (T. Gutoit, Trans.). Stanford, CA: Stanford University Press.

Fairclough, N. (2001). *Language and power* (2nd ed.). London, UK: Longman.

Fang, Z. H. (2003). "Feng" yu zhongguo wenhua zhong de "shehuikexue"—guanyu zhongguo shehuikexue fangfalun de yige tansuo [Feng-wind and social sciences in Chinese culture: On Chinese social science methodology 风与中国文化中的"社会科学"—关于中国社会科学 方法论的一个探索]. *Tianjin Shehui Kexue (Tianjin Social Science)*, 6, 12–17.

Foucault, M. (1973). *The order of things: An archaeology of the human sciences*. New York, NY: Vintage Books. (Original work published 1966)

Foucault, M. (1984). Nietzsche, genealogy, history. In P. Rabinow (Ed.), *The Foucault reader* (pp. 76–100). Harmondsworth: Penguin.

Hsu, E. (2007). The experience of wind in early and medieval Chinese medicine. *Journal of the Royal Anthropological Institute (N.S.)*: S117–S134.

Jullien, F. (2004). *Detour and access: Strategies of meaning in China and Greece*. New York, NY: Zone Book.

Kern, M. (2001). Ritual, text, and the formation of the canon: Historical transitions of "Wen" in early China. *T'oung Pao*, Second Series, 87(1), 43–91.

Kern, M. (2008). Cong chutu wenxian tan 'Guofeng' de quanshi wenti: yi 'Guanju' wei li [Hermeneutic issues regarding "the airs of the states" as seen from excavated manuscripts: The case of guanju 從出土文獻談《國風》的詮釋問題：以《關雎》為例] In *Zhonghua Wenshi Luncong*, 89(1), 253–271.

Kim, T. (2014). The intellect, mobility and epistemic positioning in doing comparisons and comparative education. *Comparative Education*, 50(1), 58–72.

Kuriyama, S. (1994). The imagination of winds and the development of the Chinese conception of the body. In A. Zito & T. E. Barlow (Eds.), *Body, subject, and power in China* (pp. 23–41). Chicago, IL and London, UK: Chicago University Press.

Liu, S. H. (2011). *Liushahe ren zi [Liushahe on Chinese words 流沙河認字]*. Hong Kong: Commercial Press.

Low, C., & Hsu, E. (2007). Preface and introduction. *Journal of the Royal Anthropological Institute (N.S.)*, Siii–S16.

Nancy, J. L. (2007). *The creation of the world or globalization* (F. Raffoul & D. Pettigrew, Trans. with an introduction.). New York, NY: State University of New York Press.

Nova, A. (2011). *The book of the wind: The representation of the invisible*. Montreal and Kingston, London, UK and Ithaca, NY: McGill-Queen's University Press.

Paraskeva, J. M. (2016). *Curriculum epistemicide: Towards an itinerant curriculum theory*. New York, NY: Routledge.

Shuowenjiezizhu 说文解字注 *[Annotations on Shuowen jiezi]*. (1981). Shuowen jiezi written by Xu Shen 許慎 (58–147 CE) and annotations collated by Duan Yucai 段玉裁 (1735–1815). Shanghai: Shanghai Guji Press.

Sousa Santos, B. (2007). Beyond abyssal thinking: From Global lines to Ecologies of knowledges. *Review (Fernand Braudel Center)*, 45–89.

Sun, L. K. (1991). Contemporary Chinese culture: Structure and emotionality. *The Australian Journal of Chinese Affairs, 26,* 1–41.

Tan, C. (2015). Education policy borrowing and cultural scripts for teaching in China. *Comparative Education, 51*(2), 196–211.

van Dijk, T. A. (Ed.). (2007). *Discourse studies (Vol. I-5).* Los Angeles, CA, London, UK, New Delhi, Singapore, Washington, DC: Sage Publications.

Wu, K. M. (1997). *On Chinese body thinking: A cultural hermeneutic.* Leiden, The Netherlands and New York, NY: Brill Academic Publishing.

Yang, H. (2005). "Yifengyisu" mingti kaoyuan: zai zhongguo meixueshi shiyexia [On the origins of the proposition of "transforming social customs (wind and customs)": Based on the perspectives of Chinese aesthetical history 移风易俗命题考源: 在中国美学史视野下] (Unpublished doctoral dissertation). Zhejiang University, China.

Zhang, X. L. (2013). *Fujian Tiandixin—Rujia zailin de yunyi yu daolu.* [*Revealing the heart of heaven and earth: On meaning of and path toward authentic Confucianism* 复见天地心- 儒家再临的蕴意与道路]. Beijing: Oriental Publishing House.

Part I
Overcoming "Epistemicide" in Cross-cultural Educational Studies

1 "Epistemicide" as an Effect of Comparative Paradigms and Globalized Discourses

According to Giorgio Agamben (2009), method especially in human sciences is a "matter of ultimate or penultimate thoughts" (p. 7) that follows, not precedes, practical application and can "legitimately be articulated only after extensive research" (ibid.). Following his understanding, method and theory are constitutive of each other such that method has full theoretical force in (re)ordering the selection of research paradigms, theoretical perspectives, objects of examination, and specific analytical methods. In this light, Part I (Chapters 1–3) offers a retrospective reflection upon the overall situating, as well as the methodological-theoretical lens, of the book, yet not as some a priori constructs selected beforehand but as some thoughts and reflections gained along and after doing the whole research project extensively.

This book situates itself in comparative or cross-cultural studies and addresses the issue of epistemicide (Paraskeva, 2016). In particular, Chapter 1 unpacks and delimits the broad issue of epistemicide as a hidden effect of two factors, namely, the developmental comparative paradigms used as a "norm" in cross-cultural studies and the globalization of Western-Eurocentric discourses as epistemic rules into the rest of the world. It examines the twentieth-century-and-after China studies and its education/curriculum reforms as the examples of epistemicide, and cautions against a cultural relativist stand in re-engaging ancient and modern Chinese thought in the twenty-first century. As an overcoming gesture, the following two chapters propose an archaeological-historical mode of inquiry borrowed from Martin Heidegger, Michel Foucault, and Giorgio Agamben (Chapter 2); and an ontological language–discourse perspective from Martin Heidegger and Michel Foucault (Chapter 3). In a word, this book deploys an archaeological-historical and language lens to address the issue of epistemicide in the studies of China's education, curriculum, and knowledge on a cross-cultural landscape.

"Epistemicide" or Epistemological Crisis on International Intellectual Landscape

"Curriculum epistemicide," a term coined by João M. Paraskeva (2011, 2016), describes a form of Western imperialism, which he claims now reaches a "quasi-irretrievable point" (2016, p. 3) and continues to intersect with the daily praxis of schools in and beyond the West. By epistemicide, it means that the prevailing West-Eurocentric Anglophone discourses and practices around the world have suppressed and eliminated the existence of alternative forms of knowledges in developing countries, even though the latter may be "shockingly and unknowingly the pillars of [the] Western epistemological path" (p. 46). The crisis does not necessarily anchor upon "the so-called superiority of the Western modern Eurocentric epistemological perspective, but shockingly on the eugenic claim that such an epistemological claim is unique and the only cognitive possible" (p. 3). Such a eugenic claim glorifies a blunt lie, or a false idea, of a Western "monolithic episteme" (p. 46). As a human rights issue, such a claim concerns a matter of social and cognitive justice, revealing the hegemonic nature of West-Eurocentric modernity not merely as a product of a neoliberal economic dynamic albeit its driving force. Rather, the hegemony is implicated within an ideological terrain entailing culture and politics as an effect of coloniality of knowledge and being. Coloniality, according to Maldonado-Torres (2007), refers to the memory or legacy of the colonialism, which defines culture, labor, inter-subjective relation, and knowledge production well beyond the limits of colonialism and long after the end of a colonial administration.

What legitimizes such a eugenic claim, among other themes, is a dichotomous inclusion-exclusion style of reasoning as a defining feature and yoke of the modern Western mode of thinking, which Sousa Santos (2007) puts as "abyssal thinking." Expressed in the field of knowledge is the "monopoly of the universal distinction between true or false" (p. 47) in modern science, marginalizing philosophy and theology as two alternative knowledge systems. Santos (2007) maintains this "abyssal thinking" constitutes a system of visible and invisible distinctions, with the latter grounding the former. It presumes a radical line between "this (visible) side" and "that (invisible) side" such that the invisible "vanishes as reality, becomes nonexistent, and is indeed produced as nonexistent" (p. 45), nonexistent in any relevant or comprehensive way of being. That is, whatever analytically comes out as nonexistent is radically excluded ontologically. This abyssal thinking, partly accountable by the Western logocentric metaphysics, conflates an analytical categorization of the visible and the invisible with an ontological inclusion-exclusion. Henceforth, the "impossibility of the co-presence of the two sides of the [division] line" (ibid.), say, identity and difference, self and others, presence and absence, marks the most fundamental characteristics of abyssal thinking as the modern Western thinking mode.

This abyssal thinking is then functionalist, and it inevitably ferments, grounds, and fosters a coloniality of Western knowledge and being to the extent that some counter dominant critical theories turn out to be as functionalist as the hegemonic functionalism they criticize. As an example, Paraskeva problematizes the critical progressive curriculum scholarship of, say, Michael Apple (1990), Basil Bernstein (1977), Henry Giroux (1980, 1983),

William Pinar (1980), and Michal Young (1971). Even though engaged in a laudable struggle for curriculum meaning and justice, this scholarship ends up "being a Eurocentric anti-Eurocentric critique" (p. 45), not just failing to heed the colossal epistemic diversities beyond the West-Eurocentric domain but also producing the latter as nonexistent. Even the critical, post-modern, and post-structural theories are not sufficient to disrupt the coloniality of power and being since they too are basically "an anti-Eurocentric/Western critique from a Eurocentric/Western fundamentalist position" (p. 76).

As an effort to address this functionalist fundamentalist anti-European critique and cleanse the coloniality of West-centric knowledge, power, and being, Santos (2007) proffers a notion of "post-abyssal thinking," which Paraskeva characterizes as a decolonial style of thinking. A post-abyssal thinking presumes a radical co-presence between the visible and the invisible, and is "sentient of the wor(l)ds behind and beyond the Western epistemological platform, wor(l)ds that are non-monolithic" (Paraskeva, 2016, p. 86). Namely, it recognizes an ecological co-existence of varying epistemological forms of knowledge around the world. As a form of decolonial thinking, it doesn't ask to begin anew in the old West-Eurocentric cartography of knowledge, but to find an entirely new ecological beginning in a distinct space of knowledge. It delinks itself from the yoke, the spell, or the rhetoric of modernity, democracy, post-modernity, or post-colonialism, all grounded in the Occident, hoping to bring to the foreground "a silenced and different genealogy of thought" (p. 80).

Toward that agenda, Paraskeva proposes an Itinerant Curriculum Theory (ICT) as a new "never stable gathering epistemological point" (p. 11), itinerant in the sense of going beyond a dichotic skeleton of West–Rest, yet not romanticizing the indigenous cultures and knowledges. As a decolonial struggle for a social and cognitive justice, ICT upholds the understanding that "critical knowledge starts by the critique of knowledge" itself (Sousa Santos, 1999, p. 205; cited in Paraskeva, 2016, p. 8). ICT not merely explores the classical significant curriculum question of "what/whose knowledge gets taught at schools (see, e.g., Apple, 2000), but "fights for (an)other knowledge outside the Western epistemological harbor" (p. 43), knowledge and epistemologies largely marginalized and discredited in the current world order.

Reframing "Epistemicide" as an Effect of Comparative Paradigms and Globalized Discourses

Paraskeva's unpacking of curriculum epistemicide is highly relevant to my project in two ways. First, epistemicide also enthralls China's modernity as an effect of its modernization and currently globalization process, expressed as the destruction of its language, knowledge, and education, or put simply, the entire Confucian culture, especially since China's New Cultural Movement in the 1920s. Second, epistemicide is the very issue or concern this book aims to address by providing a paradigmatic case study. I comply with Paraskeva's unpacking of epistemicide as a coloniality matrix of knowledge, power, and being, and fully embrace the necessity to bring to the foreground (an)other forms of knowledge in its genealogy. *Moving one step further though, this book explores how it is paradigmatically possible first to discern and then render visible and intelligible in English wor(l)d these other forms of knowledge on a cross-cultural landscape.*

Toward that agenda, this book confines its dissection of the issue of epistemicide as an effect of two factors, namely, a "normative" paradigm in comparative cultural studies and a globalizing Western–Northern discourse in the rest of the world in the fundamentalist name of internationalization, modernization, and globalization. The former refers to using a Western framework to map out non-Western historical-cultural sensibilities. As Chakrabarty (2000) rightly argues, a thought is related to a place, henceforth, Western epistemological frameworks and methodologies are indispensable yet insufficient in interpreting non-Western contextualized historical-cultural thought and practice. An uncritical appropriation of the West as a reference point in comparative cultural studies is a hidden form of "New Imperialism" (Tikly, 2004), or "mental colonialism" (Nguyen, Elliott, Terlouw, & Pilot, 2009), causing an epistemological crisis or epistemicide. As a result, the non-West is often constructed in and imagined through the eyes of the West as what the West is not, or outside of the Western bracket (Said, 1979; Saussy, 2001), not relevant to and even contradictory from what the non-West factually is. Please note that my using of these broad notions like tradition, culture, Chinese, East, and West in its singular form is just for the convenience of analysis and based on the understanding that all these English terms themselves are empty linguistic signifiers rather than essential entities. Moreover, the singular form doesn't signify a totality either, as the historical and actual movements and events these terms help to embody or point at are never singular and unitary.

Apart from using the West-based comparative paradigm as a gauge in cross-cultural studies, a globalizing of the West-Eurocentric discourses in the rest of the world also contributes to the issue of epistemicide in the name of modernization and globalization. Globalization often features a one-way export of knowledge, education, and scholarship from the global centers and their standardization and dominance to the developing countries (Shi-xu, 2016). Furthermore, these Western knowledge, education, and scholarship are often adamantly promoted by the scholars in non-Western societies without realizing the possible issue of epistemicide (see, e.g., Zhang X., 2013). Yet, these Western epistemological theories and frameworks often subjugate and discredit the creation of alternative knowledge in developing countries, producing an "academic aphasia" (Shi-xu, 2016) in the latter. As such, globalization disrupts and transcends an essentialized geographical West/global vs. non-West/local construct toward a metamorphosed confrontation between local historical-cultural traditions and a globalized

Western modernity, a confrontation of never merely innocuous or contested interconnections or hybridities (Lawless, 2014; Ossewaarde, 2014).

Globalized discourses are never merely language terms in use, but embody the West-Eurocentric epistemological principles, say, an instrumental logic and a binary subject–object style of reasoning as an effect of the Enlightenment movement or the specters of Western modernity. The most salient yet hidden feature of globalized discourses is the modern mode of signification, that is, meaning is generated through and delimited to a signifier–signified relay-play of concepts and ideas. This mode of signification presumes language as an enclosed system, subjected to a trap of philology, which assumes the a priori existence of grammatical arrangements in a language for what can be expressed in it. This conceptual mode of signification, along with a modern treatment of language as a representational system, has become a naturalized "planetary" (Heidegger, 1978) style of reasoning, from which we modern people are yet to emerge (Foucault, 1973). Imprisoned by it, other historical-cultural styles are eclipsed, and alternative productions of meaning and knowledge are invalidated. For example, Blumenfeld-Jones (2016) claims that the Protestant discourse–language derived from the Hellenic and subsequently Christian thinking has structured and ordered the Western world, marginalizing and excluding a Judaic rabbinic interpretive paradigm. The section below unpacks how espistemicide happened in post-nineteenth-century China, largely due to a West-based comparative paradigm and the modernization and Westernization of Chinese language.

Epistemicide Enslaves the Chinese Intelligentsia Since the Mid-nineteenth Century

It widely concurs that the Chinese culture itself burgeons out of a unique civilization with an understanding of cosmology, onto-epistemology, philosophy, and language far distinct from the Indo-European languages and cultures. The term "Chinese culture" itself is an agglomeration of varied schools of thought rather than one objective entity with fixed predicates, henceforth inherently dynamic and diverse intra-culturally throughout its history.

This being said, Indian Buddhism can be seen as the first outside culture that gets assembled and assimilated into the Chinese culture and later as a form of Chinese Buddhism (Zen) from the first-century East Han Dynasty to the mid-seventh-century Tang dynasty. Islam civilization is the second that entered into China from the seventh to the thirteenth century in late Song dynasty. Both intercultural encounters and negotiations are peaceful and mutually informing, without jeopardizing a sense of ethnocentric superiority the imperial China had indeed enjoyed for over two millennia (see, e.g., Zhang H., 2014). However, this ethnocentric superiority was blasted in 1840 when China was forced to enter into its modern trajectory by the British gunboat and opium drugs, signaling the start of the Western imperial colonialization of modern China.

The Sino-British Opium War (1840–1842), the Sino-Japanese War (1894–1895), and the Siege of the International Legations (1900–1901) morally and psychologically devastated the late Qing Dynasty Confucian intellectuals-officials, dividing them into the thought camps of liberals, radicals, and conservatives. Liberals, like Hu Shi 胡適 (1891–1962) who studied in the Philosophy Department at the Columbia University, USA, try to reconstruct the Chinese traditional culture via the Western-introduced democracy and science. Radicals like Chen Duxiu 陳獨秀 (1879–1942), Li Dazhao 李大釗 (1889–1927), and Lu Xun 魯迅 (1881–1936) thoroughly deny, and call for an eradication of, the Chinese traditional culture and thought as "backward" gauged through what they view as the "advanced" Western science and technology. Conservatives like Zhang Zhidong 張之洞 (1837–1909) and Liang Shuming 梁漱溟 (1893–1988) contend to realize the ideals of democracy and modernization based on the Chinese culture, as expressed in a well-known claim of "Chinese culture as body and Western culture as function" (*zhongxue weiti, xixue weiyong* 中學為體西學為用). In the second half of the nineteenth century, a few industrial movements were launched as endeavors to defend the Qing Dynasty and the Confucian culture from the imperialist powers under the slogan of "learning from the West to resist the West and to strengthen China" (師夷長技以制夷/自強). Nevertheless, all the efforts were ultimately demolished by the towering Western military powers.

Accordingly, the Chinese thought and culture have undergone an unparalleled degree of epistemicide since the mid-late nineteenth century then in the name of modernization and now globalization. Paraskeva (2016) claims what legitimizes the Eurocentric epistemicide is the bind of eugenic claim with a category of race, henceforth legitimizing racial discrimination and even genocide. However, different from the Western colonialism in South America and India where indigenous culture kind of survived, what is extraordinary about China is the collective self-aligned demolition of the Chinese cultures by the Chinese intelligentsia themselves, a cultural absurdity in the world civilization history rarely accounted for so far (Zhang X., 2013, p. 65). That is, the Chinese intelligentsia especially during and after the 1920s New Cultural Movement has collectively constructed a colonial mentality, namely, backward Chinese Confucian tradition vs. advanced Western modernity of democracy and science. Worse still, they gave such mentality a eugenic value and even aligned themselves to it, acquiescing those Western-Eurocentric epistemological claims as *the* globalized standard reference. With this self-legitimized mentality, they collectively maintain an overall negative attitude toward its tradition, calling to demolish their own backward Confucian culture and system as a precondition for China to go modern for an entire century.

As a consequence of such self-aligned epistemicide, modern Western ideology and epistemology, say, its abyssal binary mode of thinking, conceptual style of reasoning, scientism, presentism, and technology, have since imprisoned modern China's thought and practice, marginalizing and excluding the Chinese Confucian culture and system as feudal dross. Such a developmental gauging framework still holds sway, although in a more surreptitious form, in the current international positioning of China, West, and the China–West relationship, an epitomized expression of which is the *China Threat* versus *China Harmonious Rising* discourses, as well as President Xi's latest *China/ese Dream* slogan.

Even though Confucian tradition re-emerges since the late 1980s, its living conditions and structure, say, the Confucian family structure, the Chinese language, and social structure are hard, if not impossible, to reconstruct, let alone revive as a predominant originary source and living fountain of the whole Chinese thought (Zhang X., 2013). Zhang X. (2013) argues that Confucian scholars in current China need to recognize this hegemonic epistemicide issue, without which it is tough for them to embrace an alternative paradigm, alternative to the East–West developmental trope, to explicate "the existential-cultural-textual Confucian Being" (p. 11) nurtured within the Confucian primordial Text. Below I further clarify Zhang's unpacking of the effectuation of such epistemicide with the radical Chinese intelligentsia during the New Cultural Movement and demonstrate its impact on China's current education/curriculum reform discourses.

Epistemicide as Backward-East vs. Advanced-West Comparative Paradigms

The New Cultural Movement is often conflated with the May Fourth Movement in 1919, the so-called Renaissance or the Enlightenment in China (Yu, 2004; Hu, 1926; Schwarcz, 1986). The latter specifically refers to the students' patriotic movement as a protest against the then Chinese Northern Warlords Government that failed to protect China's interests in the post-World War I Versailles Treaty. However, the New Cultural Movement was incurred by the establishment of a radical journal in 1915, titled *New Youth* 新青年 (originally called *Youth Magazine* 青年雜誌 and changed to *New Youth* in 1916). This movement immediately gained the support of the then influential revolutionary thinkers such as Chen Duxiu, Li Dazhao, Lu Xun, Hu Shi, Cai Yuanpei 蔡元培, all having some personal experiences with the overseas science and technology. This New Cultural Movement accelerated the Westernization of the Chinese culture and system under the lofty flags of Western progressive "democracy" and "scientism." What is "new" about this cultural movement is that it severs the modern China nation-state from its Confucian cultural foundation by attributing China's defeat under the Western gunboat to its own "backward" culture, and to save the China nation needs to discard its own culture as a precondition (Zhang X., 2013). The Chinese radicals vehemently despised, opposed, and even called for the sheer eradication of what they claimed as the *deep-rooted and human-eating feudalist (mainly Confucian) rites-teaching*. In a word, the majority of the Chinese intelligentsia underwent a transformation in its subjectivity from Confucian cultural upholders/agents to depreciators.

Zhang X. (2013) maintains three factors have contributed to the happening of such collective self-demolition of Confucian culture by the intelligentsia: Yan Fu's 嚴復 deformed translation of Darwinism, a eugenic ordering principle, and the neighboring nation of Japan invoked as a "successful" exemplar. Yan Fu (1854–1921) translated the British biologist Thomas Henry Huxley's (1825–1895) book *Evolution and Ethics*, the latter a clarification of Charles Darwin's (1809–1882) evolution theory. According to Zhang (2013), Yan's translation manipulates Huxley's text to the extent that Yan rephrased Huxley's argument that "the only adaptable species will survive" as "only the powerful will survive" and even "the powerful will eat the weak and the wise will manipulate the silly" (see, p. 66, pp. 102–106). These deformed claims foreground *power* as a deciding factor in the ecological competition among species and glosses over Huxley's second point of ethical negotiation. This mentality of "only the powerful can survive" became an ordering principle to re-gauge the Chinese culture and system since then, *powerful* in the sense that *power* can be embodied and measurable materially, ideographically, institutionally, or epistemologically. Yan's claim was repackaged as a eugenic one when Chen Duxiu, in his *New Youth* article, claims that the weak or the inadaptable should be eliminated, justifying the Western science and democracy as the universal norm, as the life–death divisive line.

In Zhang's viewpoint, Japan played a significant role in molding the radical mentality of such Chinese radical expatriates as Lu Xun who inveighs the Confucian Chinese history and culture as "man-eating feudal dross." It also makes itself a "successful" example of development gained by discarding what they claimed the backward Chinese medicine for Western science and technology. Using Japan as a model, the Chinese medical practice was institutionally abandoned in 1929, giving its place to the Western medicine.

After the New Cultural Movement, the canonical Confucian culture was further disastrously eradicated during the Proletarian Cultural Revolution (1966–1976) as the "four olds"—old thought, culture, customs, and habits. This sweeping categorization of tradition as sheer backward rubbish gives its way to a strategic differentiation of tradition into essentially good and partially backward after the 1978 opening up and reform policy. The rising of the nationalistic Confucianism since the late 1980s invites tradition to creep back and gradually win out as honored and prized long tradition to be rejuvenated and promoted worldwide, a signal of which is the current global spreading of over 300 Confucius Schools. As the current Chinese catchphrase 與時俱進 (to progress with the time) puts, tradition needs to and more importantly *can* also advance with the times/era in the current globalized and globalizing world.

The Chinese language (*hanzi* 漢字) is the soul of the Chinese culture. However, the New Cultural Movement radicals belittled it as "the dirtiest and worst pit of the middle ages in the world" (漢字真正是世界上最齷齪最惡劣最混蛋的中世紀的毛坑) (Qu, 1931/1989, p. 247), a "tuberculosis carried by the Chinese masses who would die without removing the pathogens" (漢字也是中國勞苦大眾身上的一個結核，病菌都潛伏在裡頭。倘不首先除去它，結果只有自己死) (Lu, 1935), and thus "the first thing on the to-be-abolished list of Confucianism" (欲廢孔學不可不先廢漢文) (Qian, 1918). With the Western alphabetical languages as their eugenic standard, the radical intelligentsia inveighed the Chinese non-alphabetical language as backward, not easy to read and write, not clear in meaning, and not rigorous with its grammar, and henceforth not adaptive to the twentieth new century (Qian, 1918). Lu Xun (1935), a most radical thinker, critiqued the Chinese language as a powerful weapon for the feudal rulers to fool its subjects in China's man-eating history and exhorts the then Chinese youth to read foreign literature instead. A concurred call emerged to simplify and Romanize the Chinese language, which was partly enforced in 1955. Mao Zedong declared in 1951 that the Chinese language must undergo some reformation to jump on the popular *phonetic-language* wagon of the West (cited in Zhang, 2013, p. 80). This is a best example of a self-aligned epistemicide that eugenically lauds the Western science and democracy as the *only* universal truth and framework to exclude and even slaughter the Others.

Debates on China's modern education and curriculum reforms also fall prey to this East-Tradition versus West-Modernity paradigm through a few marked events. The Confucian Imperial Civil Examination (*keju* 科舉), a system of recruitment for civil officials based upon their competence in making meanings out of the Confucian classics, was abolished in 1905, and the Confucian reading-classics was ended in 1912 when Cai Yuanpei became the then Minister of Education. When Jinshi Daxuetang 京師大學堂, the precedent of Beijing University, was established in 1898 as a modern institute of the Confucian *taixue* 太學 and *guozijian* 國子監, and as the last imperial dynasty's endeavor to confront the Western cultural colonialism, it had eight disciplines prioritizing the Confucian Classics (*jingke* 经科) as number 1. However, Cai Yuanpei, as the 1917 president, abolished the Classics Discipline as a gesture for the university to go modern.

China's first modern curriculum system was established in 1922 when the Ministry of Education of the Republic of China issued the "School System Reform Decree" as an effect of the New Education Reform Movement in the context of the New Cultural Movement (see, e.g., Zhang H., 2014). Since the early twentieth century, China's school curriculum has been the experimental sites for varied foreign education reforms, including the Deweyian pragmatism (advocated by Jiang Menglin 蔣夢麟 and Tao Xingzhi 陶行知, John Dewey's students at the Teachers College), the Japanese school curriculum and American Batson model, the Soviet educator I. A. Kairov's knowledge–instruction and management model from the 1950s, and the current American social constructionism model focused on the child's humanistic and autonomous quality development since the 2001 Eighth Curriculum Standard Reform.

This Eighth Curriculum Reform is a best epitomic caricature of the East-tradition versus West-modernity developmental paradigm debate, which revolves around the (un)feasibility or (il)legitimacy of transplanting other cultural models on China's schooling soil in negotiation with the Chinese indigenous culture. This 8th Curriculum Reform ignites the well-known South-North debate between Shanghai East Normal University base led by Zhong Qiquan and Beijing Normal University base led by Wang Cesan. It is a theoretical debate between the social constructionism focused on a de-centralized child-autonomy and life-practice-related-knowledge training and the former Soviet knowledge-based centralized school-book-knowledge-only instruction curriculum paradigm (see, e.g., Wang C., 2004; Zhong & You, 2004; Zhang H., 2014).

Paraskeva (2016) claims that colonialism and coloniality are the two sides of the coin of epistemicide (p. 56). Colonialism, as Maldonado-Torres (2007) argues, speaks to the political and economic relation between the colonizer–nation/people and the colonized–nation/people. However, coloniality is the memory or legacy of the colonialism, which defines culture, labor, inter-subjective relation, and knowledge production well beyond the limits of colonialism and long after the end of a colonial administration. It "continues to be reborn through neoliberal hegemony as a pervasive power that has strong epistemological ties" (Paraskeva, p. 57). Below is a further unpacking of how such coloniality is expressed in post-socialist China's education and curriculum reform discourses as hegemonic styles of reasoning.

Globalized Discourses as Epistemicide in China's Education and Curriculum Reforms

Since the early twentieth century, the Chinese language started to become devoured by Western-introduced terminology and epistemology (Zhang X., 2013; Wang S., 2012) to the extent that Liu (1994) even argues the Chinese modernity is a translated modernity. Namely, when the modern Western terms enter into China, either traditional Chinese terms are re-invoked, or neologisms of monographical Chinese characters are coined, as their semantic glosses. Either way, the mode of translation often transfigures or overwrites the original cultural-historical senses as well as the epistemological meanings and rules nurtured within each monographical and ideographic Chinese character (*hanzi* 漢字) and the Chinese thought. For example, the modern Chinese term *wenhua* 文化, as a gloss of the English "culture," is re-invoked from its historical Yijing statement *yiwenhuatianxia* 以文化天下, literally saying "transforming (the world below the sky) with letters/literacy (not with weapons)." However, re-invoked as a semantic equivalent of "culture," *wenhua* becomes a modern concept signifying things like language and customs, eclipsing its original historical-cultural sensibilities nourished in the Yijing thought. This is what I mean by epistemicide as a result of the globalizing discourses since discourses are never merely language in use. Rather, discourses embody the epistemological rules grounding and structuring the way we think and act.

Since the early twentieth century, China's educational and curriculum discourses have also become Westernized at an unparalleled pace (Wu, 2014; Curran, 2014; Hayhoe, 2014), yet so far rarely recognized by educational policy makers, scholars, and school teachers. For example, such Western discourses as "learning outcome/competency, student-centered learning, lifelong learning, learning autonomy, teacher professionalization, task-based teaching, and professional development community" have already become the catchphrases in current China. Underpinning these discourses is an instrumental learning logic that orders education as an outcome-based and measurable process toward an industrial use end. Two examples will show us how these discourses and its predominant learning logic are eclipsing the cultural-educational sensibilities nurtured within such Chinese terms as *shide* 師德 (teaching and virtue), *shifan* 師範 (teaching and modeling), and *suyang* 素養 (pure and nurturing) in ordering the modes of being of teaching, learning, and teacher–student engagement. In other words, how is it possible for the globalized discourses and now internationalization to become the apparatus of the hidden form of epistemicide? Through them, modern Western epistemologies have been expanding the very process and significance of "what is to think" (Paraskeva, 2016, p. 241), a form of coloniality that continues to define the culture and knowledge production in post-colonial or de-colonialist landscapes.

The first example is China's National Teacher Training Plan for Grades 1–12 In-Service School Teachers initiated in 2010 by the Ministry of Education and Finance. The plan (2010–2015) has a total budget of 0.55 billion RMB (approximately 84 million US dollars) and aims to "train a batch of *seed teachers* 種子教師 who could play a *key modeling* role 骨幹示範作用 in further promoting quality education and teacher training" in China (MOE, 2010, National Training Notice). In 2012, a 583-page *National Training Curriculum* was compiled, covering 67 modules for training K–12 subject teachers, classroom management teachers, as well as teacher-trainers. Between 2010 and 2015, over 7 million frontline school teachers were trained, forming a large cohort of teacher-trainers at provincial, municipal, county, and school levels (MOE News Brief, 2015). From 2016 on, the Plan aims to train principals from mid-west suburban schools, hoping to systemize teacher training as a regular practice. In a word, China has now formed a nationwide "multi-leveled, multi-disciplinary, and multi-functional teacher training network" (MOE, 2010, National Training Notice).

I have elsewhere (2017) examined this *National Training Curriculum* as entangled discourses, or styles of reasoning, of Confucian cultural theses, modern Tyler curriculum rationality, and a representational-conceptual mode of signification. Put simply, the Confucian notion of *shide* 師德

(literally teaching + virtue) as a way of being woven into a Confucian "teaching-virtue-modeling-transforming" grid of intelligibility has already given its way to a modern reconceptualization of it as a form of knowledge that can be anticipated, learned, and evaluated along a self-justified Tyler curriculum rationale. The *National Training Curriculum* text depicts *shide* as a concept, semantically relating itself to the ideas of "mission, responsibility, professional idealism, self-cognition, career development, teacher–student relationship, cooperation with fellow teachers, pressures, home-school communication." That is, the notion of *shide* has already become an empty linguistic signifier, grammatically divided into and also re-assembling the above set of segments as signified, and the evaluation of *shide*-training is effectuated by collecting technological evidence of various kinds that may be fitted into these segment categories.

This mode of signification foregrounds language as an enclosed symbolic system that assumes a priori existence of grammatical arrangements in a language, and infer meaning from the horizontal grammatical arrangements within and between sentences. Imprisoned, we no longer listen to the epistemological murmuring of the Chinese notion of *shide* 師德 (literally teaching + virtue) as a way of being woven into a Confucian "teaching-virtue-modeling-transforming" grid of intelligibility. This semantic transfiguration of Confucian notions into modern concepts as a form of epistemicide is best expressed by the current Chinese intelligentsia's persistent, albeit unconscious, attempt to define China's latest *suyang* curriculum reform, which is my second example.

With the latest global-wise twenty-first-century educational reforms spearheaded by OECD's core competencies and US core skills, China also jumped on the twenty-firstcore competencies/skills wagon to hopefully and proactively keep Chinese students and talents globally competitive. The signature document, titled *Core Suyang Definitions for Chinese Student Development*, was released in September 2016 as a product of a three-year state-commissioned research project which involved a cohort of up to 100 university researchers across China. This team consulted 15 international and regional twenty-first-century student development schemes, interviewed 608 people from 12 professions, surveyed 566 experts, scholars, school principals, and entrepreneurs, and held 60 consultation meetings and 20 discussion meetings (Ministry of Education, 2016).

This *Core Suyang Definitions*, involving three domains, six core categories, and 18 key definitions (complete version available at http://aic-fe.bnu.edu.cn/xwdt/skxx/17740.html) claims to hopefully fulfill three missions: to enact China's human-based educational mission of *establishing people with virtue* (*yideshuren* 以德樹人) proposed at the Third Plenary Session of the 18th CCP (Chinese Communist Party) Central Committee; to enhance China's educational competitiveness across the globe; and to initiate a new round of China's quality-based curriculum reform (Ministry of Education, 2016). The Chinese core *suyang* primarily refers to "the necessary character traits (*pinge* 品格) and key competencies that 21st-century students will need to adapt to their lifelong development and the development of the society" (ibid.). These combined character traits and key competencies are to cultivate an "all-around person" and claim to align with the Chinese (Confucian) cultural tradition of "learning, body/self-cultivation, and governing" (see, e.g., Lin, 2016).

This latest curriculum reform bespeaks a double vision of post-socialist China development, going global and re-vitalizing the Chinese culture. Accordingly, the cultural term *suyang* is re-invoked as a replacement of *suzhi*, commonly glossed as *quality* in quality education, foregrounding China's explicit focus on character traits as a theme distinct from OECS's competency scheme and the US twenty-first-century learning outcome outline. However, the way how the well-established Chinese scholars endeavor to define *suyang* belies a self-aligned confinement to the planetary signifier–signified mode of signification as a form of epistemicide. Worse still, they relentlessly try to define *suyang* through the contours of English notions of competency, skill, and literacy (see, e.g., Chu, 2016; Zhong, 2016; Cui, 2016; Li & Zhong, 2015; Zhang H., 2016; Liu, 2014). Here is an example by a well-known curriculum scholar in China:

> *Suyang* has competence or competency as its English gloss with a Latin root of competere. Etymologically, competence/competency signifies a gathering of varied abilities or powers, enabling a person to cope with a situation. With competere, com- means together, petere means to seek, drive forward. Put together, competere means to strive together (to cope with situations). To sum up, *suyang* in the first place signifies the comprehensive competencies needed when coping with a situation appropriately. Essentially, *suyang* is a state of being or competency of human beings.
>
> (Zhang H., 2016, my translation)

The above discursive reasoning entails a grammatical and semantic slippage from *suyang* to *competence*, which is justified by a presumed transparency principle of translation. Namely, a signifier–signified understanding of language legitimizes the assumed equivalence between the signifiers of *suyang* and *competence* in referring to the same semantic signified. Even though what is etymologically and grammatically clarified is *competence*, *suyang* is vicariously defined through the semantic contours of *competence*. What is etymologically said with *competence* is relayed to *suyang*. Furthermore, the scholar concludes "to sum up, *suyang* in the first place signifies the comprehensive competencies needed when coping with a situation appropriately. Essentially *suyang* is a state of being or competency of human beings." Here "a state of being" and "competence/ability" are categorically distinct, yet they are grammatically conflated with a particle of "or." What grounds such a semantic relay is a signifier–signified mode of reasoning, the linking of one idea with another through grammatical representation, which treats *suyang* as an empty signifier with its signified, i.e., the idea of competence. As a result, what is said is not *suyang* itself, but *suyang* as a gloss of competency through competency.

This is the taking-place of epistemicide or epistemological colonialism, expressed as a discourse-reasoning trope through translation that confronts China's academia and its education/curriculum reform, among other fields. The epistemological crisis is confined to what Foucault says as the trap of philosophy and a signifier–signified style of reasoning. To be specific, the very effort of defining *suyang* as a concept to be filled up with semantic signified itself presumes the a priori existence of *suyang* as a modern concept, not as a historical assemblage of the Chinese monographic characters of *su* + *yang* (素+养). Having fallen into such a trap, the epistemological quest is delimited to "what does *suyang* mean semantically?" or "what *is* suyang?", and we no longer delve into the saying and being of *suyang* itself. Accordingly, we treat *suyang* as an empty signifier, a receptacle, trying to fill it up with varied signified of competency, skill, and literacy, the so-called Western curriculum superdiscourses (Autio, 2006, 2007, 2014).

Seen this way, the popularization of Western superdiscourses does speak volumes about one of the most important aspects of the modern Western coloniality. A homogenization of thesaurus in the non-Western world indeed paves a "specific" understanding of how curriculum and education, among other topics, are said and reasoned, which possibly causes a self-aligned "academic aphasia" (Shi-xu, 2016) in the non-Western world. By self-aligned, it means the intelligentsia would not realize the brain-washing themselves. Beneath such a Westernization of Chinese discourses is a replacement of style of reasoning, namely, the traditional Confucian exegesis that traces meaning to the historical Classics for the originary saying of each Chinese character (to be further clarified in Chapter 3), by the modern conceptual mode of signification, which presumes meaning-making within the synchronic arraignments of language system. The pre-modern Chinese ways of knowing and thinking were perceived as unintelligible and backward as against the "universal" latter. As Paraskeva (2016) observes,

> The production and reproduction of hegemonic forms of knowledge are precisely the institutionalizations of a linguistic or cultural epistemicide that cannot be delinked from the modes and conditions of production, especially today, that more than ever before, have been treated as a commodity.
>
> (p. 241)

In this light, "language does play a key role in the decolonial turn" (p. 237) in that it provides a significant way to expose the issue of coloniality for new openings.

Re-engaging Ancient and Modern Chinese Thought in the Twenty-First Century: Caution Against a Cultural Relativist Stand

Over the past few decades, some Chinese scholars, mostly with cross-cultural intellectual experiences and some homegrown, started to address the epistemological crisis in China studies regarding its knowledge, discourses, culture, and education, among other topics. Whether in the name of re-vitalizing the Chinese culture or not, one common strategy is to re-invoke ancient Chinese wisdom, including Yijing, Confucian, Daoist, and Buddhist schools of thought, as "originary" (re)source of the entire Chinese thought, hoping to envision new paradigms to hopefully explicate the Chinese styles of reasoning beyond the Western framework so as to shed new light on today's thinking and practices in China and beyond.

I borrow the term "originary" mainly from Heidegger (1969) who treats the past as an "originary" source in such a way that it is not reducible to what has been thought. It always nourishes something that has not been thought, which in turn sets free traditional thinking. To Heidegger, the force of conversing with the historical tradition is not to be sought in something that has already been thought but in what has not yet been thought, even though what has been thought prepares what has not yet been thought. This past "prevails throughout the tradition in an originary way, is always in being in advance of it, and yet is never expressly thought in its own right and as the Originary" (pp. 48–49). Agamben (2009) takes this "originary" source as a point "where something remains obscure and un-thematized," a point an archaeological inquiry would often retrace and take up, further revealing what is unsaid in the originary source (p. 8).

Here I focus on two areas, philosophy and education, the former as the originary source of knowledge and system of reason, which further grounds the latter. In the field of philosophy, Zhang Xianglong 張祥龍 (1992, 1996) unpacks an intrinsic connection between Heidegger's thinking and the Chinese Daoism in what he terms "the horizontal-regional way of thinking," as an alternative to the mainstream Western yet already planetary conceptual or dichotomous way of thinking. This horizontal-regional way of thinking signifies a reciprocal belonging of yin-yang-like bipolar opponents, traceable and nurtured within the Chinese Dao which indeed criss-crosses the Chinese Yijing, Confucian, and Daoist thinking. Recently, Zhang Xianglong (2013) calls for a rethinking of modern China's destruction if not demolition of its Confucian culture as an effect of the Western colonialism and imperialism, effectuated by the radical intelligentsia of the New Cultural Movement in the name of pursuing the advanced Western modernity to replace the backward Chinese Confucian culture and system. Only by exposing such self-aligned collective epistemicide, can we modern Chinese Confucian scholars constrain and clear this Western coloniality in a way for some originary Confucian thinking to re-emerge. As case studies, Zhang (2013, 2015) explicates the Confucian living family structure and its concomitant inter-generational familial relationship (parental love or filial piety) as a possible originary horizon for Confucian thinking, which can complement the mainstream Western presentism and logocentric metaphysics.

Also inspired by Heidegger's critique of the Western logocentric metaphysics as embodied in its language and grammar, Wang Shuren 王樹人 (2012) since the 1980s has been explicating a Chinese xiang-style of reasoning (象思維) as an alternative to the mainstream Western(ized) conceptual style of reasoning and a subject–object binary logic. Drawing upon Heidegger's notions of Dasein and Ereignis, Wang unpacks the Chinese xiang-style of reasoning as its originary source, first embodied in the Yijing hexagram image, lines, and numbers and further expanded in Laozi's Dao and Zhuangzi's texts. This xiang-style of reasoning is coeval with the conceptual style of reasoning, albeit in the modern era the former has been marginalized and concealed by the latter. Only by suspending and bracketing the latter can the former self-reveal by itself. Compared to the conceptual style of reasoning, the xiang-style of reasoning is holistic, non-conceptual, embodied and experienced intuitively, and their movement can be analogically interpreted through the Dao De Jing statement, "to know the white, one has to remain with the black" (知其白守其黑) (Chapter 28). An onto-hermeneutic Yijing notion *guan* (observing), Wang claims, could help attune one to the xiang-style of reasoning to approach the ontological Dao. This book will expand on the Yijing *guan-observing* as an onto-epistemological theme that orders the genesis of Chinese knowledge, thought, and education in Chapter 4.

Zhang Zailin 張再林 (2008, 2015) proposes an ontological Chinese "body-Dao" (*shendao* 身道), namely, Dao is coeval with the material living and being, which is akin to what the Taiwanese–American scholar Wu Kuang-Ming 吳光明 (1997) calls "body-thinking" in contradistinction to the mainstream Western Platonic mind-thinking. By body-thinking, it means body ontologically thinks, and thinking embodies itself in bodily engagements. It is not that thinking has a bodily dimension; rather, thinking is body experiencing and vice versa. Similarly, by an ontological "body-Dao," Zhang Z. (2015) vociferates a double dimension of the ancient Chinese thought, attributable to the Yijing thought as its originary source and expressed for example in the co-movement between the two trigrams of *qian* (sky) and *kun* (earth). Specifically, the *kun*-trigram foregrounds an intuitive and submissive following and attuning to the Dao movement whereas the *qian*-trigram accents an incessant self-strengthening through hard work. The former is further elaborated in the Chinese Daoist thinking while the latter in the Confucian thinking, and their mutual reciprocity has guaranteed their respective growth and sustainability in historical China (see, pp. 285–291).

Intriguingly, these scholars leverage upon the post-modern or post-structural critique of the mainstream Western thinking as a method to help them re-approach the Chinese styles of thought in its genealogy. Such a methodological gesture, however, also runs a risk of applying the Western frameworks as a "norm" to gauge the non-Western epistemologies. Paraskeva's unpacking of the fundamentalist bent within the critical curriculum studies is a good alert for us here, a precaution against romanticizing non-Western epistemologies and reinstating a functional relativist cultural stand back into the epistemological crisis on a cross-cultural landscape. Ahmad (2008) for example claims that our task is to de-mystify the very category of non-modern Western epistemologies in the way it emerges "in metropolitan universities [as] something of a counter-cannon and which—like any cannon, dominant or emergent—does not exist before its fabrication" (p. 45).

Original as these research projects are in seeking new paradigms for understanding the Chinese thought and culture and to address the epistemological crisis in current China as a continued effect of Western coloniality, these dimensions have not informed educational researchers to rethink or re-envision education and knowledge in China. For example, even though "body" starts to come back to the Asian educational field, it gains curriculum scholars' attention mainly through Foucault's *Discipline and Punishment* or the Western art-based educational research paradigm. The given-ness of the Chinese educative "body" as an object itself has rarely been problematized ethnographically and historically in the Chinese context.

In the field of education studies, some scholars start to recognize that Confucian educational culture, as a prototype of modern China's educational thinking and practice, is not always compatible with the Western epistemologies. Lee and Kerry (2017) compares the similarities and differences between the Chinese and European theories of teaching and learning. Henceforth, transplanting uncritically Western educational theories, concepts, pedagogies, discourses, practices, as well as research methodologies into the Chinese context may cause tensions and problems (Schulte, 2012; Tan, 2015; Yang, 2007, 2011; Bai, 2010; Cai & Jin, 2010; *Comparative Education* 47(3), 2011). For example, grafting American academic practices in current China's modern education has resulted in an unbalanced rush for economic catch-up and a go global mentality at the cost of neglecting its Confucian cultural context (Yang, 2011). A melding of China's powerful examination tradition, the central neoliberal notion of human capital, and the competitive market resulting from decentralization and financial diversification has generated an "ironic impasse"; and beneath the masks of modernization and student-centeredness, inequalities thrive (Bai, 2010). Overall, a returning to or reviving of a contextual understanding of traditional Confucian value is called for to restore China's current education back to its health (Evers & Mason, 2011).

Many comparative studies have also identified factors such as students' hard work, parents' high expectation, lots of practice, respect for teachers, discipline in class, a focus on moral values, and a didactic teaching as attributes or indicators of a Confucian educational culture (Tan, 2011, 2013, 2015; Cai & Jin, 2010). A high value on all the above contributes to students' educational success in Asian countries, say, Shanghai students' outstanding PISA performance in 2009 and 2011, the so-called PISA-shock to the rest of the world. Tan (2015) argues that such cultural beliefs on teaching are traceable to a Confucian worldview on knowledge and knowledge acquisition as expressed in *Xueji* (Record of Learning), a Confucian classical text with only 1,229 Chinese characters within 22 sections. She describes *Xueji* as the epistemological basis for such cultural views that philosophically justifies the teacher-dominated pedagogy still valued in current China, which also adjudicates the mediated assimilation of the Western student-centered learning in the Chinese indigenous contexts.

The Shanghai PISA-shock has made the Chinese Confucian educational culture a "new reference society in the global education policy field," engendering a "looking east" fad (Sellar & Lingard, 2013) and a "two-way policy transfer" (Forestier & Crossley, 2015) between Asian countries and the West. For example, in the summer of 2015, the Bohunt School in the United Kingdom invited five teachers from China to teach four weeks using traditional Chinese teaching methods as an experimental Chinese school. Although the didactic teaching, strict discipline in class, long school hours, and rote memorization were strongly resisted by the British students at least at the very beginning, the Chinese school nevertheless well outperformed its British counterparts in the exams of all the subjects taught. The BBC covered the experiment as a documentary titled "Are our kids tough enough?" (2015), and its broadcasting did incur another wave of global discussion on the Chinese (Confucian) style of teaching and learning, and its apparent (in)compatibility with the Western student-centered pedagogy.

The Chinese Confucian style of teaching and learning, albeit in its full strive to go global, is often stereotypically depicted as being "hierarchical, rigid, and lacking creativity and imagination" (Di, 2016, p. 42). However, with the reviving nationalist Confucianism and Shanghai students' recent excellent PISA performance, Confucian educational culture has re-emerged as a hot topic nationally and internationally, and with a shifting paradigm. Scholars, especially Asian-American scholars, have started to re-invoke Chinese ancient cultures, say, Yijing, Confucian, Daoist, and Buddhist thought, for new implications to enrich and inform the educational scholarship in North America. For example, Jing Lin et al. (2016) and Jing Lin (2013) have been investigating a Confucian paradigm to inform the emerging contemplative education scholarship in the United States. Mei Hoyt (2016) has been unpacking the mindful Buddhist body for implications for mindful education in classrooms. Hongyu Wang (2014) has been investigating Daoist thought to complement peace education and neo-Daoist Chinese psychology and Jung for reciprocation. Seungho Moon (2015) has unpacked Daoist notion of *wuwei* (non-action) to revise American education reform.

Furthermore, other scholars have begun to reject stereotypical labels of Chinese educational philosophy and pedagogy as "hierarchical, rigid, and lacking creativity and imagination" (Di, 2016, p. 42). These labels are at best simplistic (mis)interpretations from a Western perspective, which do not genuinely reflect the complexity and diversity of Confucius' or the early Confucian educational thinking. Instead, as Di (2016) reviews, scholars argue the stereotypical Chinese "rote memorization" can be multilayered and multidimensional (Marton, Dall'Alba, &Tse, 1996; Pratt, Kelly, & Wong, 1999) and effectuates a deep and strategic, not surface, learning (Chalmers & Volet, 1997; Nield, 2007), legitimizing a "paradox of the Chinese learner" (Watkins & Biggs, 2001).

Against one Western criticism of Confucianism as hierarchical, one-dimensional and conservative, Sigurdsson (2017) evokes a relational-social "transformative self-critical attitude" in the early Confucian philosophy to broaden and enrich the Western individualistic concept of critical thinking. With such a critical attitude, a Confucian learner makes "ongoing and never wholly attainable effort to transform oneself to become fully human" (p. 139), overcoming an initially exclusive ego toward becoming a relational-social being. Wu (2011, 2014) elaborates the teacher–disciple dialogues in *Lunyu* as a critical pedagogical form which can transfigure the monotonous didactic pedagogy in current China. The author (Zhao, 2015) has alternatively re-envisioned a (Chinese) teacher–student relationship along a Confucian harmonizing co-belonging, exploding a power-based hierarchical versus egalitarian ordering pendulum. The Chinese 2016 moral education curriculum has re-invoked a Chinese Daoist co-being with sensibility (Zhao & Sun, 2017).

Two newly edited collections are noteworthy in terms of reconnecting modern China with its classical educational root so as to re-envision current Chinese education in a global context: Di and McEwan's (2016) *Chinese Philosophy on Teaching and Learning: Xueji* (學記) *in the Twenty-First Century* with a new translation of the classical text, and Zhao G. and Deng's (2016) *Re-envisioning Chinese Education: The Meaning of Person-Making in a New Age*. Albeit far from being exhaustive of Confucian literature on teaching and learning, these two books sufficiently reiterate the key characteristics of the Confucian philosophy of education as rooted and expressed in *Lunyu*, *Xueji*, and *Daxue*, among which I pinpoint the below four themes for two purposes. First, these four themes provide a basic yet latest understanding of the gist of Confucian teaching and learning to readers of English. Second, I lay them out as a backdrop to foreground the contribution and significance of my unpacking of Confucius' educational vision as expressed in *Yijing* in Chapters 4 and 5.

Here are the four themes of Confucian educational thinking. First, there exists a congruence between Confucian education and state governance such that "the Confucian state was a large-scale metaphorical school where the ruler–subordinator relationship was reframed to that of the teacher–learner" (Han, 2013, p. 57). Seen this way, the notions of Confucian teaching and learning, though often expediently conflated with modern notions of teaching and learning, is much broader than the modern delimiting psychology–cognition-based learning of individuals (Jarvis, 2010). That is, Confucianism is embedded within a relational Chinese cosmology that pinpoints a congruence of personal, social, political, and cosmic order and governance. Second, Confucian ideals of learning entail not only an acquisition of knowledge but more important a learning of Dao (Chen, 2016), through which a person can transform oneself into a consummate person (*junzi* 君子) who embodies both "inner sagehood and outer kingliness" (*neisheng waiwang* 內聖外王) (Ke, 2016). Furthermore, Confucian teaching and learning are enacted through relational roles each person assumes in family and community, constituting what Ames (2011, 2016) calls a "Confucian role ethics," and Confucian state governance is ideally attained when each person is transformed to maintain a proper self-governance.

Third, Confucian teaching and learning are constitutive of each other as the two halves of a whole, an overriding theme expressed in *Xueji* (Di and McEwan, 2016). Etymologically, the ancient Chinese characters for teaching (*xiao* 教) and learning (*xue* 學) are almost homophonous and homographic, sharing a "kid" graph 子 and a graph for a hand holding a bamboo brush 聿, with the extra graph 冂 in learning (*xue* 學), gesturing a sense of being blind/unenlightened. This holistic understanding of teaching and learning challenges means-end thinking and re-integrates teaching and learning into a dynamic movement wherewith one accelerates and deepens the other (Ames, 2016). Finally, unlike the Western Socrates-like teacher who sets an example or model in the distance, the Confucian *junzi*-like teacher *is* an exemplary model of engagements, "a person who is directly working with his pupils, as both learner and teacher, in shaping conduct" (McEwan, 2016, p. 69). This modeling sense symbolizes a Chinese teacher or teaching such that learning is to imitate and follow what teachers do.

To summarize, Confucian learning is primarily to *transform oneself* into a consummate person, and Confucian teaching as governing is to *transform others*. Then how is it possible for such a "transforming" theme to construe and construct Confucius' vision of teaching and learning? What images can be evoked to help understand Confucius' vision of teaching as governing and governing by transforming? My unpacking in Chapter 3 of Confucius' "wind-pedagogy" as expressed in *Yijing* aims to answer these unexplored questions.

These research projects, informative as they are, are done along with a common what-is logic, mapping out the features, contents, and scripts of what is called Confucian education culture. It doesn't historicize Confucian educational culture in its historical context. It treats canonized Confucian culture as a tradition, not as an event or happening. This book aims to complement and supplement this set of scholarship by a historical-archaeological and language perspective to address the epistemicide issue as an effect of both comparative paradigm and globalized discourses. The next two chapters move onto unpacking these two methodological-theoretical perspectives, which can constrain the double challenges in mapping out Chinese educational sensibilities on a global landscape: (a) largely globalized modern language, and (b) a rising nationalistic Confucian ideology. Then how is it possible to read the Confucian values back in history and re-envision it in present China's education as an intersection of past and present as well as East and West? This calls for a better understanding of the broader comparative studies as a method and a field.

References

Agamben, G. (2009). *The signature of all things: On method*. New York, NY: Zone Books.
Ahmad, A. (2008). *In theory*. London, UK: Verso.
Ames, R. T. (2011). *Confucian role ethics: A Vocabulary*. Hong Kong: Chinese University Press.
Ames, R. T. (2016). On teaching and learning (Xueji 學記): Setting the root in Confucian education. In X. Di & H. McEwan (Eds.), *Chinese philosophy on teaching and learning: Xueji (學記) in the twenty-first century* (pp. 21–38). Albany, NY: State University of New York Press.
Apple, M. (1990). *Ideology and curriculum*. New York, NY: Routledge.
Apple, M. (2000). *Official Knowledge: Democratic education in a conservative age*. New York, NY: Routledge.
Autio, T. (2006). *Subjectivity, curriculum and society: Between and beyond the German didaktik and Anglo-American curriculum studies*. New York, NY: Routledge.
Autio, T. (2007, February). Towards European curriculum studies: Reconsidering some basic tenets of building and didaktik. *Journal of the American Association for the Advancement of Curriculum Studies, 3*. Retrieved August 8, 2017, from http://ojs.library.ubc.ca/index.php/jaaacs/article/viewFile/187654/185757
Autio, T. (2014). The internationalization of curriculum studies. In W. F. Pinar (Ed.), *The international handbook of curriculum research* (2nd ed., pp. 17–31). New York, NY: Routledge.
Bai, L. M. (2010). Human capital or humane talent? Rethinking the nature of education in China from a comparative historical perspective. *Frontiers of Education in China, 5*(1), 104–129.
BBC. (2015). Are our kids tough enough? Retrieved from www.bbc.co.uk/programmes/b06565zm
Bernstein, B. (1977). *Class, codes and control* (Vol. 3). London, UK: Routledge and Kegan Paul.
Blumenfeld-Jones, D. (2016). The violence of words, words of violence: Keeping the uncomfortable at bay, a Jewish perspective. *Journal of Curriculum Theorizing, 31*(1), 4–12.
Cai, B., & Jin, Y. (2010). Woguo jichujiaoyu gaige de xianshi jingyu yu weilai jueze [Realistic circumstances and future choices of reform in basic education in China 我国基础教育改革的现实境遇与未来抉择]. *Journal of Shanghai Normal University* (Philosophy & Social Sciences Edition), *39*(1), 92–102.
Chakrabarty, D. (2000). *Provincializing Europe: Postcolonial thought and historical difference*. Princeton, NJ: Princeton University Press.

Chalmers, D., & Volet, S. (1997). Common misconceptions about students from South-East Asia studying in Australia. *Higher Education Research & Development*, 16(1), 87–99.

Chen, L. (2016). The ideas of "educating" and "learning" in Confucian thought. In X. Di & H. McEwan (Eds.), *Chinese philosophy on teaching and learning: Xueji (學記) in the twenty-first century* (pp. 77–96). Albany, NY: State University of New York Press.

Chu, H. Q. (2016). Hexinsuyang de gainian yu benzhi [The concept and meaning of core suyang 核心素养的概念与本质]. *Huashidaxuebao [Journal of east China Normal University]*, 34(1), 1–3.

Cui, Y. H. (2016). Suyang: yige rangren huanxi rangrenyou de gainian [Suyang as a contested concept 素养：一个让人欢喜让人忧的概念]. *Huashidaxuebao [Journal of east China Normal University]*, 34(1), 3–5.

Curran, T. D. (2014). A response to Professor Wu Zongjie's 'Interpretation, autonomy, and transformation: Chinese pedagogic discourse in a cross-cultural perspective'. *Journal of Curriculum Studies*, 46(3), 305–312.

Di, X. (2016). The teaching and learning principles of Xueji (學記) in the educational practice of the world today. In X. Di & H. McEwan (Eds.), *Chinese philosophy on teaching and learning: Xueji (學記) in the twenty-first century* (pp. 39–60). Albany, NY: State University of New York Press.

Di, X., & McEwan, H. (Eds.). (2016). *Chinese philosophy on teaching and learning: Xueji (學記) in the twenty-first century*. Albany, NY: State University of New York Press.

Evers, C. W., & Mason, M. (2011). Context based inferences in research methodology: The role of culture in justifying knowledge claims. *Comparative Education*, 47(3), 301–314.

Forestier, K., & Crossley, M. (2015). International education policy transfer- borrowing both ways: The Hong Kong and England experience. *Compare: A Journal of Comparative and International Education*, 45(5), 664–685.

Foucault, M. (1973). *The order of things: An archaeology of the human sciences*. New York, NY: Vintage Books. (Original work published 1966)

Giroux, H. (1980). Beyond the correspondence theory: Notes on the dynamics of educational reproduction and transformation. *Curriculum Inquiry*, 10(3), 225–247.

Giroux, H. (1983). *Theory and resistance in education: Towards a pedagogy for the opposition*. New York, NY: Bergin and Garvey.

Han, S. (2013). Confucian states and learning life: Making scholar-officials and social learning a political contestation. *Comparative Education*, 49(1), 57–71.

Hayhoe, R. (2014). Hopes for Confucian pedagogy in China? *Journal of Curriculum Studies*, 46(3), 313–319.

Heidegger, M. (1969). *Identity and difference* (J. Stambaugh, Trans. with an Introduction). New York, NY, Evanston, IL and London, UK: Harper & Row Publishers. (Original work published 1957)

Heidegger, M. (1978). Letter on humanism. In D. F. Krell (Ed.), *Basic writings* (pp. 213–265). London, UK: Routledge.

Hoyt, M. (2016). Teaching with mindfulness: The pedagogy of being-with/for and without being-with/for. *Journal of Curriculum Theorizing*, 31(1), 126–142.

Hu, S. (1926). The renaissance in China. *Journal of the Royal Institute of International Affairs*, 5(6), 265–283.

Jarvis, P. (2010). *Adult education and lifelong learning: Theory and practice*. London, UK: Routledge.

Ke, X. (2016). Person-making and citizen-making in Confucianism and their implications on contemporary moral education in China. In G. P. Zhao & Z. Y. Deng (Eds.), *Re-envisioning Chinese education: The meaning of person-making in a new age* (pp. 116–129). New York, NY: Routledge.

Lawless, K. (2014). Constructing the "other": Construction of Russian identity in the discourse of James Bond films. *Journal of Multicultural Discourses*, 9(2), 79–97.

Lee, J. C. K., & Kerry, K. J. (Eds.). (2017). *Theorizing teaching and learning in Asia and Europe*. Oxon and New York, NY: Routledge.

Li, Y., & Zhong, B. C. (2015). Tan "hexinsuyang" [On core suyang 談"核心素養"]. *Jiaoyuyanjiu [Eduacation Research]*, 428(9), 17–23.

Lin, J. (2013). Education for transformation and an expanded self: Paradigm shift for wisdom education. In J. Lin, R. L. Oxford, & E. J. Brantmeier (Eds.), *Re-envisioning higher education: Embodied pathways to wisdom and social transformation* (pp. 23–32). Charlotte, NC: Information Age Publishing.

Lin, J., Culham, T., & Oxford, R. (2016). Developing a spiritual research paradigm: A Confucian perspective. In J. Lin, R. Oxford, & T. Culham (Eds.), *Toward a spiritual research paradigm: Exploring new ways of knowing, researching and being* (pp. 141–170). Charlotte, NC: Information Age Publishing.

Liu, L. H. (1994). *Translingual practice: Literature, national culture, and translated modernity China 1900–1937*. Stanford, CA: Stanford University Press.

Liu, X. L. (2014). Cong "suzhi" dao "hexinsuyang"—guanyu "peiyang shenmeyang de ren" de jinyibu zhuiwen [From shushi to core suyang: Further explorations on the cultivation of school subjects 从"素质"到"核心素养"—关于"培养什么样的人"的进一步追问]. *Jiaoyukexueyanjiu [Educational Science Research]*, 3, 5–11.

Lu, X. (1935). Guanyu xin wenzi [On new Chinese writing and language 關於新文字]. *Ke Guan*, 1(3), 13.

Maldonado-Torres, N. (2007). On the coloniality of being. *Cultural Studies*, 21(2–3), 240–270.

Marton, F., Dall'Alba, G., &Tse, L. K. (1996). Memorizing and understanding: The keys to the paradox? In D. A. Waktins & J. B. Biggs (Eds.), *The Chinese learner: Cultural, psychological and contextual influences* (pp. 69–83). Hong Kong and Melbourne, Australia: Comparative Education Research Centre and Australian Council for Educational Research.

McEwan, H. (2016). Conduct, method, and care of the soul: A comparison of pedagogies in Confucian and Western thought. In X. Di & H. McEwan (Eds.), *Chinese philosophy on teaching and learning: Xueji (學記) in the twenty-first century* (pp. 61–76). Albany, NY: State University of New York Press.

Ministry of Education. (2016). Zhongguo Xuesheng Fazhan Suyang [Core Suyang Definitions for Chinese Student Development 中国学生发展素养]. Retrieved September 13, 2016, from www.jyb.cn/basc/sd/201609/t20160914_673105.html

MOE. (2010). National training notice on implementing the national teacher training plan. Retrieved from www.gov.cn

MOE News Brief. (2015). National training plan achievement in its 5-year implementation. Retrieved from www.gov.cn

Moon, S. (2015). Wuwei (non-action) philosophy and actions: Rethinking "actions" in school reform. *Educational Philosophy and Theory, 47*(5), 455–473.
Nguyen, P., Elliott, J., Terlouw, C., & Pilot, A. (2009). Neocolonialism in education: Cooperative learning in an Asian context. *Comparative Education, 45*(1), 109–130.
Nield, K. (2007). Understanding the Chinese learner: A case study exploration of the notion of the Hong Kong Chinese learner as a rote or strategic learner. *Journal of Hospitality, Sport, Leisure, and Tourism Education, 6*(1), 1–10.
Ossewaarde, M. (2014). The national identities of the 'death of multiculturalism' discourse in Western Europe. *Journal of Multicultural Discourses, 9*(3), 173–189.
Paraskeva, J. M. (2011). *Conflicts in curriculum theory: Challenging hegemonic epistemologies*. New York, NY: Palgrave Macmillan.
Paraskeva, J. M. (2016). *Curriculum epistemicide: Towards an itinerant curriculum theory*. New York, NY: Routledge.
Pinar, W. (1980). Life history and education experience. *Journal of Curriculum Theorizing, 2*(2), 159–212.
Pratt, D. D., Kelly, M., & Wong, W. S. S. (1999). Chinese conceptions of "effective teaching" in Hong Kong: Towards culturally sensitive evaluation of teaching. *International Journal of Lifelong Education, 18*(4), 241–258.
Qian, X. T. (1918). Zhongguo jinhou de wenzi wenti [The writing and language issue in China from now on. 中國今後的 文字問題]. *Xin Qingnian [New Youth], 4*(4), 350.
Qu, Q. B. (1931/1989). Putong zhongguohua de ziyan de yanjiu [Study on Chinese language. 普通中國話的字眼的研究]. In *Qu Qiubai Wenji [Collected works by Qu Qiubai Volume 3]* (pp. 240–250). Beijing: Renmin Wenxue Chubanshe.
Said, E. W. (1979). *Orientalism*. New York, NY: Vintage.
Saussy, H. (2001). Outside the parenthesis (those people were a kind of solution). In H. Saussy (Ed.), *The Great Walls of discourse and other adventures in cultural China* (pp. 146–182). Cambridge, MA: Harvard University Press.
Schulte, B. (2012). World culture with Chinese characteristics: When global models go native. *Comparative Education, 48*(4), 473–486.
Schwarcz, V. (1986). *The Chinese enlightenment: Intellectuals and the legacy of the May Fourth Movement of 1919*. Los Angeles, CA: University of California Press.
Sellar, S., & Lingard, B. (2013). Looking East: Shanghai, PISA 2009 and the reconstitution of reference societies in the global education policy field. *Comparative Education, 49*(4), 464–485.
Shi-xu. (2016). Cultural discourse studies through the Journal of Multicultural Discourses: 10 years on. *Journal of Multicultural Discourse, 11*(1), 1–8.
Sigurdsson, G. (2017). Transformative critique: What Confucianism can contribute to contemporary education. *Studies in Philosophy and Education, 36*(2), 131–146.
Sousa Santos, B. (1999). Porque e que e tao dificil construir uma teoria critica. *Revista Critica de Ciencias Sociais, 54*, 197–215.
Sousa Santos, B. (2007). Beyond abyssal thinking: From global lines to ecologies of knowledges. *Review, XXX*(1), 45–89.
Tan, C. (2011). Framing educational success: A comparative study of Shanghai and Singapore. *Education, Knowledge and Economy, 5*(3), 155–166.
Tan, C. (2013). *Learning from Shanghai: Lessons on achieving educational success*. Dordrecht, The Netherlands: Springer.

Tan, C. (2015). Education policy borrowing and cultural scripts for teaching in China. *Comparative Education*, 51(2), 196–211.
Tikly, L. (2004). Education and the new imperialism. *Comparative Education*, 40(2), 173–198.
Wang, C. S. (2004). A critical reflection on the thought of "despising knowledge" in Chinese basic education. *Beijing University Education Review*, 8(4), 5–23.
Wang, H. (2014). *Nonviolence and education: Cross-cultural pathways*. New York, NY and London, UK: Routledge.
Wang, S. R. (2012). *Huigui yuanchuang zhi si [Returning to the originary source of thought 回归原创之思]*. Nanjing: Jiangsu People's Publishing House.
Watkins, D., & Biggs, J. B. (2001). *Teaching the Chinese learner: Psychological and pedagogical perspectives*. Hong Kong: Comparative Education Research Centre, The University of Hong Kong.
Wu, K. M. (1997). *On Chinese body thinking: A cultural hermeneutic*. Leiden, The Netherlands and New York, NY: Brill Academic Publishing.
Wu, Z. J. (2011). Interpretation, autonomy, and transformation: Chinese pedagogic discourse in a cross-cultural perspective. *Journal of Curriculum Studies*, 43(5), 569–590.
Wu, Z. J. (2014). "Speak in the place of the sages": Rethinking the sources of pedagogic meanings. *Journal of Curriculum Studies*, 46(3), 320–331.
Yang, R. (2007). Comparing Policies. In M. Bray, B. Adamson, & M. Mason (Eds.), *Comparative education research: Approaches and methods* (pp. 241–262). Hong Kong: Comparative Education Research Centre, University of Hong Kong and Dordrecht: Springer.
Yang, R. (2011). Self and the other in the Confucian cultural context: Implications of China's higher education development for comparative studies. *International Review of Education*, 57, 337–355.
Young, M. F. (Ed.). (1971). *Knowledge and control: New directions for the sociology of education*. London, UK: Collier-Macmillan.
Yu, Y. (2004). Wenyifuxing hu? Qimengyundong hu?—yige shixuejia dui wusiyundong de fansi [Neither Renaissance nor Enlightenment? A historian's reflections on the May Fourth Movement 文艺复兴乎？启蒙运动乎？—一个史学家对五四运动的反思]. In Y. Yu (Ed.), *Chongxun Hu Shi licheng: Hu Shi shengping yu sixiang zairenshi* (pp. 242–268) *[Re-thinking Hu Shih's experience: Hu Shih's life and thought 重寻胡适历程：胡适生平与思想再认识]*. Guilin, China: Guangxi Normal University Press.
Zhang, H. (2014). Curriculum studies and curriculum reform in China. In W. F. Pinar (Ed.), *Curriculum studies in China. Curriculum studies in China: Intellectual histories, present circumstances* (pp. 29-67). London: Palgrave Macmillan.
Zhang, H. (2016). Lun hexinsuyang de neihan [On the connotations of core suyang 论核心素养的内涵]. *Quanqiujiaoyuzhanwang [Global Eduacation]*, 45(4), 10–24.
Zhang, X. L. (1992). *Heidegger and Taoism* (Unpublished doctoral dissertation). State University of New York, Buffalo.
Zhang, X. L. (1996). *Heidegger sixiang yu zhongguo tiandao: zhongji shiyu de kaiqi he jiaorong [Heidegger and Chinese Taoism 海德格尔思想与中国天道：终极视域的开启和交融]*. Beijing: Shenghuo-Dushu-Xinzhi Sanlian Shudian.
Zhang, X. L. (2013). *Fujian Tiandixin—Rujia zailin de yunyi yu daolu. [Revealing the heart of heaven and earth: On meaning of and path toward authentic*

Confucianism 复见天地心—儒家再临的蕴意与道路]. Beijing: Oriental Publishing House.

Zhang, Z. L. (2008). *Zuowei Shenti Zhexue de Zhongguo Gudai Zhexue* [Traditional Chinese philosophy as body philosophy 作为身体哲学的中国古代哲学]. Beijing: Chinese Social Science Publishing House.

Zhang, Z. L. (2015). *Zhongguo Gudai Shendao Yanjiu* [Body-Dao in Ancient China 中国古代身道研究]. Beijing: SDX Joint Publishing Company.

Zhao, G. P., & Deng, Z. Y. (Eds.). (2016). *Re-envisioning Chinese education: The meaning of person-making in a new age.* New York, NY: Routledge.

Zhao, W. (2015). Voluntary servitude as a new form of governing: Reinstating kneeling-bowing rites as educational pain and shame in modern Chinese education. In T. Popkewitz (Ed.), *The "reason" of schooling: Historicizing curriculum studies, pedagogy and teacher Education* (pp. 82–96). New York, NY: Routledge.

Zhao, W., & Sun, C. (2017). "Keep off the lawn; grass has life too!": Re-invoking a Daoist ecological sensibility for moral education in China's primary schools. *Educational Philosophy and Theory.* doi:10.1080/00131857.2017.1323623

Zhong, Q. Q. (2016). Jiyu hexinsuyang de kechengfazhan: tiaozhan yu keti. [Curriculum development on core competencies: Challenges and tasks. 基于核心素养的课程发展：挑战与课题.] *Quanqiujiaoyuzhanwang [Global Education]*, 45(1), 3–25.

Zhong, Q. Q., & You, B. (2004). Famei de nailao—renzhen duidai qingshizhishi de jiaoyu sichao duhougan [Moldy cheese—critical reflection on the thought of despising knowledge in Chinese basic education 发霉的奶酪—《认真对待"轻视知识"的教育思潮》读后感], *Quanqiujiaoyuzhanwang [Global Education]*, 33(10), 3–7.

2 An Archaeological-Historical Mode of Inquiry

Chapter 1 unpacks the material happening of epistemicide through a developmental comparative paradigm and a Westernization of the Chinese language since the twentieth-century China. This chapter moves a step further to scrutinize the "comparative" rationale as the reasoning undergirding the developmental comparative paradigm. In so doing, it brings in two strategies to overcome the developmental framework. First is to track "difference at its limit" as an entry point, just as how Michel Foucault envisions his book project of *The Order of Things*. Second is to turn to a historical-archaeological mode of inquiry to ethnographically historicize a cultural system of knowledge and its conditions of possibility within its own context. In so doing, this chapter proffers a new way of thinking about the distinctions of difference in comparative studies. This unpacking of difference also paves a way for further rethinking about the issue of difference, expressed as the teacher–student ordering in Chapter 5 and the identity–difference (re)ordering in Chapter 6.

Theoretical-Methodological Complexity of Comparative Studies

Comparative and international education, as a "vibrant multidisciplinary field" (Crossley, 1999), continues to attract increased attention from researchers and policy makers worldwide, so does a concomitant debate on its muddling-muddled definitions, methods, roles, boundaries, and purposes (Bray, 2010). Increased efforts on consistent contextual reconceptualization, fresh insights, and comparative methodologies have been called for to hopefully bridge and/or juxtapose new and existing various cultures and traditions, promoting more fruitful, systemic, historical, thematic, inter (intra)-cultural, inter (intra)-national and multidisciplinary dialogues and collaborations (Bray, 2010; Bray, Adamson, & Mason, 2007; Crossley, 2008; Evans & Robinson-Pant, 2010; Schriewer, 2006).

The special issues of the leading journals *Compare* (2010), *Comparative Education* (2008), and *Comparative Educational Review* (2009) maintain that twenty-first century comparative and international education research should place its due or more emphasis on its methodological theory and issues, since the comparison focus has mostly been on the cross-national educational organizations, systems, and practices. Debates on comparative methodology raged in the 1960s and 1970s but are, to some regret, largely absent in the current mainstream comparative research (see Bray, 2010; Little, 2010; Evans & Robinson-Pant, 2010). Henceforth, the below directions are anticipated to re-engage comparative educational studies in the twenty-first century.

First, new cultural values and ways of teaching and learning, as neglected units for comparison, should be better understood (see, e.g., Bray et al., 2007; Little, 2010; Evans & Robinson-Pant, 2010). Second, a much-ignored philosophical dimension should be (re)taken up to help researchers better reflect upon how to healthily extricate in English and dialogue non-Western epistemological sensibilities with the West on an equal footing (Crossley & Watson, 2009; Millgan et al., 2011). For example, a recent review of five top journals in philosophy of education and comparative education reveals only a handful of articles published in the last decade that might be termed as the comparative philosophy of education (Millgan et al., 2011). Finally, a more nuanced synchronic theoretical and empirical excavation of the processes of cross-sections of indigenization, appropriation, and translation in new settings should replace a simplistic diachronic, influence-oriented "educational transfer" problematic (Popkewitz, 2007; Sobe & Ness, 2010).

Recently, quite a few research projects have emerged that comply with these new directions in comparative or cultural education fields. For example, Kim (2014) examines the positioning issue in comparative studies. Bernadette Baker, by herself (2017) and with colleague (e.g., Hattam and Baker, 2015), pushes further the otherwise commonsensical epistemological comparisons between different cultural contexts into the onto-philosophical groundings as conditions of possibilities for the varied forms of knowledge, say, the scientific and the embodied knowledge.

These arguments about the nature, roles, paradigms, and philosophical underpinnings of comparative educational studies are, however, not new to its broader field of comparative study. Comparative study, as Schriewer (2006) reviews, is trans-disciplinary from its very inception in the Western academia around the late eighteenth and early nineteenth century along with the emergence of a field-or-problem-focused horizontal scheme of ordering scientific activity, and a methodological emphasis on the radical re-evaluation of empirical evidence. It saw its beginning in comparative anatomy, that is, the quintessential reference discipline at the turn of the nineteenth century, and then gradually found its inception in newly emerging disciplines such as comparative linguistics (William Jones on Indo-European predecessor language), comparative anthropology (South American structured human and social science based on comparative and historical research, Wilhelm von Humboldt), and comparative geology (Alexandra Humboldt), comparative language (Franz Bopp), and comparative education (Marc-Antonio Jullien de Paris).

Comparative study is also philosophical in its engagement with epistemological and ontological problems within a whole network of power interests and identity issue. For example, around the mid-nineteenth century when European nations started to command their power on the land of Near Orient and later on Far Orient, comparative approach easily became an expedient tool for the West, through their viewpoints of Marxist historicism and linear progressive time, to construct "the Orient" as "inferior, exotic, backward," waiting to be ruled and transformed. China, as an independent country from the West for thousands of years, entered into the scope of comparative study with the arrival of missionaries around the seventeenth and eighteenth centuries, and as shown in Chapter 1, has since been consciously and unconsciously embroiled within the catch-up-with-the-West mentality.

A consequence of such a comparative mentality is, as Chapter 1 argues, what Paraskeva (2016) defines as "epistemicide," an epistemological crisis, on the international epistemological landscape, often depriving the non-West of its very agency in originating and constructing its knowledge and practices. Edward Said's (1979) *Orientalism* is an incisive example of this. "As a way of coming to terms with the Orient that is based on the Orient's special place in European Western experiences" (p. 5), *Orientalism* represents the Orient from the European's vision and rationale and thus deprives the locals of their voice and power. In other words, the Orientalism has nothing to do with the local people's cultural praxis, whether there is a correspondence or lack thereof between the represented Orientals and the real Orientals. Through this strategy, "European culture gained in strength and identity by setting itself off against the Orient as a sort of surrogate, an even underground itself" (Said, 1979, p. 3).

Trenchant as it is, this kind of critique of Western colonialism and neo-colonialism tends to deploy Western philosophical discourses, especially critical theory and post-structuralism, to expose and attack Western hegemonic practices in the non-Western world (Young, 2001). Thus, what is not exposed is "how educational development that eschews neo-imperialist tendencies might proceed" (Milligan et al., 2011). This endeavor calls for a more robust comparative philosophical dialogue to translate and integrate the Western and non-Western worldviews (Libbrecht, 2007), or a "dialogical philosophy," which is "not the imposition of one philosophy or one mode of understanding, but the forging of a common universe of discourse in the very encounter" (Panikkar, 1988, p. 132), where both relevant differences or irrelevant in-differences, as well as similarities rather than forced uniformity, abide and flourish.

Then, what does it really mean to *compare*, and more important, how can we do a more robust comparative or dialogical philosophy, that is, to compare without necessarily and unconsciously placing one, mostly the Western, epistemological framework on top of the other cultures and thus enclosing the others into its developmental reason within a binary-contrastive logic? To put differently, how is it possible to render intelligible and in modern English those non-Western contextual and historical sensibilities without using the English (Western) metaphysical frameworks and globalized (Westernized) language as a normative identity to frame the other cultures as mirrored contrastive differences? How can comparative thinking flatten out the binary tropes in our analysis, including but not confined to the similarity–difference, equality–difference, identity–difference, and self–others myths?

"Comparison" Enthralled Within a Binary Identity–Difference Value Judgment

The Oxford English Dictionary says, "to compare is to mark or point out the similarities and differences of (two or more things); to bring or place together (actually or mentally) for the purpose of *noting the similarities and differences.*" This general definition, however, doesn't tell us how to select two things for comparison practically or how to conceptualize difference in the first place, difference as a starting point leading to similarities or as a perceived result based upon a gauging similarity/identity. Put aptly, the knotty identity–difference or difference–identity ordering priority is at the core of how-to-compare inquiry and this requires further philosophical thinking on the method as well as on the notion of difference.

Schriewer (2006) argues that there are two common methods of comparison, that is, comparing essences and comparing relations, dependent on how differences and similarities may be gleaned, filtered, and made intelligible. The essence-comparison method consists in relating "observable facts" as such, regarding their actual concreteness with pre-existing resemblances and thus differences would only remain at a "descriptive level" with no theoretical strength. The relation-comparison method "consists in relating relationships or even patterns of relationships to each other" through "systematically exploring and analyzing socio-cultural differences concerning establishing the credibility of general concepts, theoretical propositions or statements of equivalence" (p. 310). In other words, this social-scientific comparison method bears a positivist bent and "seeks out the relation between hypothetically presumed and empirically explored relationships" (ibid.). To clarify, detailed empirical evidence and theoretical hypothesis build into and substantiate each other. Seen this way, "the similarities (of proportions, relations, or functions) do not turn out to be informative but through showing the (empirical) differences" (Masson-Oursel, 1923, p. 22, quoted in Schriewer, 2006) or "difference can't be made in kind, but have to be made intelligible" (Jullien, 2004, p. 11).

Some important comparative inquiries have been conducted to render intercultural differences and similarities visible through de-familiarizing the Western logocentric rationale and de-mystifying the "exotic" Oriental life and experiences. Just as the title *Detour and Access* artistically indicates,

Jullien (2004) renders visible his own Western taken-for-granted tacit "mode of interpretation" through detouring into the subtlety of the Chinese meaning-making rhetoric as an outsider. Jullien says "with China in full view, and Greece on the periphery, perhaps I am really trying to approach Greece" (p. 10). In *Double Exposure: Cutting across Buddhism and Western Discourses*, Fauer (2004) "examine[s] some of the constraints that bear upon so-called rational thought and tend[s] to make it lose the thread of its arguments or to undermine its claims," by "grafting certain Asian concepts onto our own modern or postmodern discourse" (p. 19). By so doing, he hopes to render it (Buddhism) philosophically operational by stripping it of its false Oriental aura. In *Provincializing Europe*, Chakrabarty (2000) claims that Western categories related to political modernity along the line of historicism and the political are both indispensable and inadequate both theoretically and practically to think through the experiences of political modernity in non-Western nations. Henceforth he imbues a Heideggerian life-worlds understanding into his reading on Marxism historicism to narrate the native experiences in India with the hope that the margins could help to renew the Western rationale.

Actually, to scholars upholding the contextuality of concepts, what is indispensable and inadequate of Western cultures in thinking through the non-Western cultures is not just those categories related to political modernity but Western-specific epistemological frameworks in general. For example, Stephen Angle (2012) argues that the Chinese notion *daode* 道德 (with *morality* as its English gloss) is culturally incommensurable with the English notion *virtue* as they are embedded within distinct conceptual grids of discourse historically. What helps to gloss over the cultural nuances is the rule of transparency presumed in translation. Therefore, a grafting of Western notions and practices into other cultures is a misplaced strategy in the first place and often results in tension or problems, if not an epistemological crisis.

Analytically, this indispensability–inadequateness complex raises a practical conundrum (Popkewitz, Khurshid, & Zhao, 2014) issue in intercultural dialogue, both theoretically and practically, which has enthralled most, if not all, comparative (philosophical) inquiries in the last century. By conundrum, it means that as long as discourse pairs like margin/periphery vs. center, West vs. non-Western operates within a binary-contrastive logic, the analytics may very well end up, though inadvertently, reinforcing the oppositional boundaries with periphery and non-Western cultures as differentiated from the West center. However, the conundrum is not enclosed. Porous interstices exist here and there that are possible to expand.

What grounds the binary logic is not a dualistic way of thinking per se, but rather, its concomitant dichotomy evaluation. This binary-contrastive logic, Saussy (2001) argues, remains with Ferdinand de Saussure who describes the mechanism of language as turning entirely on identities and differences, the former being merely the counterparts of the latter. Saussure argues that terms are defined not positively but negatively, "their most exact characteristic is that of being what the others are not. The idea or the phonic substance contained in a sign matters less than what is going on in the other signs around it" (cited in Saussy, 2001, p. 151). The proof is that the value of one term can be modified without any change occurring in its sound or its meaning, simply because of a modification in some neighboring term. What makes it possible for there to be such a determining relation among the properties of neighboring sign is, in Saussure's account, "the fact that they all inhabit the same linguistic space and vie for existence like adjacent bubbles in a fluid; their relations cannot but be systematic" (cited in Saussy, 2001, p. 151).

Thus, Saussy further argues, if we put China and the West as oppositive, relative and negative entities, tacitly fashioning a system of relevant difference, our language, in the strict Saussurian sense of that term, runs on ahead of us. To put differently, the Western post-structural representation of China, namely, the binary logic doesn't exist in China with common stock yin-yang as its counter example, can't stand on its own. Lots of binary pairs exist in Chinese way of thinking, and the question is how to de-construct them concerning its historical self.

Difference, Zhang Longxi (1998) argues, is a favorite bet in modern popular relativism that takes in comparing and understanding the East–West cultural relation at the cost of neglecting the notion of a shared common ground. Camouflaged as a critique of Western colonialism and imperialism, relativism seems to be morally superior to Euro-centrism; however, Zhang argues, cultural relativists may very well make much the same argument as his opponents in the value conviction that the non-West is an entirely different and alien creature from the West. Whatever their divergence is and as long as they bracket their egocentric and binary value judgment for a *Zhuangzi*-like equalization regard, universalists and relativists would have more productive conversations in comparative studies. Here Zhuangzi is a Chinese Daoist thinker who maintains all things in the cosmos are equally different and differently equal, namely, epistemologically judged as different but ontologically remaining to be equal.

Zhang (1998) further argues that since difference and similarity are mutually defined and always coexist in things as well as our experiences of them, it is, therefore, an impertinent question to ask whether one should emphasize difference or similarity in comparative study of cultures. When crucial differences between Chinese and Western cultural and political backgrounds are ignored, it is imperative to point out the danger of such oversight; but when China and the West are set up in a rigid and mutually exclusive dichotomy, it is then necessary to point out the many similarities, what is shared common in languages, literature, and cultures of the East and the West. Therefore, comparative studies call for genuine efforts at understanding that does not reduce China to a fantastic mirror image of Western desires, fantasies, and stereotypical notions.

Then, how is it possible to constrain and expand these porous interstices of the analytical conundrum of value judgment? How is it possible to argue for the possibility of a genuine East–West dialogue, both geographically and culturally, beyond a binary logic? How to encounter, in the first place, an entry point for a possible dialogue? How to revision the ordering of identity and difference? How to approach the politics of translation? In the next part, I adumbrate the particular strings of thought, say, Heidegger's historical mode of inquiry, Derrida's aporia, and Foucault's difference at limit, that have helped pave my thinking path in this book project.

How Can a Cross-cultural Dialogue Become Possible in the First Place?

Heidegger grapples with the essence of the Western metaphysical thinking throughout his lifetime. One of his strategies is to go back to the Greek language and thought as the historical root of the Western thought for new openings. According to Heidegger (1977a), the European epistemological models of metaphysics and science, say, a technological and calculative way of thinking, have already imprisoned the entire contemporary world. With such a planetary mode of thinking, he holds a mixed attitude toward the validity and possibility of a genuine East–West dialogue (Ma, 2008). On the one hand, Heidegger (1966/1996) occasionally wonders whether or not one day the ancient traditions of a "thinking" in Russia and/or China, which has not been submerged into the current technological and calculative mode of thought, will awaken so that man would have a free relationship to the technical world. In *On the Way to Language* (1959/1971), he recalls a dialogue with a Japanese scholar, and at the end, he couldn't help wondering:

> Whether in the end—which would also be the beginning—a nature of language can reach the thinking experience, a nature which would offer the assurance that European-Western saying and East-Asian saying will enter into dialogue such that in it there sings something that wells up from a single source.
>
> (p. 8)

On the other hand, however, Heidegger claims that all of the then so-called East–West dialogues are far from deep and genuine. Instead, they are merely ontic and inauthentic assimilations and intermixtures, encountered and pursued through the European conceptual constructs. For Heidegger, it may take another 300 years for profound and genuine East–West dialogues to possibly occur at all (see, Ma, 2008). His reason is that Western scholars can't get out of their inborn way of thinking, and the Eastern scholars are already too enthralled by the Western binary logic to see their tradition in their authentically traditional way. Heidegger claims "contemporary Indians, Chinese and Japanese can usually bring to us what is experienced by them only through our European way of thinking" (as cited in Ma, 2008, p. 69) to the extent that Asian thought is no longer available in its authenticity. "What is authentic has already been distorted by a dualistic European metaphysical system" (ibid.).

Heidegger further claims that an East–West encounter in a real sense would be possible only after the current Western historical calculative Being has its genuine encounter with its Greek and pre-Socratic first beginning so that it could be brought back to its originary beginning where a more genuine Being is laid bare and visible. According to Heidegger (1969), an originary beginning nourishes something that has not been thought, which is not reducible to what has already been thought and can further sets free traditional thinking from further systemization and development of gained ideas. An originary past prevails throughout the tradition in what is preserved, "is always in being in advance of it, and yet is never expressly thought in its own right and as the Originary" (pp. 48–49). In the *Spiegel* interview, he clarifies his claim that "the Germans bears a unique destiny" as below:

> I could explain what was said in the quotation in the following way: it is my conviction that a reversal can be prepared only in the same place in the world where the modern technological world originated, and that it cannot happen through any takeover by Zen Buddhism or any other Eastern experiences of the world. There is need for a rethinking which is to be carried out with the help of the European tradition and of a new appropriation of that tradition. *Thinking itself can be transformed only by a thinking which has the same origin and calling.*
>
> (1966/1996, my emphasis)

In his seminars, Heidegger often warns his students to pay more attention to his trajectory of thinking and think what is still to be thought, rather than holding to what he says as fixed truth. He says that reflection on language and Being has determined his path of thinking from early on, and therefore their exposition has stayed as far as possible in the background (1971). He characterizes the question of language and Being as a gift of that light ray that fell upon him just as what Friedrich Hölderlin says, "For as you began, you will remain." For him, thinking is concerned with Being concerning its difference from beings. He goes from what is as yet un-thought, from the difference between Being and beings as difference (the ontological difference) to that which is to be thought, the oblivion of that difference. Oblivion belongs intrinsically to difference. This strategy helps him move forward by the step back into the realm of the essence of truth that has never yet come to light.

Well, what Heidegger says about the planetary domination of Ge-stell seems sensible in a broad sense. For example, the Western binary metaphysical way of thinking has indeed become dominant in the current Chinese logic in that nature, humans, and education are mostly treated as standing reserve waiting to be employed. I believe a historical return to China's first beginning would also be one, maybe inevitable but certainly helpful, stepping stone for a possible genuine dialogue with the current China's and Western modes of thinking. Still, how is it possible to encounter an entry point as a signpost that is not yet submerged into the current planetary thinking and language but meantime can guide an inquiry into the current back toward its traditional beginnings? Heidegger says that the question of language and Being is a gift of that light ray that fell upon him. His strategy is predominantly a historical encounter with the pre-Socratic way of thinking. His strong interest in the Chinese classical text, *Laozi* (*Dao De Jing*), or in the Japanese notions of *iki* or *takoba* is mainly targeted to see whether his ontological understanding of Western language as House of Being, a nearness to the Greek first beginning, is also discernible in Chinese or Japanese cultural beginnings (see, Ma, 2008; Zhang X. L., 1992, 1996; Zhang W., 2006). But he doesn't think about possible cross-cultural difference at its limit, that is, radical difference or indifference, as a possible spur for him to further meditate on the Western logic. But Michel Foucault does and in a very strategic way, to which we now turn.

Difference at Its Limit as Strategic Foothold for Comparative Study

Foucault takes up difference at its limit-state as a disruptive and liberating entry point on his journey to reflect upon his cultural way of thinking. In its preface to *The Order of Things* (1966/1973), Foucault said the book arose out of the Borges' quote on Chinese animal taxonomy. This Chinese classification set Foucault into a good laughing though not without a certain uneasiness. This uneasiness comes less from "the oddity of unusual juxtapositions" (p. xvi) of these animals than from the removal or lack of an "operating table" (p. xvii), a common locus as a residence for ordering and holding together, in the commonsensical Western eyes, these largely incongruous animals. This exotic Chinese ordering of space, Foucault said, also marks the "limitation of our own, the stark impossibility of thinking *that*" (p. xv) in that it does not "distribute the multiplicity of existing things into any of the categories that make it possible for us to name, speak and think" (p. xix). And this unthinkable difference at its limit "disturbs and threatens with collapse our age-old distinction between the Same and the Other" (p. xv). To put aptly, the imaginary Chinese space is a sheer shock to the Western ethnocentrism developed along a notion of linear time.

This difference at its limit concerning thinking marks a state of aporia with both a disruptively paralyzing and a productively liberating power for Foucault. Aporia, Derrida (1993) narrates, is a possibly paralyzing but fascinating experience when one gets stuck or paralyzed in a place or at a certain border where there is no longer any problem (neither a projection ahead nor a protection behind to shield oneself), where one doesn't know where to go—an experience and a word that often imposes itself on Derrida with formalizable regularity (pp. 12–13).

Following Derrida's way of thinking, I would like to treat difference at its limit as limitrophy of difference, namely, a thickening at the edges, which points to "examples of forms of expression, narrativizations, and/or modalities of operation that incidentally or decidedly challenge some basic premises on which claims to scientific rationalities have been predicated" (Baker, 2013, p. 15). In other words, like Foucault, I will take up the difference at its limit, examine the limit point that enables comparison as an act, re-approach why such an act might arise as a problem and examine the formation of norms upon which the task of comparison would depend—the norm that constitutes binary logic, on but not limited to, word and things, mind and body, and identity and difference.

Here a tentative understanding of the relation between the English terms "limit/end" and "limitless/endless" might help. The suffix "less" indicates a negation, so limitless means no limit and endless no end. However, how can we experience the relation between limit/end and limitless/endless? Can we usually have an experience or perception of limit/end before a limitless/endless, or vice versa? I feel only when we come to this end/limit, and confront it directly can we come to the possible endless/limitless. Imagine wandering through a maze to the seemingly final door and not knowing what is beyond that door. Only when the last door is opened, crossed, and traversed, can we find that the door is open to an endless space.

Furthermore, coming across the difference at its limit is a throw of dice, more of a matter of momentous enlightenment through a cultural encounter with some others: my seeing the Chinese "wind" and "body" as detailed in Introduction is such an experience. They desiccate the modern signifier–signified logic and drive my project toward an archaeological-historical dimension.

From Cross-Cultural Conversation to Archaeological-Historical Dialogue

When I say cross-cultural comparison, this cross-cultural involves not only an international dimension, but also a historical dimension. As culture is inherently and historically hybrid in its form and content, any juxtaposition of various cultural forms involves a comparative perspective. Seen this way, the central notion of difference in cross-cultural comparative studies needs to be rethought and re-configured from a produced differentiation through the gauge of sameness to a source of potentiality for opening up healthy dialogues.

Agamben (2009) argues,

> Every inquiry in the human sciences—including the present reflection on method—should entail an archaeological vigilance. In other words, it must retrace its trajectory back to the point where something remains

obscure and un-thematized. Only a thought that does not conceal its own unsaid—but constantly takes it up and elaborates it—may eventually lay claim to originality.

(p. 8)

This archaeological-historical mode of inquiry involves an epistemological shift from viewing time, history, and tradition as being some static, irreversible, and irreducible essences (data) to re-configuring them as happening, events, movement, and moments of arising possibly external to any timeline. The aim of disrupting the fixed and canonized tradition and history is to set back into motion the original inner happenings of the presently silenced "wind-body" rationale by tracing its way back to its self-laid grounds to found itself anew out of them. This new founding and finding are expected to shed new light on and render accessible the otherwise enclosed present educational reforms and discourses in China (and all around the world) largely on the Enlightenment development paradigm. To that end, this historical-archaeological mode of inquiry also engages a comparative exposition of the Chinese cultural epistemological positions and evaluations on language, meaning, difference, history, and tradition in order not to read the Western and modern epistemological frameworks into the historical Chinese context taken-for-granted.

In *What Is a Thing* (1967), Heidegger treats the question of what is a thing as a historical inquiry, distinct from the usual history of ideas mode of inquiry, namely, historical reporting of the various opinions, viewpoints, and propositions, about the thing through the centuries. His argument is that the latter history-of-ideas reporting of the thing already presupposes the static existence of the thing and thus is "an explicit shutting down of history, whereas it is, after all, a happening" (p. 43). Therefore, a historical enquiry doesn't ask about "the formula and the definition of the essence of the thing," instead, it asks about the "basic positions, the happening and the movements," taken by the historical being, of which the formula and the definition are only the residuum and sediment (p. 44).

Furthermore, the happenings and movements are not necessarily the already established and past actual movements, but could also be in a form of *acquiescence* (my italics) no longer going on in the present yet still constituting as a basic form of the presence of the history. This is because

what we normally know as past, and first represent, is mostly only the formerly 'actual,' what once caused a stir or even made the noise which always belongs to history but which is not history proper. What is merely past does not exhaust what has been.

(p. 44)

The purpose of this historical mode of inquiry, Heidegger further argues, is to bring the question of what is a thing out of its quiescence by inserting its historical, Platonic–Aristotelian, determinations of the thing, the proposition and the truth into specific possibilities not in order to acknowledge how it was before, but to pose for decision how essentially it still is today. Put differently, the detour into the past is aimed to access the present, and this is a shared methodology among authentic historical-archaeological inquiries.

This historical-archaeological mode of inquiry, or History of the Present, is granted a privilege over all the other disciplines in Foucault's discussion about today's human sciences in the last chapter of *The Order of Things*. Concerning that strong take, Foucault clarifies in his interview *On the Ways of Writing History* (1998) that

> for centuries now discourses are linked in a historical fashion in that we acknowledge things that were said as coming from a past in which they were succeeded, opposed, influenced, replaced, engendered and accumulated by others, (i.e., with a history).
>
> (p. 292)

That is also why, he said, in studying an ensemble of theoretical discourses concerning language, economy and living beings in *The Order of Things*, he didn't try to establish the a priori possibilities or impossibilities of such knowledge but do a historian's work by showing the simultaneous functioning of these discourses and the transformations that accounted for their visible changes. The transformations, he later argues, involves complex periodization and also an embroiled intersection between a vertical (discourse and non-discourse/institutional connections) and a horizontal lens (discursive regularity among various fields/domains of knowledge).

A focus on the transformations and change as an object of analysis along with a claim that history is happening rather than static entities based upon one another are further elaborated in Foucault's *Nietzsche, Genealogy, History* (1984). Genealogy, as an examination of both descent and emergence (moment of arising) and opposed to a search of "origin" which presupposedly precedes the external world of accident and succession, examines the "historical beginning—numberless beginnings whose faint traces and hints of color are readily seen by an historical eye" (p. 365) and cultivates "the details and accidents that accompany every beginning" (p. 364). History is the concrete body of a development with its vicissitudes and a genealogist "needs history to *dispel* the chimeras of the origin" (my italics) (p. 364) and be able to recognize the *events* of history and diagnose the illnesses of the body like a doctor rather than a metaphysician who would seek its soul in the distant ideality of the origin. "Genealogy, as an analysis of descent, is thus situated within the articulation of the body and history. Its task is to expose a body totally imprinted by history and the process of history's destruction of the *body*" (Foucault, 1984, p. 366, my emphasis).

In *Philosophical Archaeology* (2009), Agamben strategically picks up the French word *conjurer* for the English word *dispel* in the above quote and further builds on its two opposite meanings: to evoke (evocation) and to expel (expulsion) into his further argument on genealogy as consisting in "conjuring up and eliminating the origin and the subject" (p. 84). Put in other words, one has to "account for the constituting of the subject within the weavings of history to get rid of it once and for all" (p. 84), or the analysis of descent permits the dissociation of the self, its recognition, and displacement as an empty synthesis, in liberating a profusion of lost events. A precaution is that this constitution takes place in non-place of the origin.

Agamben borrows Overbeck's notion *prehistory* to further unpack the "non-place of the origin" (p. 84). Overbeck argues that authentic historical enquiry must necessarily engage the dimension of what he calls prehistory—the history of the constitution, emergence, or the moment of arising—which is "of incomparable value for the history of every living being and, more generally, of life" (as cited in Agamben, 2009, p. 85). For him, this means that every historical phenomenon necessarily splits itself into prehistory (the history of the moment of arising) and history when the limits dividing it from the world can no longer be shifted. Historical inquiry, as an engagement with this constitutive heterogeneity, can be done in the form of the critique of tradition or the critique of sources that deals not with a meta-historical beginning, but with the mode in which the past (the possible source) has been constructed in a tradition and the very structure of historical inquiry.

When the past is constructed into a tradition, tradition thus becomes a master, and it does so in such a way that what it transmits is made so inaccessible, proximally and for the most part, that it rather becomes concealed and accordingly mars access to those primordial sources where tradition partly burgeons from. In other words, the primordial sources become lost or silenced in the present time when tradition is canonized. Therefore, a returning to the past, a liberating of these lost events, a renewed access to the sources as a moment of arising, requires a "destruction of tradition" (Agamben, 2009, p. 88).

Furthermore, Agamben (2009) argues,

> [I]t is not possible to gain access in a new way, beyond tradition, to the sources without putting in question the very historical subject who is supposed to gain access to them. What is in question, then, is the epistemological paradigm of inquiry itself.
>
> (p. 89)

Archaeology can be provisionally a practice in any historical investigation that has not to do with origins, but with the moment of a phenomenon's arising, and must, therefore, engage anew the sources and traditions. It cannot confront tradition without deconstructing the paradigms, techniques, and practices through which tradition regulates the forms of transmission, conditions access to sources, and in the final analysis, determines the very status of the knowing subject (p. 89).

This is what I mean by seeking an epistemological comparison cross-culturally so that one will not easily read one cultural system of epistemology into and replace the cultural other. Meantime, historical and epistemological dimensions are interwoven in a mutually informing way and can only be separated for analytic convenience.

Archaeology concerns knowledge constitutive in its condition of possibility rather than a history of ideas or sciences. It is an inquiry that, by going back upstream in the history of discursive formations, knowledge, and practices, seeks to discover "on what basis knowledge and theory became possible" (p. 93). This going back to the prehistory and source to expose the present contains a temporal paradox or "future anterior" in Agamben's words in that prehistory doesn't necessarily designate a chronological timeline in the past or ancient, but alongside and immanent with the present. In this sense, the archaeologist retreats toward the present in that

> every historical phenomenon split[s] in accordance with the fault line separating in it a before and an after, a prehistory and a history, a history of the sources and a historical tradition that are in actuality contemporaneous, insofar as they coincide for an instant in the moment of arising.
>
> (p. 95)

Furthermore, a presumption of the unitary prehistoric stage before a historical split doesn't mean that we could project upon the presupposed "primordial instinct" the characteristics defining the split spheres already known to us. For example, the features of a unitary sacred and profane at a more archaic stage can't be the sum of the defining features of the split spheres as the sacred and human body could be constellated in a dynamic prehistoric unity at a more archaic stage so that the feasibility of the defining notions and categories in the current separate domains in education, governance, and human body known to us is questionable. Likewise, Manfred Porkert (1974), in his endeavor to map out the theoretical foundations of Chinese medicine, realizes that there are no corresponding modes of thought for some Chinese classical medical terms in the western culture. To try to render them intelligible to the English world, he creates a series of new words not analogical with modern Western science and technology, rather than dismissing these non-analogous parts simply as primitive as against the Western "norm."

Archaeological-Historical Mode of Inquiry as a Defining Feature of This Book

To sum up, an archaeological-historical mode of inquiry involves two interrelated conditions as effects. First, it suspends the rational value or objective form of knowledge toward a problematization of the positivity of knowledge itself. Second, it engenders a transformation of the inquirer's very mode of being, as the problematization often entails a suspension and transformation, not reproduction, of the naturalized viewpoints, presumptions, styles of reasoning with which the inquirer unavoidably starts and stands upon. As Agamben (2009) argues, in archaeological inquiry, "it is not possible to gain access in a new way, beyond tradition, to the sources without putting in question the very historical subject who is supposed to gain access to them" (p. 89).

In compliance with these two conditions–effects, this book henceforth intends to fulfill two missions. First, as a paradigmatic exemplar to address the paradigm challenge, as well as a concomitant epistemological crisis, in comparative studies by historicizing the events of language, education, and curriculum in modern China. Second, as an exemplary case of post-foundational *study* by scrutinizing and theorizing my intellectual research journey itself as a Daoist onto-un-learning experience.

With a focus on knowledge's conditions of possibility, this book distinguishes itself from other books on China's education and curriculum mostly focused upon explicating its content, features, knowledge, as well as changes thereof along a what-is question or a history-of-ideas logic. In contrast, this book aims to discover on what basis knowledge and styles of reasoning about China's education and curriculum become possible, and within what space of order are they constructed. It explicates the historical-cultural a priori that makes it possible for teaching, learning, and the teacher–student difference in past and present China to be said and enacted as they were and are. In other words, this book doesn't track the historical vicissitudes of China's education and curriculum reform; rather, it gets deeper into the epistemological field, examining the positivity of knowledge as well as the historical-cultural principles as conditions of possibility for today's educational thinking and practice in China on a cross-cultural landscape.

As an exemplary case of post-foundational *study*, this book recounts and scrutinizes my intellectual research journey as an educational experience in a way to problematize, expose, and turn in my subjectivity about the objects of language, knowledge, educative body, and teacher–student ordering. The transformation of my mode of being as a researcher, as one key to the post-foundational paradigm of inquiry, often happens in aporia moments when my naturalized viewpoints, styles of reasoning, and presumptions are paralyzed. For example, encountering the etymological/analytic definition of the Chinese wind-character, *feng* 風, as "the wind blows and insects get germinated and hatched within eight days" in China's first comprehensive dictionary is one such aporia moment when I found myself in the hands of language, not vice versa. This aporia moment turned over an otherwise naturalized subject–object ordering between me and language toward a relational movement between two co-beings. This transformed inter-subjectivity enabled me to *see* "wind" as a signature language of China's education, and Confucius' "wind-pedagogy" as expressed in *Yijing* as another originary re(source) of the entire Confucian educational culture. Neither point has so far been discerned, let alone scrutinized in scholarship on Confucius and Confucian educational culture in China and beyond.

Re-invoking an Archaeological-Historical Inquiry in (China's) Educational Studies

The field of education lacks a historical perspective in general (Phillips, 2014), even though it is highly needed to reclaim some "historical-philosophical-cultural motifs" (Kazamias, 2009, p. 37) as the very root of education to re-humanize the currently predominant neoliberal order (Baker, 2009; Popkewitz, 2013). Since Herbert Kliebard's (2004) classical historicization of the American curriculum from 1893–1958, historical unpacking of educational thinking and practices in the Foucauldian sense of the history of present has emerged, if not flourished, as a new field. For example, Bernadette Baker's (2009) edited book, titled *New Curriculum History*, indexes the challenges in locating the irreducible "heritage" of transnational curriculum studies that meanwhile does not centralize curriculum, education, knowledge, and power as boundary fields or reproduce the second-order normativity embedded in the a priori definitions of these terms. Thomas Popkewit edited books by himself (2015) and with colleagues (Popkewitz, Diaz, & Kirchgasler, 2017) that problematize the "reason" of schooling by historicizing the conditions of possibilities of curriculum, pedagogy, teacher education, and the sociology of knowledge in varied cultural (con)contexts.

In China's educational studies, historical investigations have been conducted less in the archaeological sense, but more along the history-of-the-idea diagram. For example, Thomas Lee (2000) puts together an introductory encyclopedia of the history of China's education over the past two millennia. Zhang Hua (2014) unpacks modern China's two major curriculum reforms which happened from 1922–2012. With the emerging somatic turn and the contemplative turn in educational studies, ancient Chinese wisdom, the Yijing, Buddhist, Daoist, and Confucian thinking, is frequently re-invoked as an alternative style of reasoning to inform and dialogue the latter (see, e.g., Lin, 2013; Lin, Culham, & Oxford, 2016; Hoyt, 2016; Wang, 2014; Moon, 2015; Zhao & Ford, 2017). However, most of these studies tend to treat the ancient Chinese thought more as fixed sets of ideas, knowledge, or beliefs to be recovered than as historical and contextual events, moments of arising, the murmuring of which is still visible in current China's educational thinking and practices. Such an idealization or objectification runs the risk of further rigidifying, not liberating, of the ancient Chinese wisdoms, since a returning to the past, a liberating of these lost events, a renewed access to the sources as moment of arising, requires a "destruction of tradition" (Agamben, 2009, p. 88). Therefore, a returning to or reviving of a contextual, or archaeological-historical, understanding of traditional cultural value is called for to restore China's current education back to its health (Evers & Mason, 2011).

An archaeological-historical perspective reconfigures time, history, and tradition no longer as some static, irreversible, and irreducible essences (data) but as happening, events, movement, and moments of arising possibly external to any timeline. The aim of disrupting the fixed and canonized tradition and history is to set back into motion the original inner happenings of the presently silenced "wind-body" rationale by tracing its way back to its self-laid grounds to found itself anew out of them. Henceforth, an archaeological-historical inquiry implodes an (my) otherwise naturalized canonization and compartmentalization of Chinese wisdom into distinct Yijing, Confucianism, Daoism, and Buhhism schools of thought. Instead, I re-treat them as historical and primordial sources of Dao, where the varied forms of thinking burgeon from, yet not reduce or condense to, like a river of *wen* 文 that nourishes the latter to happen, coagulate, and move along. To use Agamben's (2009) words, I treat them as an originary thought "where something remains obscure and un-thematized," which "does not conceal its own unsaid and can constantly be taken up and elaborated for new openings" (p. 8).

For example, due to some salient distinctions between Confucius' or Confucian thinking before the Han Dynasty (202 BCE—220 CE) and the canonized institutional Confucian thinking ever since then till the collapse of the last dynasty in 1911, Confucian thinking, or Confucianism, is "notoriously hard to define" (Sigurdsson, 2017, p. 135). Furthermore, since Confucius (551–479 BC) mostly "transmits/comments but not writes" (*shuerbuzuo* 述而不作) (*Lunyu: Shu'er*), his thought is scattered throughout the so-called *Four Books and Five Classics* (*sishuwujing* 四書五經). Nevertheless, Confucian philosophy of education, as the gist of Confucius' thought (Chen, 2016), is commonly believed to be primarily "rooted" (Ames, 2016) in the canonized classics of *Lunyu* (*The Analects* 論語), *Xueji* (*On Teaching and Learning* 學記), and *Daxue* (*The Great Learning* 大學). In other words, these texts are treated as a "cultural script" (Tan, 2015), which defines the way teaching and learning are currently re-configured in China and other East Asian countries with Confucian Heritage Culture (CHC).

An archaeological-historical perspective disrupts such a shared understanding of Confucian educational thinking or the root-origin metaphor in particular. The history-of-ideas reporting and unpacking of the features, content, and viewpoints and propositions about Confucian educational thinking already presuppose the static existence of the thing, and this is "an explicit shutting down of history, whereas it is, after all, a happening" (Heidegger, 1967, p. 43). Therefore, a historical enquiry doesn't ask about "the formula and the definition of the essence of the thing"; instead, it asks about the "basic positions, the happening and the movements," taken by the historical being, of which the formula and the definition are only the residuum and sediment (p. 44). With this in mind, this book aims to unpack the ancient Chinese system of thought, the Yijing, as a grounding epistemology for education and knowledge, among others, to be thought as it is by Confucius and others. My unpacking of Confucius' educational vision becomes another originary, not the only original, source of Confucius' educational thinking, originary in the sense that it can constantly be tapped for new openings. Besides, an archaeological-historical perspective disrupts a past–present–future timeline, which reconfigures the mode of signification not just within a synchronic dimension, but also a diachronic one (Wu, 2016). This disrupts the presentism as a signature of the Western mode of signification and representation. I will further out this point more in Chapter 4 on the Chinese (con)textures of *wen* (letters and language).

Thus, with an archaeological-historical mode of inquiry into knowledge's conditions of possibility, this book does not provide another (re)presentation of the semantic meanings as well as syntactical organizations of these distinct objects of language, education, curriculum, and knowledge in China. Nor does it laud the success, or lament the failure, of current China's education and curriculum reforms, or proffer a salvation future for it. Rather, it treats language, education, curriculum, and knowledge as theoretical constructs, as material events and happenings, and examines their conditions of possibility from a historical and cross-cultural perspective. Specifically, how is it possible for Chinese people to say, reason, and act about these issues as they do, and furthermore to rethink them in alternative ways? Alternative to some "normative" ordering principles like a West-based comparative framework, a planetary mode of signification and representation, a signature instrumental learning logic, and a binary subject–object style of reasoning. These "normative" principles, largely as an effect-expression of the Western Enlightenment rationale, crisscross and structure such distinct fields as comparative studies, language philosophy, social and human sciences, and educational research paradigms. This book, cross-disciplinary and multidimensional, clears the grounding presumptions and limits of these "normative" principles as a (pre)condition toward exploring a new perspective to re-understanding China's education, curriculum, and knowledge both in the past and at present.

This chapter, a penultimate reflection on method after extensive research, makes possible, intersects, and follows my first seeing of the prevailing yet silent Chinese schooling wind and body discourses. Reading Agamben, Foucault, and Heidegger gives me an intuition that such an aporetic wind-body language can function as a window as well as a positive difference-at-limit entry point in cross-culturally rendering visible some unsaid cultural sensibilities of Chinese education. Furthermore, their shared understanding that a historical or archaeological mode of inquiry entails a transformation of the researcher's subjectivity prepares a way for me to loosen up and subsume my mode of being into encountering Chinese language, body, and difference. Seen this way, a historical dialogue with the classical wind and body language as a way of reasoning becomes a stepping stone for me to map out the Chinese sensibilities in its reasoning about teaching, learning, and teacher–student engagement without falling within the global technological language and frameworks. With such an understanding, I move onto the next chapter on language as another perspective to help overcome the epistemicide issue in comparative studies in general.

References

Agamben, G. (2009). *The signature of all things: On method*. New York, NY: Zone Books.

Ames, R. T. (2016). On teaching and learning (Xueji 學記): Setting the root in Confucian education. In X. Di & H. McEwan (Eds.), *Chinese philosophy on teaching and learning: Xueji (學記) in the twenty-first century* (pp. 21–38). Albany, NY: State University of New York Press.

Angle, S. (2012). *Contemporary Confucian political philosophy: Toward progressive Confucianism*. Cambridge, MA: Polity.

Baker, B. (Ed.). (2009). *New curriculum history*. Rotterdam, The Netherlands: Sense Publisher.

Baker, B. (2013). *William James, sciences of mind, and anti-imperial discourse*. New York, NY: Cambridge University Press.

Baker, B. (2017). To show is to know? The conceptualization of evidence and discourses of vision in social science and education research. *Curriculum Inquiry*, 47(2), 151–174.

Bray, M. (2010). Comparative education and international education in the history of compare: Boundaries, overlaps and ambiguities. *Compare*, 40(6), 711–725.

Bray, M., Adamson, B., & Mason, M. (Eds.). (2007). *Comparative education research: Approaches and methods*. Hong Kong: The University of Hong Kong, and Dordrecht: Springer.

Chakrabarty, D. (2000). *Provincializing Europe: Postcolonial thought and historical difference*. Princeton, NJ: Princeton University Press.

Chen, L. (2016). The ideas of "educating" and "learning" in Confucian thought. In X. Di & H. McEwan (Eds.), *Chinese philosophy on teaching and learning: Xueji (學記) in the twenty first century* (pp. 77–96). Albany, NY: State University of New York Press.

Crossley, M. (1999). Reconceptualising comparative and international education. *Compare: A Journal of Comparative Education*, 29(3), 249–267.

Crossley, M. (2008). Bridging cultures and traditions for educational and international development: Comparative research, dialogue and difference. *International Review of Education*, 54, 319–336.

Crossley, M., & Watson, K. (2009). Comparative and international education: Policy transfer, context sensitivity and professional development. *Oxford Review of Education*, 35(5), 633–649.

Derrida, J. (1993). *Aporias* (T. Gutoit, Trans.). Stanford, CA: Stanford University Press.

Evans, K., & Robinson-Pant, A. (2010). Compare: Exploring a 40-year journey through comparative education and international development. *Compare: A Journal of Comparative and International Education*, 40(6), 693–710.

Evers, C. W., & Mason, M. (2011). Context based inferences in research methodology: The role of culture in justifying knowledge claims. *Comparative Education*, 47(3), 301–314.

Fauer, B. (2004). *Double exposure: Cutting across Buddhism and Western discourses* (J. Lloyd, Trans.). Stanford, CA: Stanford University Press.

Foucault, M. (1973). *The order of things: An archaeology of the human sciences.* New York, NY: Vintage Books. (Original work published 1966)

Foucault, M. (1984). Nietzsche, genealogy, history. In P. Rabinow (Ed.), *The Foucault reader* (pp. 76–100). Harmondsworth: Penguin.

Foucault, M. (1998). On the ways of writing history. In M. Foucault & J. D. Faubion (Eds.), *Aesthetics, method, and epistemology* (pp. 279–334). New York, NY: Publisher Press.

Hattam, R., & Baker, B. (2015). Technologies of self and the cultivation of virtues. *Journal of Philosophy of Education, 49*(2), 255–273.

Heidegger, M. (1939/2004). *On the essence of language: The metaphysics of language and the essencing of the word, concerning Herder's Treatise on the origin of language* (W. T. Gregpry & Y. Umma, Trans.). Albany, NY: State University of New York Press.

Heidegger, M. (1996). Spiegel interview with Martin Heidegger. In *Philosophy Today, 20,* 268–284. (Original work published 1966).

Heidegger, M. (1967). *What is a thing?* (W. B. Barton, Jr., & V. Deutsch Trans. with an analysis by E. T. Gendlin.). Chicago, IL: Henry Regnery Company.

Heidegger, M. (1969). *Identity and Difference* (J. Stambaugh, Trans. with an Introduction). New York, Evanston, and London: Harper & Row Publishers. (Original work published 1957).

Heidegger, M. (1971). *On the way to language* (P. D. Hertz, Trans.). San Francisco: A Division of Harper Collins Publishers. (Original work published 1959)

Heidegger, M. (1977). *The question concerning technology and other essays* (W. Lovitt, Trans. with an introduction.). New York, NY: Harper Torchbooks.

Heidegger, M. (1996). Spiegel interview with Martin Heidegger. *Philosophy Today, 20,* 268–284. (Original work published 1966)

Hoyt, M. (2016). Teaching with mindfulness: The pedagogy of being-with/for and without being-with/for. *Journal of Curriculum Theorizing, 31*(1), 126–142.

Jullien, F. (2004). *Detour and access: Strategies of meaning in China and Greece.* New York, NY: Zone Book.

Kazamias, A. M. (2009). Forgotten men, forgotten themes: The historical philosophical cultural and liberal humanist motif in comparative education. In R. Cowen & A. M. Kazamias (Eds.), *International handbook of comparative education* (Vol. 1, pp. 37–58). New York, NY: Springer.

Kim, T. (2014). The intellect, mobility and epistemic positioning in doing comparisons an comparative education. *Comparative Education, 50*(1), 58–72.

Kliebard, H. M. (2004). *The struggle for the American curriculum, 1893–1958.* New York, NY & London, UK: Psychology Press.

Lee, T. H. C. (2000). *Education in traditional China: A history.* Leiden, The Netherlands: Brill Academic Publishing.

Libbrecht, U. (2007). *Within the four seas: Introduction to comparative philosophy.* Leuven, Belgium: Peeters.

Lin, J. (2013). Education for transformation and an expanded self: Paradigm shift for wisdom education. In J. Lin, R. L. Oxford, & E. J. Brantmeier (Eds.), *Re-envisioning higher education: Embodied pathways to wisdom and social transformation* (pp. 23–32). Charlotte, NC: Information Age Publishing.

Lin, J., Culham, T., & Oxford, R. (2016). Developing a spiritual research paradigm: A Confucian perspective. In J. Lin, R. Oxford, & T. Culham (Eds.), *Toward a*

spiritual research paradigm: Exploring new ways of knowing, researching and being (pp. 141–170). Charlotte, NC: Information Age Publishing.
Little, A. W. (2010). International and comparative education: What's in a name? Compare, 40(6), 845–852.
Ma, L. (2008). Heidegger on East-West dialogue: Anticipating the event. New York, NY: Routledge.
Millgan, J. A., Stanfill, E., Widyanto, A., & Zhang, H. (2011). Philosophers without borders? Toward a comparative philosophy of education. Educational Studies, 47, 50–70.
Moon, S. (2015). Wuwei (non-action) philosophy and actions: Rethinking "actions" in school reform. Educational Philosophy and Theory, 47(5), 455–473.
Panikkar, R. (1988). What is comparative philosophy comparing? In G. J. Larson & E. Deutsch (Eds.), Interpret-ing across boundaries: New essays in comparative philosophy (pp. 116–136). Princeton, NJ: Princeton University Press.
Paraskeva, J. M. (2016). Curriculum epistemicide: Towards an itinerant curriculum theory. New York, NY: Routledge.
Phillips, D. (2014). "Comparatography", history and policy quotation: Some reflections. Comparative Education, 50(1), 73–83.
Popkewitz, T. (2007). Alchemies and governing: Or, questions about the questions we ask. Educational Philosophy and Theory, 39(1), 64–83.
Popkewitz, T. (Ed.). (2013). Rethinking the history of education: Transnational perspectives on its questions, methods, and knowledge. New York, NY: Palgrave Macmillan.
Popkewitz, T. A., Diaz, J., & Kirchgasler, C. (Eds.). (2017). A political sociology of educational knowledge: Studies of exclusions and difference. New York, NY: Routledge.
Popkewitz, T. P., Khurshid, A., & Zhao, W. (2014). Comparative studies and the reasons o reason: Historicizing differences and "seeing" reforms in multiple modernities. In L. Vega (Ed.), Empires, post-coloniality and interculturality: New challenges for comparative education (pp. 21–43). Rotterdam, The Netherlands: Sense Publishers.
Popkewitz, T. S. (Ed.). (2015). The "Reason" of schooling: Historicizing curriculum studies, pedagogy, and teacher education. New York, NY and London, UK: Routledge.
Porkert, M. (1974). The theoretical foundations of Chinese medicine: Systems of correspondence. Cambridge, MA: MIT Press.
Said, E. W. (1979). Orientalism. New York, NY: Vintage.
Saussy, H. (2001). The Great walls of discourse and other adventures in cultural China. Cambridge, MA and London, UK: Harvard University Asia Center.
Schriewer, J. (2006). Comparative social science: Characteristic problems and changing problem solutions. Comparative Education, 42(3), 299–336.
Sigurdsson, G. (2017). Transformative critique: What Confucianism can contribute to contemporary education. Studies in Philosophy and Education, 36(2), 131–146.
Sobe, N. W., & Ness, C. (2010). Comparative history of education: William Brickman and the study of educational flows, transfers, and circulations. European Education, 42(2), 57–66.
Tan, C. (2015). Education policy borrowing and cultural scripts for teaching in China. Comparative Education, 51(2), 196–211.

Wang, H. (2014). *Nonviolence and education: Cross-cultural pathways*. New York, NY and London, UK: Routledge.
Wu, Z. (2016). Person-making through Confucian exegesis. In G. P. Zhao & Z. Y. Deng (Eds.), *Re-envisioning Chinese education: The meaning of person-making in a new age* (pp. 93–115). New York, NY: Routledge.
Young, R. (2001). *Postcolonialism: An historical introduction*. Malden, MA: Blackwell.
Zhang, H. (2014). Curriculum studies and curriculum reform in China. In W. F. Pinar (Ed.), *Curriculum studies in China: Intellectual histories* (pp. 29–67). New York, NY: Palgrave Macmillan.
Zhang, X. L. (1992). *Heidegger and Taoism* (Unpublished doctoral dissertation). State University of New York, Buffalo.
Zhang, X. L. (1996). *Heidegger sixiang yu zhongguo tiandao: zhongji shiyu de kaiqi he jiaorong [Heidegger and Chinese Taoism* 海德格尔思想与中国天道：终极视域的开启和 交融]. Beijing: Shenghuo-Dushu-Xinzhi Sanlian Shudian.
Zhang, X. L. (1998). *Mighty opposites: From dichotomies to differences in the comparative study of China*. Stanford, CA: Stanford University Press.
Zhang, W. (2006). *Heidegger, Rorty, and the Eastern thinkers: A hermeneutics of cross-cultural understanding*. Albany, NY: State University of New York Press.
Zhao, W., & Ford, D. R. (2017). Re-imagining affect with study: Implications from a Daoist Wind-Story and Yin—Yang movement. *Studies in Philosophy and Education*, 1–13. doi:10.1007/s11217-017-9577-0

3 An Ontological Language–Discourse Perspective

Besides the developmental comparative paradigm, Westernization of the Chinese language since the early twentieth century also contributes to the material happening of epistemicide in structuring the knowledge system and educational reform in modern China. This chapter moves a step further to scrutinize the principles and rationales of signification and representation that reduce modern languages, both English and Chinese, into an enclosed linguistic system. With such representational system, meaning is generated mainly through analyzing the synchronic grammatical arrangements within statements. To constrain such a representation rationale, this chapter brings in an ontological language–discourse perspective for educational studies in China and beyond. This perspective calls for a reconceptualization as well as demystification of the Chinese language, no longer with some Western notions and frameworks, but by historicizing it back to its own historical strata. In so doing, it constructs a diachronic hermeneutics to understand the tones and contextures that subsist in the Chinese individual characters and words. This chapter prepares a way for further mapping out the conditions of possibility of China's entire knowledge system and educational thinking as expressed in *Yijing* in the next chapter.

Language/Discourse in Education and Curriculum Studies

Language and discourse are two popular yet contested notions. It goes without saying that almost all research uses language–discourse as its means or object of examination. In linguistics and sociolinguistics, language usually refers to a self-justified linguistic system and discourses are specific language terms in use. In Western philosophy and literary studies, language is closely linked with the grounding issues of metaphysics, signification, and representation. For example, the linguistic (pro)nouns and grammatical subject–verb–object structure presume and foster *presence* as the grounding principle of the whole Western logo-phono-centric thinking. In *The Logic of Sense*, Gilles Deleuze (1990) proposes a verb of pure *becoming* to elude the present-based identity and also implode the binary division structure of past and future. In educational or cultural studies, language is often treated as a given or fabricated cultural sign, competency, or medium that interconnects with the issues of power, identity, equity, and hegemony in colonialism, post-colonialism, multiculturalism, and diversity at both policy and curriculum levels (see, e.g., Ciscel, 2010; Cayir, 2015; Coyne, 2015; Gallucci, 2014; Hamid & Jahan, 2015; Iliycheva, 2010; Kim, 2016; Martin-Jones, Kroon, & Kurvers, 2011; McCormick, 2012).

With Michel Foucault and other post-modern or post-structural thinkers, language and discourse are no longer treated merely as a given linguistic system or term impregnated with fixed semantic meanings. Rather, language–discourse becomes a theoretical construct, an embodiment of historical-cultural styles of reasoning, which orders as well as delimits our thinking about social-political reality and truth. Unpacking language–discourse this way is to render visible the broader landscape of thought and practice, and the theoretical-methodological force of such a language–discourse perspective is just beginning to gain scholars' attention in comparative cultural studies of education and world order. Blumenfeld-Jones (2016), for example, pinpoints that the Protestant language–discourse derived from the Hellenic and subsequently Christian thinking has structured and ordered the Western world, marginalizing and excluding a Judaic rabbinic interpretive paradigm. Horlacher (2016) historicizes the German notion of *Bildung* as an educational language–discourse and explores how this notion gets deployed in other linguistic and cultural contexts, say, the Scandinavian countries and the English-speaking world, to impart varied educational aspirations and styles of reasoning.

Daniel Tröhler's *Languages of Education* (2011/2013) is another example to the point. Treating *language* as an embodiment of some historical–ideological–cultural "modes or modalities of thinking, talking, or writing about education" (p. 1), it provides an original narrative on how the rooted religious languages of Protestantism and republicanism, in confrontation or negotiation, have historically, ideologically, and politically structured the schooling in Germany, the United States, and Switzerland. Tröhler's invocation of *language* as a theoretical regulating system draws upon the well-known *langue–parole* distinction made by the Genevan linguist Ferdinand de Saussure (1857–1913), with *langue* designating a rather stable language system and *parole* spoken verbal utterances and speech. Tröhler explains that he prefers the contested concept of "language" over other controversial terms such as paradigm, weltanschauung, ideology, architecture, culture, and mentality, partly because "language" is comparatively old, internationally accepted, and tangible.

To Tröhler, employing the notion of "language" as a theoretical construct has three benefits. First, it enables his research to transcend the national limits most educational studies are confined to. Second, since language unavoidably intersects with the issues of ideology, culture, and power, examining language enables him to get down to the fundamental historical-cultural ideological core of varied educational arguments, proposals, systems, and concepts in their historiography. Third, a focus on *langue* rather than *parole* distinguishes his book from Israel Scheffler's book, *The Language of Education* (1960), which to Tröhler remains within the realm of paroles in the tradition of analytic philosophy by analyzing the characteristic slogans and metaphors in public communication. Focused on contextualized religious and political languages (*langues*) rather than arguments (*paroles*), Tröhler's book conducts a transnational archaeology of educational arguments in a historical, analytical, and comparative way, adding new nuances to what counts as educational theories. Van Brummelen (2013) comments that Tröhler's reconceptualization of language as theoretical regulating systems can be mobilized as "an historical tool that gives us insights that go beyond Whig and Marxist interpretations" (p. x).

In the field of curriculum studies, Dwayne E. Huebner back in the 1960s already alerts us to the language issue, which he re-asserts in the 1990s remains to be the problem in the American curriculum research and praxis (see Pinar's Introduction in Huebner, 1999, p. xxii). Actually, what Huebner means by the language problem continues today in the form of globalized discourses and on a global landscape, namely the Tyler Rationale language of learning objectives, experiences selection, organization, and evaluation. This Tylerian curricular language, mainly from the fields of social sciences and psychology (see, also Autio, 2017), has a demonic force and bespeaks two tyrannical myths, one of learning and the other of purpose, to the extent that "mysteries are reduced to problems, doubts to error, and unknowables to yet-to-be-discoverables" (Huebner, 1999, p. 104). Curriculum workers, once locked into such a language system as they mostly are, can't tackle with mystery or doubt or unknowables that go with the existing temporal activities within a classroom.

To break from this Tylerian tyrannical myth, Huebner vociferates that the language of learning and purpose must be cast aside and new questions to be asked. Toward that intention, curricular workers need to search for a new language, a language that has not been bogged down to the instrumental logic, which would enable them to describe the educational activities as accurately as possible and also to become conscious of the five different values nurtured within varied types of language. These five possible value schemes that go with our curricular language are technical, political, economic, scientific, esthetic, and esthetic, the last two of which Huebner argues are often largely, if not completely, ignored in the then curriculum activities. This is still true with today's educational practices largely enthralled by a predominant learning logic, an instrumental trope, and managerial governance.

This is actually one form of epistemicide expressed as the predominance of scientific learning rationale in the educational field. It has happened as an effect of the replacement of philosophy by psychology and learning science as the grounding principle of education (Autio, 2017). Empirical research in education is mostly the quantitative exploration by standardized questionnaires resulting in statistically verified statements (Tröhler, 2011/2013, p. 16). These scientific learning discourses have now become globalized across the world, and as a hidden form of epistemicide, they have also marginalized other cultural styles of reasoning. For example, the Tylerian learning language has also become the catchphrase of China's current educational and curriculum reforms as manifested in Chapter 1, imprisoning the thinking and practices of Chinese policy makers, curriculum theorists, and practitioners. However, also as shown in Chapter 1, globalization discourse as epistemicide has not been well recognized in the field of education and curriculum.

Nevertheless, in the field of critical cultural discourse studies, scholars like Shi-xu and Zongjie Wu, also my former colleagues at Zhejiang University in China have been critiquing the Westernization of Chinese discourse and styles of reasoning. For example, Shi-xu (2005, 2014, 2015, 2016) has been constructing a paradigm for Chinese discourse studies in general. Zongjie Wu (2011, 2014, 2016) has been in search of an appropriate language to re-talk about China's reason, knowledge, education, and pedagogy to loosen up their imprisonment by a Western Enlightenment rationale. In his earlier years, he uses Mikhail Bakhtin's notion of heteroglossia to dissect the Westernized discourses in current China's teacher education reform. In recent years, he has been examining Confucian cultural and educational heritage through some material and spatial imprints. Wu (2016) argues that the purpose of Confucian person-making was primarily to

> Establish a language instead of knowledge so that learners could speak/act in the place of the sages. This linguistic perspective, hardly explored today, may offer an alternative way of thinking, an intellectual tool to reconstruct visions of person-making pedagogy that resonate with the Western and Eastern pasts.
>
> (p. 98)

My intellectual training first started in linguistics, sociolinguist, and critical discourse studies with Shi-xu and Zongjie Wu, and later moved to a Foucauldian–Heideggerian discourse/language studies during my doctoral studies. With such a cross-disciplinary training background, I treat language-discourses interchangeably as an ontological being that embodies and delimits our styles of reasoning, and stand with Heidegger that "the reflection on language (is) a decisive *way* toward the leap into the completely other, namely being-historical thinking" (1939/2004, p. 5, cited in Ma, 2008, p. 41). It is also because of my background training in both discourse and curriculum studies that this book foregrounds an ontological language–discourse perspective, a perspective with its theoretical significance not much documented in educational studies in general.

Modern Representational Language: Re-reading Foucault's *The Order of Things*

As mentioned in Preface, my cross-cultural intellectual journey genuinely started with re-reading Michel Foucault's classic, *The Order of Things*

(1969/1973). This book, Foucault claims, was inspired by the ancient Chinese animal taxonomy that strikes him as utterly unthinkable within the Western epistemology. Intrigued by and somewhat flipping around Foucault's *way* of picking up a research project, I couldn't help wondering how far it would be possible for me as a native Chinese to first discern and then render intelligible such Chinese historical-cultural sensibilities cross-culturally, sensibilities unthinkable to Westerners and yet tacitly common-sensical to Chinese. A rendering that unfolds in the English language yet still exhibits the Chinese epistemological sensibilities as they are. A rendering that goes with and beyond using the Western categories and frameworks as a reference point and yet not getting entrapped within a stagnant cultural relativist stand.

Such an intention partly helped me discern the literal, prevalent, yet silent wind-schooling discourses, that is, "school/teaching/learning wind," as a culturally unique sensibility that I actually grew up with yet had never really *seen*, except as naturalized linguistic metaphors, until I went to the United States for doing my doctoral studies. Culturally unique in that the literal English gloss of "school wind" and the discursive "wind-education" interlock don't seem to make direct sense to the English readers. Can "school wind" represent the winds blowing within schools? If yes, then how can it be associated with teaching and learning? If not, then what kind of other winds can it register than the natural-physical wind blowing around? I intuitively felt such a "school wind" falls out of the modern Western(ized) signifier–signified representational or conceptual style of thinking, but failed to express clearly why it is so. Puzzled and also intrigued, I re-turned to Foucault's *The Order of Things*, particularly exploring his thinking about the notion of representation in relation to language as a sign system, asking how such representational way of thinking becomes contextually possible in the Western history of thought, and pondering how far it is justified to use the Western terms of "representation" or "non-representation" to describe the Chinese language.

With such a focused agenda, I came up with the below detailed epistemic picture of ordering between words and things, or man and nature, on the one hand, and an operationalization of the representational mode of thinking on the other hand. The Western cultural and historical words–things or man–nature ordering becomes an expedient point that makes it possible for me to re-approach the Chinese language as a being. The representational mode of thinking that Foucault succinctly critiques and that still enthralls the modern conceptual thinking becomes a trap that I need to constantly caution myself against slipping into throughout my whole research project, as it is so easy to fall back within before I know it. It becomes a blockage that has to be cleared toward my embarking on a new thinking path. For this reason, excuse me that I have to keep the below re-capitulation of Foucault's thinking as long as it is.

To avoid confusion with two other English books already published under the title of *Words and Things*, the English translation of Foucault's *Les*

Mots et Les Choses finally adopts the author's alternative title *The Order of Things*, claimed as his originally preferred title (1973, Publisher's note, p. viii). However, I find its French title, *Les Mots et Les Choses* (*words and things* in English), indeed capitulates very concisely one key theme running throughout Foucault's whole book, namely, the vicissitudes in the Western epistemological understandings of the juxtaposition and movement between words and things, along the dynamics of a profound kinship, divorced separation, and/or superimposition with varied rules of organization. One of Foucault's strategies is to examine the transformed organizations of the *sign* at different historical periods, treating it as both a constituent as well as an effect of the distinct rules and forms of *episteme* that historically order empirical beings and living things.

From the Stoic time up until the Renaissance period (roughly the end of the sixteenth century), Foucault argues that Western knowledge imbricates words and things in "profound kinship" (p. 43) insofar as words/languages, being natural (God's) written signs/marks of things, embody the virtues of things they designate, intermediated by the form of similitude/resemblance and through the principal figures of convenience, emulation, analogy, and sympathy. "It signifies exactly *in so far as* it resembles what it is indicating (that is, *a* similitude)" (p. 28, my italics). It is worthy to note here that Foucault uses "*in so far as*" and "*a*" to rightly accent an "almost the same" (p. 64) rather than an overlapping "homology" between the signatures (words) and what it indicates (things). In the latter case, things would become naturally transparent and immediately knowable. Thus, "the similitudes that form the graphics of the world are (always) one 'cog' out of alignment with those that form its discourse" (p. 30) and although "the signatures and what it denotes are of exactly the same nature," they obey "a different law of distribution" (p. 29).

Embedded within such a complicated system of duplication, the epistemological question for the sixteenth century poses itself as "how it was possible to know that a sign did in fact designate what it signified" (p. 42). By seeking out and interpreting the form of similitude! Foucault says:

> To search for meaning is to bring to light a resemblance. To search for the law governing signs is to discover the things that are alike. The grammar of beings is an exegesis of these things. And what the language they speak has to tell us is quite simply what the syntax is that binds them together.
>
> (p. 29)

In other words, hermeneutics (related to the meaning of signs) and semiology (related to the location, constitution, and laws of signs) are superimposed through the law of resemblance. To know is to discover and make speak the signs as well as the rule of resemblance. Nature and the word are intertwined through analogy, rather than signification, and spin into one infinite single text. The very existence of language as a totality intersects with the "loci and forms of the cosmos" (p. 37).

At the end of the Renaissance, however, things and words were to be separated from one another. To be specific, "the peculiar existence and ancient solidarity of language as a thing inscribed in the fabric of the world" (p. 43) were dissolved in its new "functioning in representation" (ibid.) wherein language functions only as purely transparent and neutral representative signs, being separate from things. Here the Renaissance unitary and triple system of signs (with the rule of resemblance connecting the mark and that which is marked) gave its way to a strictly binary arrangement between "the idea of one thing and the idea of another thing" (p. 63) with no more intermediary figure. Signs no longer exist as material marks waiting in silence to be recognized and rendered visible; they are now constituted only by an act of knowing and perform their signifying function within knowledge itself. Reduced to a bond established inside knowledge between the ideas of things, their sign relation is no longer guaranteed by order of things in themselves. In other words, the uniform layer where things and words were endlessly interwoven vanished in the early seventeenth century; the epistemological question becomes "how a sign could be linked to what it signified" (p. 43), and the answer is provided through analysis of representation.

According to Foucault, presupposed as a logical necessity within such a newly emerged binary arrangement is that "the sign is a duplicated representation doubled over upon itself. It is at the same time *indication* and *appearance*, a relation to an object and a manifestation of itself" (p. 65, italics original). In other words, the sign is the "*representativity* of the representation in so far as it is *representable*" (ibid., italics original). Seen this way, words are virtual elements of discourse, and all language was posited and had value only as "discourse," that is, as "the spontaneous analysis of representation" (p. 43, p. 232) or "merely representation itself represented by verbal signs" (p. 81). Language has no content in itself, but only a representative function or role in signifying and representing something else. The words that compose languages "existed only by virtue of the representative value they possessed, and the power of analysis, of duplication, of composition and arrangement that they were accorded with regard to the things represented" (p. 280).

This representative role of language finds its expression in analysis conducted by general grammar in its purest form, general to the extent that it attempts to make visible the representative function of discourse, namely, "all the words of a language were bearers of a more or less hidden, more or less derived, signification whose original *raison d'etre* lay in an initial designation" (p. 233). Two principles undergird general grammar analysis: that of an original and common language which supposedly provided the initial batch of roots; and that of a series of historical events, foreign to language, which, from outside, bend it, wear it away, refine it, make it more flexible, by multiplying or combining its forms (invasions, migrations, advances in learning, political freedom or slavery, etc.). Language in classical period works according to principles of proposition, articulation, designation, and derivation. "The fundamental task of Classical 'discourse' is *to ascribe a name to things, and in that name to name their being.* For two centuries, [the] Western discourse was the locus of ontology" (p. 120, italics original).

Towards the end of the eighteenth century, the representative role is no longer constitutive of the word (and knowledge) in its very being. The word is displaced away from its representative functions by the introduction of some grammatical formal elements, say, inflection, vowel graduation, and consonantal changes, into the philological analysis of language in comparative grammar that is not reducible to "pure discursivity" (p. 282). Having no representative content and thus not transparent to the signification of the discourse, these grammatical formal elements with regularities of their own impose upon the sounds, syllables, and roots an organization that is not that of representation.

Such independent analysis of grammatical structures as practiced from the nineteenth century on brings back to language an autonomous organic structure and a being proper to itself that has been marred up and forgotten by representation and signification since the sixteenth century. It is the deep scission of literature in the nineteenth century from other genres of language that functions as a "counter-discourse," bringing the language back to shine in its raw being, yet in a different mode from the Renaissance. Instead of rediscovering some primary word that has been buried in the Renaissance episteme, Foucault argues the task for modern criticism now is:

> To disturb the words we speak, denounce the grammatical habits of our thinking, to dissipate the myths that animate our words, to render once more noisy and audible the element of silence that all discourse carries with it as it is spoken.
>
> (p. 298)

Foucault says that the revival of all the techniques of exegesis in the nineteenth century should be understood as an exemplar of modern criticism in exploding the trap of philology, namely, assuming the a priori existence of grammatical arrangements in a language for what can be expressed in it. To Foucault, "the truth of discourse is caught in the trap of philology" (p. 297) and to suspend this trap,

> Modern criticism does not proceed from the observation that there is language towards the discovery of what that language means, but from the deployment of manifest discourse towards a revelation of language in its crude being. Hence the need to work one's way back from opinions, philosophies, and perhaps even from sciences, to the words that made them possible, and, beyond that, to a thought whose essential life has not yet been caught in the network of grammar.
>
> (p. 298)

In a word, this critical modern criticism in literature or literary studies has as its mission to overhaul what is often considered as a "stagnant and abstract Western oncologic, specifically to loosen its grip on poetic language" (Bush, p. 47), toward "understanding the latter not as representational but as having its own being" (p. 48). It intends to suspend the entire conceptual mode of signification that goes hand in hand with the modern representational language. With such a spirit, reading is not much in what is signified than signifying itself and when translating the Chinese language terms to English, "one must follow closely what is said, not merely what is abstractly meant" (Fenollosa, 1936, p. 20). Now I show the ways this re-reading of Foucault's *The Order of Things* enabled me to work back the Chinese language from a modern representational system to a being, which can be seen as a self-reflexive Daoist onto-un-learning experience.

Working Back (Chinese) Language From a Representational System to a Being

Just a reminder that this book intends to fulfill two parallel missions. First, it provides a paradigmatic exemplar to address a comparative methodological challenge and a possible epistemological crisis that results from it. The strategy is to historicize the events of language, education, and curriculum in modern China. Second, it provides an exemplary case of post-foundational *study* by scrutinizing and theorizing my intellectual research journey itself as a Daoist onto-un-learning *way*. I coin the term "Daoist onto-un-learning" to resonate what Dao De Jing murmurs, "doing learning gains and doing Dao loses" 為學日益為道日損 (Chapter 48).

To clarify, my self-reflexive Daoist onto-un-learning way moves forward by often moving back intellectually. By moving back intellectually, I mean the signposts I pick up on my way often help me (1) recognize the presumptions my thinking stands upon and gets confined to, (2) turn them around by explicating their limits and constraints, and (3) re-situate my thinking on a more justifiable cross-cultural platform. Sometimes zooming out helps to see a broader picture just as a painting appreciator can have a fuller perspective at a certain distance from the object. Foucault's genealogical unpacking of the Western epistemological juxtapositions of words and things, from a profound kinship, through a divorced separation, toward words/language becoming a being proper to itself as a material object/thing in modern criticism, is one such significant signpost gesturing me to move both forward and backward intellectually.

As a forward signpost, it reassures me of the feasibility of my initial research agenda to re-examine the prevalent yet silent schooling wind-discourses not as mere linguistic metaphors but as a mode of being to itself. In other words, "school wind" should not be simply taken as a dead metaphor semantically meaning "school atmosphere." Instead, the expression of "school wind" itself, as well as the juxtaposition of the notions "school" and "wind," should be further problematized to listen to what has historically been said (or not) through and beside their togetherness. Besides, as a mode of being to itself, the nature of the Chinese language needs to be further investigated. For example, what features does it have as a graphic writing system to make it distinct from phonetic languages? Can I assume the grammatical arrangements of the Chinese language in the first place and search for its meaning? How can I situate the Chinese writing as a way of reasoning ethnographically to its historical context to see its ordering with Chinese people's thinking and practices?

As a backward signpost, it suspends my two thinking presumptions. First, to re-treat the Chinese language as a mode of being means a need to work the Chinese wind-language back from its common English gloss of "wind" to the Chinese character "風" (*feng*), suspending the principle of transparency presumed in trans-lingual translation. Translation instead is to explicate translucency or difference in cross-cultural studies. As Chakrabarty (2000) rightly observes,

> Translation is the stake but also the scapegoat for cross-cultural inquiry. What translation produces out of seeming 'incommensurability' is neither an absence of relationship between dominant and dominating forms of knowledge nor equivalents that successfully mediate between differences, but precisely the partly opaque relationship we call "difference."
> (p. 17)

This difference-based principle turns translation into "an exercise of intercultural translation and diatopic hermeneutics through which the reciprocal limitations of alternative conceptions of human dignity can be identified thus opening the possibility of new relations and dialogues among them" (Sousa Santos, 2009, p. 18). In other words, translation would work as epistemological support for producing emancipatory, not regulatory, knowledge and practices that are finite and incomplete by each self but put together can form a sustainable web of interconnection. Seen this way, a bracketing of the "風 = wind" equalization opens up a dialogue between these two systems of language on their distinct modes of meaning-making and the epistemological conditions of knowledge.

Second, Foucault's genealogical unpacking questions the validity of my earlier intention of using post-structural strategies like Foucault's notions of "statement" (1969/1972), Deleuze's "sense" (1969/1990), and Derrida's "differance" (1982) to describe the being of Chinese language. That is, can I say the Chinese language is a Foucauldian statement with a Deleuzian sense within Derridean deferring and deferred movement? Since Foucault has shown us that the Western language has taken its historical trip to have become an enclosed representational discourse divorced from the worldly things, and since these post-structural strategies are constructed as an effect to critique such a logocentric thinking from which modern people still haven't emerged, if I use them as *the* lens to perceive the Chinese language, am I not already subsumed in the presumption that the Chinese language too is also an *idea* enclosed system waiting to be critiqued? Maybe it is! The fact that modern Chinese people rarely take notice of the expression "school wind" itself but seek its semantic signifier could be a good point in case. However, a historical inquiry is needed for examining its history to substantiate such an assertion. To note, I am not saying that these Western strategies are irrelevant as a style of thought. It is just that they can't be used as judging reference frameworks to start with in examining the Chinese language.

Seen this way, Foucault's genealogical unpacking in *The Order of Things* helped me realize my presumptions: I was standing too close to be able to see the *Chinese* language as a thing in itself, and was seeking the truth about the Chinese language within the *English* language system! I step backward to re-envision these Western post-structural critique strategies conducted in the Western context as one shared mode of inquiry, one that treats language not only as a way of reasoning but also an object of examination and one that renders visible something in the Western language irreducible to its representational logic. Accordingly, I zoom myself out for a broader view on the Western language, no longer language enclosed upon itself but in relation to things, that is, how it has become an enclosed representational system in the first place. Such a realization enables me to re-situate myself and listen to the Chinese language as a mode of being in movement with worldly things, namely, a movement between words and things, humans and nature, or culture and nature. The texture of such a movement and the way it transforms my mode of being as an inquirer-learner in my interaction with language are what I need to look at more closely.

To sum, Foucault's *The Order of Things* (1966/1973) provides me with a significant signpost on my cross-cultural learning way. The significance lies in (a) sharpening/honing my awareness that language needs to be treated as a being/thing to itself, not as an isolated system, but in relation to other things; (b) helping me realize "the trap of philology," namely, assuming the a priori existence of grammatical arrangements in a language for what can be expressed in it; and thus (c) reorienting my project toward archaeologically rendering intelligible cultural styles of thinking as expressed in *Yijing* (*The Book of Change*) and *Dao De Jing*, "whose essential life has not yet been caught in the network of (modern) grammar" (Foucault, 1966/1973, p. 285) through the Chinese "wind" language (Chapter 4) and "body" example (Chapters 5 and 6). Before unpacking this "wind-body" example, however, I would like to de-mystify some varying Western conceptualizations on the Chinese language/writing as character, ideograph, pictograph, logograph, or kanji.

De-mystifying Western Tropes of Chinese Language Back to Its Ethnographical Context

In comparative cross-cultural studies, the Chinese language is often labeled as being non-representational, as being what the West is not, as being outside

84 Overcoming "Epistemicide"

of the Western parenthesis. But such a categorization brings out the epistemicide issue in comparative thinking which I already explored at length in Chapter 1 because the Chinese language with a distinct cultural base may not fall into the category of representation in the first place. In this section, I give an overview of how the Chinese language or writing gets conceptualized as non-phonetic ideography in the West (see, Hansen, 1993) and also de-mystify the historical moments that enabled such categorization of the Chinese writing as against the Western phonetic letters. It is also to familiarize English readers outside Sinology studies with, and meanwhile to caution them against, some common and maybe misleading Western notions on describing the Chinese writing/language. Furthermore, it prepares a ground for me to hermeneutically read the Chinese "wind-language" (*feng* 風) back into its historical (con)text in the following section, showing a diachronic dimension of the Chinese mode of signification as against the largely synchronic signifier–signified conceptual style of reasoning within the modern Western language as unpacked by Michel Foucault and Ferdinand de Saussure, among others.

To clarify this point, I draw upon two historiographical papers by Haun Saussy, Professor of Comparative Literature at the University of Chicago for insights. In *Outside the Parenthesis (Those People Were a Kind of Solution)* (2001b), Saussy argues that the Chinese language or writing has been imaginatively appropriated by such Western thinkers as Michel Foucault, Jacque Derrida, Roland Barthes, and Julia Kristeva to support their so-called post-structural thinking "under the two broad headings of *grammatology* and *the end of humanism*" (p. 146, italics original). Such "projected appropriation" (Bush, 2008, p. 39) picks up the Chinese writing as a counter-point to re-invoke critiques on the Western thinking on space, time, presence, and truth, wherein the Chinese graphic writing becomes a myth of the Other, the symmetrical opposite to the Western logo-phono-centrism. Such deconstructive vocabulary expands onto the Chinese writing system but only for its project and not in relation with China itself. To go beyond such a closure, Saussy calls for a post-deconstructive way of thinking as a method to relate the Chinese language/writing in its historical self and shows such an effort in his other paper below. By post-deconstructive, Saussy (2001a) means to "ethnographically situate [the Chinese historical texts] among the conceptions it echoes or answers" (p. 36).

In *The Prestige of Writing:* 文, *Letter, Picture, Image, Ideography* (2001a), Saussy ethnographically situates the Chinese writing, using the multilayered textures of the notion *wen* (文 patterns, letter) as his strategic example, among the conceptions it echoes or answers, and explores how these Western, sometimes contradictory, conceptions as listed in the paper title itself historically gained their currency in the Western scholarship. Specifically, Saussy situates the Chinese literary writing as "inherent pattern or civilization" and picks it up as one string of patterns woven within the multilayered textures of 文. Such a strategy enables him to rethink the Chinese characters/writing from the perspective of its constituting strokes as strokes, namely, from a syntactic (in its Greek sense of parts composing the whole) rather than a semantic (what it stands for) point of view. Relevant here is Saussy's de-mystifying explication of the ways in which the distinct transformative thinking modes of Francis Bacon in the seventeenth century (with debts to Aristotle's *On Interpretatione*), of Jean-Francois Champollion in the eighteenth century, and of Ernest Fenollosa in the early twentieth century have respectively made it possible for the distinction between phonetic letters and non-phonetic writing to come into place (Bacon), to define the Chinese writing as a categorically ideographic system (Champollion), and conversely to depict the Chinese characters and even sentence as energetic or forceful image of nature (Fenollosa).

Saussy argues that it is Bacon, with debts to Aristotle's scaffolding on the ordering of mind, language (spoken and written), and things shown in *On Interpretatione* and based upon the presumption that writing is inescapably a transcription of spoken words, who initiates a contradistinction between non-phonetic, potentially wholly conventional model of writing, and phonetic letters. The Chinese script is then chosen to serve as the chief ethnographic example because it possibly eliminated spoken words as one of the levels of mediation for the inter-ordering among mind, language, and the world. In this sense, Aristotle's semiology on mind, language, and things furnished the means for the first European interpretation of the Chinese character; and such direct notation of reality, through conventional characters and without the interference of spoken words, Saussy further argues, has later been explored by Paolo Rossi, Jacques Derrida, Mary Slaughter, and Umberto Eco in their writings.

According to Saussy, the term *ideogram* entered modern European languages with the diffusion of Champollion's decoding of the ancient Egyptian script announced in the Letter *a Monsieur Dacier* of 1822 and presented more fully in the *Grammaire egyptienne* of 1836–1841. Champollion there speaks of "ideographic writing, that is, writing that depicts the ideas and not the sounds of a language" (cited in Saussy, 2001a, p. 45), and alludes to the fact that "the Chinese also use an ideographic script" (ibid.). Champollion significantly introduced phonetic characters, that is, characters whose functions in writing are not always to convey a meaningful content, into the decipherment of Egyptian, and thus disrupted the purely semantic interpretive method relying on "mimetic reference or symbolic cross-references" prevalent up till the sixteenth century. However, when adding in a parenthetical remark (the Chinese also use an ideographic script), Champollion adapted his triple classification of symbolic values to the description of East Asian scripts, namely, the alternatives were taken as *labels* for the whole of a writing system. Thus phonetic or ideographic started to operate as mutually exclusive designations of the nature of writing-systems.

Bacon's attempt is different though when he says of the Chinese writing:

> And we understand further that it is the use of China and kingdoms of the high Levant to write in Characters Real, which expresses neither letters nor words in gross, but Things or Notions; insomuch as countries and provinces, which understand not one another's language, can nevertheless read one another's writings, because the characters are accepted more generally than the languages do extend.
> (1605, cited in Saussy, 2001a, p. 47)

Saussy clarifies that Bacon uses the term "Characters Real" here to describe how the Chinese can nevertheless read one another's writings even though they can't understand one another's spoken language, and this term was presumed necessarily to lead to "a Universal character" to ensure problem-free communication among all people. However, when Champollion assigned to the Chinese writing the category of "ideographic script," he was read as offering a restrictive definition, a definition that marked the peculiar, non-universal features of that writing, thus it is defined with a look backward to the Aristotelian tradition, as "ideographic" in the precise sense of "non-phonetic."

Such a non-phonetic pictographic writing is vehemently condemned by Hegel in the nineteenth century as a fossilized language in that it "reflects and reinforces an Oriental inability to move beyond the sensuous particular toward universal ideas and concepts" (Bush, 2008, p. 38) and thus being inferior to freer phonetic. However, the modernist Fenollosa–Pound tradition inverted such a condemnation by viewing the alphabetic and European writing as the "corpse language," and the Oriental writing as vivid and vital. In his introduction to Ezra Pound's *Selected Poems* (1928), T. S. Eliot refers to Pound as "the inventor of Chinese poetry for our time," a phrase that has been quoted frequently since (see Bush, 2008, p. 34).

In Fenollosa's book, *The Chinese Written Character as a Medium of Poetry*, first published through Pound's adaptation in 1919, expresses an unparalleled and unprecedented, though somewhat mistaken, lauding of the Chinese ideographic writing as a picture of things. According to Fenollosa, it is not just the Chinese characters, but even the Chinese subject–verb–object sentences that indeed nurture such ideogram qualities, in the sense of being an image of nature, "depicting pictographically a complex of natural actions and relations laid out in causal line" (Saussy, 2001a, p. 40). As Fenollosa put it, "[t]he type of sentence in nature is a flash of lightning. It passes between two terms, a cloud and the earth" (cited in Saussy, 2001a, p. 40; also in Saussy, 2008, p. 85). Viewing the Chinese writing as "transmitting the intuition of force," Fenollosa (1936) describes all nature as a vast interplay of verbs, not of nouns; nouns or things are merely "the terminal points, or rather the meeting points, of actions, cross-sections cut through actions, snap-shots" (p. 14, also cited in Saussy, 2001a, p. 40; also see, Saussy, 2008).

However, most linguists now prefer the term *logogram* or Japanese term *kanji* (漢字) over *ideogram* to describe the Chinese language, and *ideogram* is mercifully falling out of our vocabulary. According to Saussy (2001a), "Logograms represent the words, or—to acknowledge the vagueness of the term word—the distinct meaning-bearing units of a language through a corresponding vocabulary of distinct signs" (p. 42). Attributable to the fact that the term ideogram is often used loosely as a synonym for both the visual and semantic type of reference, a conflation has occurred in that ideograms or logograms are necessarily pictograms, the latter meaning a conventional, usually highly schematized, graphic element whose interpretation is based on a claim of visual resemblance between the graph and its referent. Seen this way, pictograph is a misconception of Chinese language (Zhang L., 1998). Ideogram marks the place of ideas, such as the place-marking symbol *o*, which has nothing to do with its graphic features. Thus, ideography is not necessarily pictography: there is a distinction between an image and a mark.

Saussy's research endeavors show the shaky ground for historically labeling the Chinese as being non-representational, as being what the West is not, as being outside of the Western parenthesis. Maybe the Chinese language doesn't fall into the category of representation in the first place. Such a categorization brings out the epistemicide issue in comparative thinking, which I already explored at length in Chapter 1. Then how is it possible to show cultural sensibilities without falling into the trap of Western frameworks? With this question, I strive to hermeneutically explicate the meaning-making intricacies with the Chinese writing, languag,e and words within its historical-ethnographical context, regenerating what is rightly nurtured within the saying of the Chinese term for language and words, *wenzi* 文字.

Regenerating the Being of Chinese Language (*Wenzi* 文字): A Diachronic Hermeneutics

The Chinese language is composed of individual *zi* 字, each containing a meaning-related graphic form, a sound, and some cultural textures and tones. As "the distinct meaning-bearing units of the Chinese language" (Saussy, 2001a, p. 42), *zi* 字 doesn't have an equivalent in the English language even though it is often translated as "word" or "character." The Chinese words/characters (*zi* 字) remain more or less the same morphologically from the Qin dynasty when the writing system/language was regulated until the nineteenth century. However, as I outlined in Introduction, since the twentieth century, the Chinese language has undergone some institutionalized simplification movements initiated by the 1920s New Cultural Movement radicals. As a result, the current writing words/characters used in mainland China are called simplified Chinese characters compared to the traditional complicated version still used in Hong Kong and Taiwan. This is one expression of the Westernization of the Chinese language in modern China.

Besides that, the modern Chinese language has since the early twentieth century been devoured by Western-introduced terminology and epistemology at an unparalleled pace and degree. Specifically, when the modern Western discourses-terms enter into China, either traditional Chinese terms are in-invoked or neologisms of monographic characters are coined as their semantic glosses. Either way, the mode of translation often transfigures or overwrites the original cultural-historical senses as well as the epistemological meanings nurtured within each Chinese character. For example, the Chinese term for education, *jiaoyu* 教育, is a cultural notion re-invoked in modern China as a gloss of the English word "education." Even though *jiaoyu* 教育 originally embraces a dual sense of teaching and nurturing, the latter sense of nurturing is mostly eclipsed in its modern usage of signifying the overall schooling system and practices in modern China. Seen this way, what Bush (2008) says makes full sense:

> It is not the words that are dead, then, but the way they are read, and this is not only something that can change over time (today's shocking catachresis is tomorrow's tired cliché), but also something that can be affected and effected by cultural position—hence precisely the regenerative value of the example of Chinese.
>
> (p. 63)

In other words, the individual words or characters are still there, nourishing their historical and etymological, that is, originary textures and tones. However, the way they are currently read as concepts along a signifier–signified mode of signification has blinded us to their originary textures and tones. It is not that we don't know the words. On the contrary, we recognize their forms easily like the aporetic wind-narratives collated in the first Chinese dictionary. However, I simply couldn't understand their originary saying because the epistemological ordering of that system of knowledge is not reducible to the modern mode of signification which resides meaning within a synchronic grammatical structure of the statements. On the contrary, the way meaning is made with ancient Chinese texts is ordered along a Confucian exegesis with which the originary saying of each Chinese character/word can only be regenerated by tracing and referring it back to the ancient Confucian Classics. Wu Z. (2016) claims such a diachronic hermeneutics as "a genealogy of Dao," which has been passed down generation after generation by the Confucian scholars till the early twentieth century.

Then what epistemological theses on knowledge, reason, and meaning ground and make possible such a diachronic hermeneutics? To answer this question, we need to further unpack the (con)textures and (over)tones of the Chinese language as a "a silenced and different genealogy of thought" (Paraskeva, 2016, p. 80) nurtured within the Chinese term for language and words, *wenzi* 文字. Both *wen* and *zi* are uniquely primordial linguistic and cultural notions grounding the genesis of the entire Chinese writing system, the interlacing form of the Confucian classical texts, as well as a diachronic

Confucian exegesis, none of these reducible to the genesis and signification of the Western thought. Now let's elaborate them one by one.

First of all, the invention of *wen* and *zi* orders the genesis of Chinese thought. Not akin to the Western "word" as God's creation, the Chinese *wen* and *zi* as writing characters were invented as primordial records or imitations of the observed footprints of natural beings. Xu Shen (c. 58–147 CE), the Chinese philologist of the Han Dynasty who compiled the first comprehensive etymological/analytic Chinese dictionary *shuowenjiezi* 說文解字, systematically sorts out the intricate textures and contextures of the Chinese characters by their graphic formation, sound, and cultural meaning, grouping them into 540 graphic classifiers and 9,353 characters (*zi* 字). In so doing, he explicates six[1] principles in which the Chinese words/characters are ordered along with *wen* and *zi*:

倉頡初作書/依類象形/故謂之文/其後形聲相益/即謂之字/文者物象之本/字者孳乳而浸多也
When Cang Jie first created writing, he resorted to the primordial forms and shapes of things. This is why the created graphs were called *wen*. Later, the writing graphs was combined with sound to make up *zi*. *Wen* is the root of the images of things, and *zi* were born and grew up in its milk
(Preface to *shuowenjiezi*, in *Shuowenjiezizhu* published by the Shanghai Guji Press, 1981, p. 1343, my translation)

Here *wen* 文 are characters constituting only one graphic element (single-bodied characters), and thus are not susceptible to further analysis into the constituent parts smaller than the graphs themselves; the *zi* 字 are characters made up of more than one identifiable graphic component (joined-bodied characters), and thus are capable of analysis into those individual parts (Boltz, 1993). Henceforth the book title *shuowenjiezi* literally says "explaining *wen* and clarifying *zi*" with *wen* as originary milk nourishing the burgeoning of *zi*. To the extent that *wen* functions as the root and primordial graphic constituents of *zi*, *wen* can be conceptualized as "plereme," which, in Luis Hjelmslev's wording, glows as a meaning-embodying material being compared to the meaningless alphabetical "phoneme" of English words (see, Saussy, 2001a). In other words, each Chinese *wen* and *zi* entails some cultural senses, textures, and tones by itself, and this accounts for the fact that Confucian exegesis involves a multilayered, intertextual, and rigorous word-by-word examination of the classical scripture for its tiny and subtle textures and tones.

Such an etymological scrutiny of *wen* and *zi* explicates their originary saying, which is hardly visible in their modern compound form of *wenzi*, naturalized as a generic term for the Chinese writing characters. For example, with a sentence like "I like the Chinese *wenzi*," *wenzi* becomes a grammatical component with no inkling of their primordial cultural saying. In other words, subsuming Chinese *wenzi* within an enclosed language system conceals its cultural being. To flip it around, working back the common Chinese terms to their constitutive individual characters/words brackets our modern grammar and implodes a common sense take of language as a linguistic object. Instead we become more attentive to the rich cultural tones nurtured within our daily life discourses like *zhidao* 知道, which, commonly put as "I know," actually denotes *zhi* 知 (to know) and *dao* 道, that is, "to know *dao*."

What Bush (2008) says echoes here in that the Chinese characters/words are not dead, and their cultural value can be regenerated through re-invoking a new way of interpretation. Inspired by and following the spirit of Xu Shen's philological exegesis, Huang and Chang (2016), for example, proffer a theory of Chinese *hanzi*-hermeneutics, hoping to alert us back to the originary linkage between Chinese words/characters and their cultural senses that has been severed since the early twentieth century. By a *hanzi*-hermeneutics, they vociferate that the linguistic function of Chinese words/characters needs to be downplayed by delinking them from the modern language grammar and system. Only when they get retreated as a relevantly independent being, can we grasp and explicate the cultural (over)tones nurtured within them (p. 4). Their proffering in some way echoes Michel Foucault's (1973) strategy for modern criticism, namely, we need to

> disturb the words we speak, denounce the grammatical habits of our thinking, to dissipate the myths that animate our words, to render once more noisy and audible the element of silence that all discourse carries with it as it is spoken.
>
> (p. 298)

Second, besides as a linguistic notion, *wen* 文 is also a unique cultural thesis that holds together and orders the form in which the ancient Chinese classical texts and their historical and multilayered commentaries and annotations are crisscrossed and interlaced in vertical columns. This crisscrossing and interlacing form can be glimpsed from Figure 3.1, the *wen* entry in Duan Yucai's (段玉裁 1735–1815) *Annotations on Shuowenjiezi* with Xu Shen's original defining entry in bold interspersed with Duan's annotations and intertextual collations in the smaller font. Within it, Xu Shen interprets *wen* 文 as *cuohua* 錯畫 (crossing lines-patterns) and *xiangjiaowen* 象交文 (depicting a phenomenal form of two lines-patterns interlacing with each other). Duan further clarifies this succinct text as put in the next box:

Cuo 錯, "cross," here stands for [its homonym] cuo 逪, "meet." "Meeting lines" are lines that cross and join. When the *Kaogong ji* 考工记 [Record of Artificers] section of the *Zhou li* 周礼 [Rituals of Zhou] says, "Green set beside red: this we call *wen*," it gives a case of meeting lines, and such meeting lines are the etymon of *wen* [Sic].

(translation from Saussy, 2001a, p. 67)

As laid out above, the being of *wen* and *zi* can be regenerated in their originary saying as single-graphed characters and individual joined-bodied characters, bracketing the otherwise generic nomenclature of *wenzi* 文字 for the Chinese writing and language. A crisscrossing of varied *wenzi* constitutes the Chinese writing and classical text now commonly called *wenzhang* 文章. Intriguingly, in the classical text of *Kaogong ji* 考工记 (Record of Artificers) which Duan Yucai resorts to in his annotation on *wen*, right after the *wen*-text of "green set beside red, this we call *wen*" is "red set beside white: this we call *zhang*" (青與赤謂之文/赤與白謂之章). In other words, *wenzhang* etymologically describes the colored patterning of clothing, which is analogically picked up later on to portray the crisscrossing interlacing form of multilayered historical texts within a Chinese classical textual space as is reductively shown in Figure 3.1. This formal–visual projection in Figure 3.1 implodes an illusion of time flying in horizontal

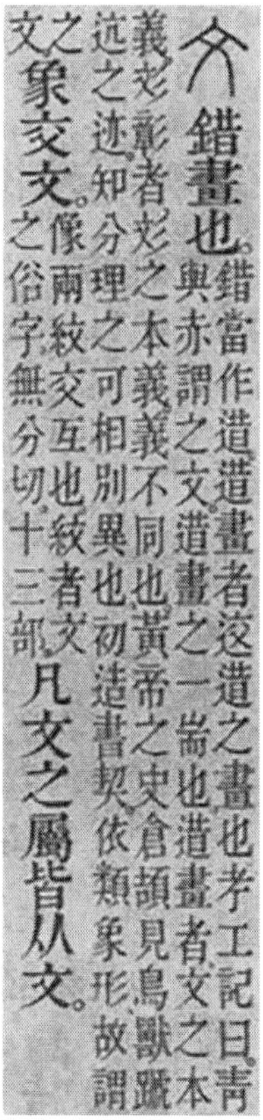
文 錯畫也。錯當作逪。逪畫者、逡逪之畫也。考工記曰。青與赤謂之文。逪畫之一耑也。逪畫者文之本義。彣彰者彣之本義。義不同也。黃帝之史倉頡見鳥獸蹏迒之迹。知分理之可相別異也。初造書契。依類象形。故謂之文。象交文。像兩紋交互也。紋者文之俗字。無分切。十三部。凡文之屬皆从文。

Figure 3.1 Wen 文 Entry in *Shuowenjiezizhu*

Retrieved from www.zgzkw.com/shuowen/imgbook/index4.htm

lines and meaning immanent in the synchronic movement. Foucault (1973) comments,

> Even [the Chinese] writing does not reproduce the fugitive flight of the voice in horizontal lines; it erects the motionless and still-recognizable images of things themselves in vertical columns. This Chinese taxonomy leads to a kind of thought without space, to words and categories that lack all life and place, but are rooted in a ceremonial space, overburdened with complex figures, with tangled paths, strange places, secret passages, and unexpected communications. There would appear to be a culture entirely devoted to the ordering of space, but one that does not distribute the multiplicity of existing things into any of the categories that make it possible for us to name, speak and think.
>
> (p. xix)

The "crisscrossing pattern" across historical strata gives a diachronic dimension to the Confucian mode of meaning-making exegesis, and this brings out the third layer of the (con)texture of the Chinese notion *wen*, which is the very "genesis of meaning in the remote past" (Wu, 2016, p. 95). It speaks to a genealogy that breaks loose the linear timeline of past, present, and future into a crisscrossing pattern. This diachronic tracing of *wen* in the ancient classics distinguishes the Chinese mode of signification from the modern Western counterpart, whereby meaning is solely generated according to the grammatical and syntactical arrangement within pre-and-after statements in the language system, namely, by a synchronic relation to others, dismissing a temporal dimension. Ferdinand de Saussure claims that there is nothing in language except difference (say, *bar* and *par*), a language which Michel Foucault argues has become an enclosed linguistic system severed from the material things they used to designate since the early seventeenth century.

The Confucian Chinese mode of signification, however, entails a diachronic dimension of tracing meaning to what was said in the past, because the past is not understood as what is over, as we currently do, but "a past of word, a meaning reservoir that could continually illuminate the present" (Wu, 2016, p. 93). In this sense, the ancient Chinese *wen* and *zi* can be treated as originary in Agabmen's sense that there is always something unsaid that could be further tapped, originary in the sense that what was said within each *wen* and *zi* "prevails throughout the tradition in an originary way, is always in being in advance of it, and yet is never expressly thought in its own right and as the Originary" (Heidegger, 1969, pp. 48–49). Their originary saying with *wen* and *zi* can't be ossified as values, ideas, and truths but can only be transmitted as living traces of the natural beings and wisdom of saints like Confucius and those before him, the relevance of which can be regenerated in its historicity. This mode of Confucian exegetical transmission is called "the genealogy of Dao (道统),

the unbroken tradition where meanings have been passed down from the ancient" (Wu, 2016, p. 94).

To sum, since the early twentieth century, the Chinese language has been Westernized by introducing more and more Western terminology and a concomitant signifier–signified mode of signification. As Bush (2008) rightly argues, what is dead is not the Chinese characters (*wen* and *zi*), but the way they are read. That is, when the Chinese *wenzi* subsumes themselves into the modern grammatical language system, their inherently nurtured cultural tones and textures get concealed. A returning to the being of Chinese characters say, by suspending their linguistic function and taken-for-granted modern conceptual meaning helps to reveal what is murmuring within the genesis of Chinese thought and meaning-making. Such a diachronic hermeneutics echoes what I mean by a Heideggerian–Foucouldian language–discourse perspective.

With a reawakened consciousness to language as a co-being rather than an object of examination, I move on to explicate a Yijing style of reasoning as onto-epistemological condition of possibility for Confucius to envision a teaching and learning movement in the next chapter. In so doing, I argue for the Chinese "wind" language to be the signature language of the whole Confucian educational heritage, and *Yijing* as another originary (re)source of the Confucian Chinese educational thinking and practice.

Transitioning From Part I to Part II: A Note

As laid out in Introduction, Chapters 1, 2, and 3 constitute Part I of the book, which proffers the overall situating of the book (comparative and cross-cultural studies), the major concerns it is to address (epistemicide), and the theoretical-methodological perspectives it employs (archaeological-historical mode of inquiry and an ontological discourse-language lens). Part II also has three chapters (Chapters 4, 5, and 6) that give concrete paradigmatic examples on how to historicize and intersect China's system of knowledge, education, and curriculum with and beyond the Western categories and frameworks. Here is a brief note on how I have laid out a methodological-theoretical ground and in anticipation of Part II in a spiral way. By that, I mean I am trying to interlace and crisscross the arguments in these chapters in a way that one foreshadows, revisits, builds, and adds onto another, rather than a linear development.

Specifically, Chapter 1 unpacks the material happening of epistemicide through a developmental comparative paradigm and a Westernization of the Chinese language since the twentieth-century-and-after China. Chapter 2 moves a step further to scrutinize the "comparative" rationale as the reasoning undergirding the developmental comparative paradigm, and Chapter 3 scrutinizes the signification and representation rationales that have enclosed the modern languages into a linguist system with meaning generated synchronically within statements. Respectively, Chapter 2 overcomes the comparative paradigm by proffering a historical-archeological mode of inquiry to ethnographically historicize a cultural system of knowledge and its conditions of possibility within its own context. Chapter 3 overcomes the representational language by calling for a re-turn to language as an ontological being and a Chinese diachronic meaning-making hermeneutics. While the theme of difference is touched upon in Chapter 2 by rethinking the comparative methods and paradigm, it will be further expanded by re-examining the Chinese teacher–student ordering in Chapter 5 and the identity–difference ordering in Chapter 6.

While the historical-archaeological mode of inquiry and the ontological language perspective will run throughout the chapters in Part II, Chapter 4 focuses on explicating the conditions of possibilities for the entire Chinese thought and a system of reason to become possible in the first place and as expressed in *Yijing*. In so doing, Confucius' educational vision is discerned, which is ordered by an ontological Chinese body-thinking. Chapter 5 picks up this discernment to further explicate the contours of the Chinese body-thinking in relation to China's current educational body events for a glimpse of the historical imprint and destruction of Chinese body. In so doing, it renders visible a binary logic that orders the Chinese teacher–student ordering and difference along a power-based pendulum. Chapter 6 further problematizes the binary logic in reasoning difference along with identity, and turns to the Chinese Daoist movement to overturn such a binary logic. Chapter 7 revisits my whole learning and un-learning research experiences as a post-foundational case of *study*, which is a newly emerged rationale in the Western scholarship often phrased as an alternative or oppositional logic to *learning*. However, I further pick up the Daoist yin-yang bipolar movement to encase the apparently binary study vs. learning logic into a dynamic movement, with one informing, confronting, and possibly transforming the other.

Note

1. The six principles are *zhishi* 指事 (single-graph word that can point to many things like 上 and 下), *xiangxing* 象形 (single-graph word that imitates what a thing looks like, say, 日 and 月), *xingshen* 形聲 (words composed of one sound-graph and one meaning-graph like 江 and 河), *huiyi* 會意 (words composed of two meaning-parts like 信), *zhuanzhu* 轉註 (interchangeable words, say, 考 and 老), *jiajie* 假借 (borrow a word for A to refer to B, say, use the elephant-word 象 for Yijing-image 像).

References

Autio, T. (2017). Reactivating templates for international curriculum consciousness: Reconsidering intellectual legacies and policy practices between Chinese, Anglo-American and European curriculum studies. In K. J. Kennedy & J. C. K. Lee (Eds.), *Theorizing teaching and learning in Asia and Europe* (pp. 38–54). London, UK: Routledge.

Blumenfeld-Jones, D. (2016). The violence of words, words of violence: Keeping the uncomfortable at bay, a Jewish perspective. *Journal of Curriculum Theorizing, 31*(1), 4–12.

Bush, C. (2008). Reading and difference: Image, allegory, and the invention of Chinese. In E. Hayot, H. Saussy, & S. G. Yao (Eds.), *Sinographies: Writing China* (pp. 34–63). Minneapolis, MN: University of Minnesota Press.

Çayır, K. (2015). Citizenship, nationality and minorities in Turkey's textbooks: From politics of non-recognition to "Difference Multiculturalism". *Comparative Education*, *51*(4), 519–536.

Chakrabarty, D. (2000). *Provincializing Europe: Postcolonial thought and historical difference*. Princeton, NJ: Princeton University Press.

Ciscel, M. (2010). Reform and relapse in bilingual policy in Moldova. *Comparative Education*, *46*(1), 13–28.

Coyne, G. (2015). Language education policies and inequality in Africa: Cross national empirical evidence. *Comparative Education Review*, *59*(4), 619–637.

Deleuze, G. (1990). *The logic of sense* (M. Lester & C. Stivale, Trans., C. V. Boundas, Ed.). New York, NY: Columbia University Press. (Original work published 1969)

Derrida, J. (1982). *Margins of philosophy* (A. Bass, Trans.). Chicago, IL: University of Chicago Press.

Fenollosa, E. (1918/1936). *The Chinese written character as a medium for poetry* (With a forward and notes by E. Pound). London, UK: Stanley Nott.

Foucault, M. (1972). The *archaeology of knowledge and the discourse on language* (A. M. S. Smith, Trans.). New York: Pantheon Books. (Original work published 1969)

Foucault, M. (1973). *The order of things: An archaeology of the human sciences*. New York, NY: Vintage Books. (Original work published 1966)

Gallucci, S. (2014). Negotiating second-language identities in and through border crossing. *Compare: A Journal of Comparative and International Education*, *44*(6), 916–937.

Hamid, M., & Jahan, I. (2015). Language, identity, and social divides: Medium of instruction debates in Bangladeshi print media. *Comparative Education Review*, *59*(1), 75–101.

Hansen, C. (1993). Chinese ideographs and Western ideas. *The Journal of Asian Studies*, *52*(2), 373–399.

Heidegger, M. (1939/2004). *On the essence of language: The metaphysics of language and the essencing of the word, concerning Herder's Treatise on the origin of language* (W. T. Gregory & Y. Umma, Trans.). Albany, NY: State University of New York Press.

Heidegger, M. (1969). *Identity and Difference* (J. Stambaugh, Trans. with an Introduction). New York, Evanston, and London: Harper & Row Publishers. (Original work published 1957)

Huang, D. K., & Chang, S. (2016). *Hanzi chanshi yu wenhua chuantong [Chinese characters hermeneutics and Chinese Culture 漢字闡釋與文化傳統]*. Taoyuan: Taiwan Changming Wenhua Chuban.

Huebner, D. (1999). *The lure of the transcendent: Collected essays by Dwayne E. Huebner* (Vikki Hills, Ed., and collected and introduced by William F. Pinar). Mahwah, NJ: Lawrence Erlbaum Associates, Publishers.

Horlacher, R. (2016). *The educated subject and the German concept of Bildung: A comparative cultural history*. New York, NY and Oxon: Routledge.

Iliycheva, M. (2010). Education and Turkish communities in Bulgaria in the years of transformation (1989–2007): A negotiated formal balance of educational outcomes. *Comparative Education*, *46*(1), 29–46.

Kim, S. (2016). English is for dummies: Linguistic contradictions at an International College in South Korea. *Compare: A Journal of Comparative and International Education*, *46*(1), 116–135.

Ma, L. (2008). *Heidegger on East-West dialogue: Anticipating the event*. New York, NY: Routledge.

Martin-Jones, M., Kroon, S., & Kurvers, J. (2011). Multilingual literacies in the global south: Language policy, literacy learning and use. *Compare: A Journal of Comparative and International Education*, 41(2), 157–164.

McCormick, A. (2012). Whose education policies in aid-receiving countries? A critical discourse analysis of quality and normative transfer through Cambodia and Laos. *Comparative Education Review*, 56(1), 18–47.

Paraskeva, J. M. (2016). *Curriculum epistemicide: Towards an itinerant curriculum theory*. New York, NY: Routledge.

Saussy, H. (2001a). The prestige of writing: Wen, letter, picture, image, ideography. In H. Saussy (Ed.), *The great walls of discourse and other adventures in cultural China* (pp. 35–74). Cambridge, MA: Harvard University Press.

Saussy, H. (2001b). Outside the parenthesis (Those people were a kind of solution). In H. Saussy (Ed.), *The great walls of discourse and other adventures in cultural China* (pp. 146–182). Cambridge, MA: Harvard University Press.

Scheffler, I. (1960). *The language of education*. Springfield: Charles C. Thomas.

Shi-xu. (2005). *A cultural approach to discourse*. Basingstoke, UK: Palgrave Macmillan.

Shi-xu. (2014). *Chinese discourse studies*. Basingstoke, UK: Palgrave Macmillan.

Shi-xu. (2015). Cultural Discourse Studies. In K. Tracy, C. Ilie, & T. Sandel (Eds.), *International encyclopedia of language and social interaction*. Boston, MA: Wiley Blackwell.

Shi-xu. (2016). Cultural discourse studies through the journal of multicultural discourses: 10 years on. *Journal of Multicultural Discourses*, 11(1), 1–8.

Shuowen jiezi zhu [Annotations on Shuowen jiezi 说文解字注*]*. (1981). *Shuowen jiezi* written by Xu Shen 许慎 (58–147 CE) and annotations collated by Duan Yucai (1735–1815). Shanghai: Shanghai Guji Press.

Sousa Santos, B. (2009). If god were a human rights activist: Human rights and the challenge of political theologies: Is humanity enough? The secular theology of human rights. *Law, Social Justice & Global Development Journal (LGD)*, (1). Retrieved from www.ces.uc.pt/myces/UserFiles/livros/278_If%20God%20were%20a%20Human%20Rights%20Activist_LawSocialJustice_09.pdf

Tröhler, D. (2011/2013). *Languages of education: Protestant legacies, national identities, and global aspirations*. New York, NY: Routledge.

Van Brummelen, H. (2013). Review article on Daniel Trohler: Languages of education: Protestant legacies, national identities, and global aspirations. *Historical Studies in Education*, 25(1), 130–132.

Wu, Z. J. (2011). Interpretation, autonomy, and transformation: Chinese pedagogic discourse in a cross-cultural perspective. *Journal of Curriculum Studies*, 43(5), 569–590.

Wu, Z. J. (2014). "Speak in the place of the sages": Rethinking the sources of pedagogic meanings. *Journal of Curriculum Studies*, 46(3), 320–331.

Wu, Z. J. (2016). Person-making through Confucian exegesis. In G. P. Zhao & Z. Y. Deng (Eds.), *Re-envisioning Chinese education: The meaning of person-making in a new age* (pp. 93–115). New York, NY: Routledge.

Part II

Paradigmatic Unpackings of China's Language, Knowledge, and Education

4 Beyond Representation
Yijing Thought and Confucius' Wind-Pedagogy

This chapter understands how education was thought in ancient texts by further unpacking the Yijing thought as the primary conditions of possibility for the entire Chinese thought and knowledge, distinct from the Western metaphysics, in three parts. First, I briefly revisit how my historicizing the current prevalent yet silent Chinese "wind-discourses" exposed me to the *Yijing* 易經 (*The Book of Change*) as an originary thought and style of reasoning not yet subsumed to the modern grammar and representation. Second, I unpack the Yijing thought in a way to mainly explicate a system of reason in ancient China that orders and correlates the disparate domains of cosmology, knowledge, culture, education, and governance onto an operating table in a Foucauldian sense. This unpacking, reductive and limited in its scope and depth, is to render visible some onto-epistemic themes, say, *wen* 文 (crisscrossing pattern), *guan* 觀 (onto-hermeneutic observing which suspends a sense of intentional and purposeful seeking toward an encountering, following, and attuning to the Dao movement within the moment), *xiang* 象 (phenomenal forms), *shu* 數 (number), and *shi* 時 (timing), that grid together the Yijing thought. These themes are chosen partly as a response to my "wind" aporia laid out in Introduction, and more importantly, as the onto-epistemological conditions that, as I show in the third part of this chapter, ground Confucius' educational vision and wind-pedagogy as expressed in his commentary on the Yijing *guan*-hexagram. In so doing, I discern a Chinese body-thinking, a theme to be further explicated in the next "body" chapter. Furthermore, I argue for re-invoking "wind" as a signature language of Chinese education and *Yijing* as another originary (re)source for the entire Confucian educational heritage, originary not in the sense of being original, but in the sense that a lot has remained unsaid in it and can be untapped to shed new light on what has already been said.

Working Back the Aporia to the *Yijing*: Wind ➔ Feng ➔ 風 ➔ 8 ➔ 觀 ☷

This project started with my serendipitous encountering of the aporetic "wind-education" discourses, prevalent yet silent in China's current schooling, aporetic in the sense that it registers a cultural linkage between the themes of "wind" and "teaching and learning" hardly intelligible to English readers but as a linguistic metaphor. Re-treating the "wind-education" discourse not as a linguistic metaphor but as a cultural epistemological linkage disturbs what Foucault calls a "trap of philology" (1973a), namely, presuming the a priori existence of grammatical arrangements within a language for what can be expressed in it. It also implodes my naturalized subject-versus-object ordering between human subjects and language object. In following the aporetic dancing "wind" to the ancient Chinese texts, I found myself again and again in the hands of language, not vice versa, which forced me to recognize the ontological being of the Chinese language itself, a being distinct from the Western phonetic languages. As I said in Chapter 3, standing too close to the Chinese language system (say, solely in pursuit of its semantic meaning) or trying to use the Western categories like "non-representational" to describe it (since the Western categories are themselves historically contextualized and produced) simply means a wrong intellectual starting point. Period.

Paralyzed, I started anew and this time by historicizing the Chinese "wind" back to its ethnographical context and situating it among the conceptions it echoes or answers in the Chinese historiography. This is a "post-deconstructive" (Saussy, 2001b) strategy that at its core resonates Foucault's (1973a) description of modern criticism as starting with "the deployment of manifest discourse towards a revelation of language in its crude being" (p. 298). Pragmatically, this strategy entails working our ways back from opinions, philosophies, and even sciences to the words or thoughts that have made them possible, and yet not been caught in the network of modern grammar. Foucault's strategy succinctly portrays my historicizing the Chinese "wind-education" discourses as a working-back journey, first from "*xiaofeng* 校風=school atmosphere" to a literal "*xiaofeng* 校風=school wind," then from "wind as air in movement" back to "*feng* 風" as "wind blows and insects get germinated and hatched in eight days" in *shuowenjiezi* and ultimately the Yijing *guan*-hexagram with an image of "wind blowing over the earth" (see Introduction for more details). Indeed, working back the Chinese "wind-discourses" enabled me to encounter the book of *Yijing* as a primordial thought and style of reasoning, a thought "whose essential life has not yet been caught in the network of grammar," and a thought ordered in another space-time and by an onto-epistemology distinct from the Western logo-phono-centrism, as to be further unpacked below.

Four points are needed here to clarify the defining features of my working-back experiences with the aporetic Chinese "wind" language. First, I unfold and understand my aporetic experiences "in [their] own terms rather than [being categorized] according to predetermined structures and theories" (Phillion, 1999, as cited in He & Phillion, 2008, p. 14). That is, I don't apply Heidegger and Foucault's strategy as an a priori given. Rather, it is my ongoing un-learning experiences that have helped me better understand the nuances of his strategy, like the *need* to suspend my naturalized treatment of the Chinese language as an enclosed grammatical structure toward opening it up as a new dwelling for meaning, and the *decisiveness* of my reflecting upon the Chinese language as a *way* to leap into a being-historical Yijing style of thinking. Second, I confront the aporetic "wind" moments as signposts and move with them in a way to un-learn my own presumptions such that they become intelligible to me again at a certain moment. To borrow Agamben's phrasing, I try not to conceal but constantly take up and elaborate what is unsaid with the Chinese "wind" hopefully to be exposed to its originary source or mode of meaning.

Third, my (un)learning experiences transform a taken-for-granted subject–object ordering between me and the language, as well as my subjectivity as an inquirer-learner, as anticipated in an authentic historical-archeological inquiry (see, Agamben, 2009). Henceforth I call this un-learning experiences as a Daoist onto-un-learning *way*. Specifically, language is no longer merely a linguistic signifying system or a tool for me to express my thought. Rather, it is a "house of Being" in the Heideggerian sense such that it speaks, and we humans dwell and respond to its call to the extent that I follow "closely what is said, not merely what is abstractly meant" (Fenollosa, 1936, p. 20). Finally, this meandering Daoist onto-(un)learning movement lacks a cause and effect linearity, a clear starting point, a theoretical framework to follow, or a destination to anticipate, and thus poses a challenge to my writing. In a way, to borrow Kierkegaard's wording, it is like our own life that has to be lived ahead but can only be understood afterwards. This is why I recount my un-learning way here and there. I will further theorize my Daoist onto-un-learning way as an exemplary post-foundational *case study* in Chapter 7.

With this brief methodological reflection, I now move to delineate the Yijing style of thought as a system of reason that orders and correlates the otherwise disparate things such as ancient Chinese cosmology, knowledge, culture, education, and governance onto an operating table in a Foucauldian sense. In other words, this Yijing style of thought grounds and conditions the way education was thought in ancient China and by Confucius in particular since the gist of Confucius' thought is a philosophy of education (Chen, 2016). Furthermore, Confucian educational thought is a "cultural script" (Tan, 2015) that largely defines the way teaching and learning are currently re-configured in negotiation with the Western-introduced educational theories and practices in the East Asian countries with Confucian Heritage Culture (CHC). This being said, I first give a brief introduction of the Yijing thought and also Confucius' role in interpreting–transmitting the originary Yijing thought in the Chinese culture.

An Introduction to *Yijing* and Confucius' Humanistic Interpretation

Chinese mythology goes that the ancient sovereign Fu Xi 伏羲 (about twenty-ninth century BCE) drew up "eight trigram images" (*bagua* 八卦), each constituting three either solid or broken "crisscrossing" (*yao* 爻) lines, to show the eight big "natural images" or "phenomenal forms" (*xiang* 象) hung up in the cosmic world: "sky" (*qian* 乾 ☰), "earth" (*kun* 坤 ☷), "sun" (*li* 离 ☲), "moon" (*kan* 坎 ☵), "thunder" (*zhen* 震 ☳), "wind" (*xun* 巽 ☴), mountain (*gen* 艮 ☶), and lake (*dui* 兑 ☱). Three Yi-text versions were developed from these "eight trigram images" in ancient China: *Lianshan* 連山 in Shengnong Yandi 神農炎帝 era around the sixteenth century BCE, *Guizang* 歸藏 in Huangdi 皇帝 era between the sixteenth century BCE–eleventh century BCE), and *Zhouyi* 周易 around the eleventh century BCE that contains *Yijing* 易經 (Yi-text) and *Yizhuan* 易傳 (Confucius' Commentaries).[1]

It is commonly believed that King Wen 文王 (1152 BCE–1056 BCE) in Zhou Dynasty juxtaposes and combines Fu Xi's eight trigrams into 64 six-lined hexagram forms, as eight is far too insufficient to demonstrate the changing dynamics of the natural-cultural world, and adds "statement" (*guaci* 卦辭) to each hexagram image; Duke Zhou 周公 (died in 1032 BCE), King Wen's fourth son, adds "statement" (*yaoci* 爻辭) to each of the six yao-line making up each hexagram. These 64 hexagrams, their constitutive six-line-juxtapositions from bottom to top, gua-statement, and yao-statement compose the Yi-text called *Yijing*. *Yizhuan* contains the so-called ten wings (*shiyi* 十翼), namely, commentaries by Confucius (551 BCE–479 BCE) and his disciples on the Yi-text. Put together *Yijing* and *Yizhuan* constitute *Zhouyi*.

Yijing, as No. 1 of the orthodox Confucian Classics and also the oldest spiritual classic on this planet (Nelson, 2011), is treated as an originary (re) source of the entire Chinese thought and civilization. As Chapter 1 shows, scholars in current China are calling for a re-invocation of the Yijing wisdom as a paradigm to regenerate the value of Chinese traditional culture that has been disparaged and destroyed ever since the 1920s New Cultural Movement in the name of modernization and now globalization (see, e.g., Wang S., 2012; Zhang Z., 2015; Zhang X., 2013). Originary in the sense that the Yijing thought is not reducible to what has been thought. It always nourishes something that has not been thought, which in turn sets free traditional thinking. *Yijing* contains unfathomable wisdom, winning it a long revered life in China and abroad with numerous exegetical commentaries and interpretations, which seems to footnote this Yi-statement: *generating and generating with no stopping is called Yi (the change)* (生生之謂《易》). As Helmut Wilhelm (1995) puts it:

> The essential thing [in interpreting the *Yijing*] is to keep in mind all the strata that go to make up the book. Archaic wisdom from the dawn of time, detached and systematic reflection of . . . the Chou era, pithy sayings from the heart of the people, subtle thoughts of the leading minds: all these disparate elements have harmonized to create the structure of the book as we know it . . . many of the treasures of the very earliest origins are brought to light, treasuries that up till then were hidden in the depths of the book, their existence divined rather than recognized.
> (p. 51, cited in Wu K., 2011, p. 78)

Confucius comments that the Yi-text can't be treated as a canon, but only a canon-in-situ (不可謂典要唯變所適) (Xici). The gist of the Yi-thought can be gleaned from its English title, *The Book of Change*, which aptly capitulates *Yijing* as basically about an ontological paradigm of "change" (*yi* 易), disclosing the dynamic "crisscrossing pattern" (*wen* 文) of the "phenomenal forms" (xiang 象) within the entire cosmic world, namely, "the cadences, rhythms, and threads running through the transformation of the myriad things" in the moment (Nelson, 2011, 336). This sense of "moment" (*shi* 時) foregrounds the everlasting dynamic movement of the whole cosmos. However, such momentary drift and direction of change can be "onto-hermeneutically observed-sensed" (*guan-gan* 观感) and "divined" (*wu* 巫) through a "image-number" (*xiang-shu* 象數) style of reasoning. There are numerous ways of interpreting the Yi-thought, but I briefly introduce the two mainstream modes. One is called "image-number" (*xiang-shu* 象数) with a focus to explicate the divinatory dimension of the Yi-thought and the other is called "meaning–rationale" (*yi-li* 義理), which is primarily initiated by Confucius to explicate a humanistic and moral implication of the Yi-thought.

Yijing "Image-Number" (*xiang-shu* 象数) *Style of Divination*

This divinatory "image-number" style of reasoning is onto-epistemologically significant. It delineates an originary and primordial cosmology wherein human beings believe themselves to be one of the ten thousand things in the cosmic world and to cohabit with the other cosmic things and life harmoniously within this world. Furthermore, they believe each cosmic thing has a divine nature and moves and interlace with each other. Even though people can divine the happening of things in the future according to the dynamic changes of the phenomenal forms or natural forms hung up in the sky, like the sun, moon, star, the purpose behind divination is to follow and comply with the cosmic change. By that point, the idea of following and attuning to the Dao movement of the cosmic world to regulate the cultural world to its optimality has not been developed forcefully. It is Confucius who later foregrounds the idea of setting up teaching–governing by observing-following the Dao movement through a "meaning–rationale" style of interpreting the Yijing.

The term *xiang-shu* 象数 (image-number) is traceable to the text of *zuozhuan* 左傳 (Commentary of Zuo). As the book commentator Du Yu 杜預 notes, "*xiang* 象 is the appeared image on a burned turtle shell and *shu* 數 is a numerical number calculated from tossing yarrow grass sticks, and their correlative combination can divine something about the future" (龜以象示筮以數告象數相因而生然後有占). Etymologically, the character *xiang* 象 (image/form) for the Yijing *xiang-shu* is borrowed from the character *xiang* 象 for the animal of elephant and is a homonym of *xiang* 像 (image). Then in what way can they, apparently disparate things to us modern people, be placed on the same epistemological operating table?

104 *Paradigmatic Unpackings*

An inspiring clue can be gleaned from Wang Anshi's 王安石 (1021–1086) *zishuo* 字說 (commenting on monographs or characters), as collated in the below entry for *xiang* 象 in the *Kangxizidian* 康熙字典 (Kangxi Dictionary):

> An elephant's trunk can have some pattern as a resonating effect of thunder while the sky image takes up some form as a resonating effect of the movement of *qi*; henceforth, the character *xiang* for *tianxiang* (sky image) borrows the character *xiang* for elephant (象牙感雷而文生天象感气而文生故天象亦用此字) www.zdic.net/z/24/kx/8C61.htm

Also, big elephants were not rare in ancient China; they lived in the South and abound in number. The pictographic form for elephant is 𧰼, so it is probably due to their strength and power that elephant is picked up as a symbol for *xiang* 象 to indicate its "phenomenal forms" in the Yi-thought (Cheng, 2011). The current Chinese term *xiangxiang* (想象) for *imagine* is literally to *think of elephants* as legend goes elephants were abundant in ancient China, and people when seeing the elephant skeletons on the road would often think of elephants. While in the northern area where elephants were less than horses in number, the term *xiang* for elephant become replaced by *ji* 驥 (horse) in the term *antusuoji* (按圖索驥 following the picture and finding the horse) (see, Duan's *shuowenjiezizhu*).

Actually, the Yijing *xiang-shu* (象數) thought still permeates China's modern life but goes largely unnoticed. For example, many Chinese daily life terms are composed of monographs derived from the Yi-text, but few people can recognize such a derived combination. A four-character Chinese term *cuozongfuza* (錯綜複雜), now simply glossed as *being very complicated*, stands for four dynamic moving re-juxtapositions among the 64 gua-hexagrams. The statement *I have numbers in my heart* (我心里有数), saying *I know the odds of what I am doing*, indicates the contour of *shu* 数 (number) traceable to the Yi-thought, but people no longer ponder over the way it is expressed in the first place, namely, why do we have numbers in our heart?

Confucian "Meaning–Rationale" (yi-li 義理) Style of Interpretation

The divinatory nature indeed distinguishes *Yijing* from all the other Confucian classics, saving it from Emperor Qin's burning of books in 213 BCE. Its original divinatory "image-number" (*xiang-shu* 象數) style of interpretation gave its way to a Confucius-initiated "meaning–rationale" (*yi-li* 義理) mode of interpretation, the latter gaining an orthodox status in the Han dynasty (206 BCE–220 CE) when Confucianism became canonized. By meaning–rationale, it means to interpret the meaning of the Yi-statements so as to understand the changing dynamics of the whole cosmic world and, furthermore, to relay such a cosmic governing rationale onto the cultural world. In other words, by following and attuning to the Dao movement of the cosmic world, the cultural world will also be regulated to its optimality. Confucius' envisioning of the *guan*-hexagram (which has nothing to do with education in itself) into a teaching and learning movement between the King and his subjects, to be further unpacked below, is a good example of his "meaning–rationale" interpretation of the Yi-text.

According to the Yi-text of *Yao*《要》excavated in 1973 from the Mawangdui Han dynasty tomb, Confucius gained access to *Yijing* in his later life and liked/studied it so much that the ropes binding the bamboo slats even broke many times. The fact that Confucius initiated the "meaning–rationale" mode of interpretation doesn't mean that Confucius doesn't divine at all. Rather, he believes that *Yi-dao* 易道 lies in a sagely and virtuous person's deep-knowing of *Yi* and *xiang* and henceforth being able to follow *the Dao-heart of the sky and earth* without using the seasons, stars, sun, and moon as signs for divination. The same Yi-text of *Yao*《要》records Confucius' response to his disciple Zigong's question on the divinatory dimension of Yi-thought:

> 易，我復其祝卜矣，我觀其德義耳也。幽贊而達乎數，明數而達乎德，又仁守者而義行之耳。贊而不達於數，則其為之巫；數而不達於德，則其為之史。史巫之筮，鄉之而未也，好之而非也。後世之士疑丘，或以易乎？吾求德而已，吾與史筮同塗而殊歸也。

> Do I like to divine with turtle shell and yard sticks like others? No, I am interested in interpreting the (moral) meaning and rationale of the Yi-statement.... Those who can divine with turtle shells but don't understand the broader movement of the natural world can only be *wu* (巫 wizard); while those who know about the natural mystery but fail to understand the way-power of the whole cosmic world can only be *shi* (史 historian). I seek the way-power and follow it through my humane deeds to the extent that we follow the same path but toward different destinations.
>
> (cited in Chen, 1999, my translation)

According to this text, Confucius differentiates himself from two other types of interpreters, namely, *wu* and *shi*, who can only pursue the Yi-thought for a divinatory purpose and don't have a virtuous cultivation (de 德) to help them understand the Dao movement (de 德) of the cosmic world as expressed in the Yijing statements. To Confucius, exemplary person (*junzi* 君子) needn't pray for good luck and fortune (*jifu* 吉福) if they are humane and virtuous both in words and deeds. In other words, Confucius does grasp a divinatory "image-number" (*xiang-shu*) mode of interpreting the Yi-thought; however, he himself focuses upon a humanistic "meaning–rationale" (*yi-li*) dimension of the Yi-thought. This humanistic mode of interpretation becomes a canonized form in the Han dynasty and also defines the "governing" nature of the whole Chinese education, but in the past 3,000 years, interpreting the 64 Yi-hexagrams, and its commentaries have never digressed from these two arts of interpretation (see Liu, 2010).

Explicating Yijing Thought as Conditions of Possibility for Confucius' Educational Vision and Wind-Pedagogy

Cheng (2011) argues for an "onto-hermeneutical" way of interpreting the Yi-text. By that, it means reading the Yi-text is not to trace authorial intentions for the sake of historical reconstruction, but to engage the reader in becoming a Yijing practitioner to observe/feel, participate in, and enact the being and interaction of cosmos, society, and self in the moment. Such a self-engaging way of reading as experiencing resonates with Fenollosa's claim, namely, reading Chinese characters and writing entails a close observation of what is said and of the textures and overtones in its saying, not merely of its semantic meaning. It further sharpens my consciousness that I need to shift my attention/observation from what I read, to how I read, and furthermore, to the interaction between me as a reader, my way of reading, and what I read, and contemplate on how such a transformed viewpoint re-shapes my mode of being as an inquirer-learner.

With this methodological caution, I unpack the Yijing thought not hoping to provide a holistic or philosophical picture of it, which, considering the unfathomable richness of the book and the narrowness of my knowledge, is not possible at all. Rather, I treat the Yi-text and Confucius' commentary text as a system and style of reasoning, hoping to explicate some epistemic principles as nodes which hold together and order such themes as cosmology, knowledge, meaning-making, language, culture, education, and governance onto a Foucauldian operating table in ancient China. *That is, I unpack the Yijing style of thought as a condition of the whole Confucian education and Chinese knowledge system.* Possible themes include *wen* 文 (crisscrossing pattern), *guan* 觀 (onto-hermeneutic observing), *xiang* 象 (phenomenal forms), *shu* 數 (number), and *shi* 時 (timing). To note, I historically/archaeologically unpack these themes for three purposes. First is to provide an alternative paradigm that can cut into the present conceptual mode of signification and modern representational language as an imprisonment of today's thinking in general. Second is to render them visible as conditions of possibility for Confucius to envision his teaching and learning movement as expressed in his commentary on the Yijing *guan*-hexagram (observation), which is rarely explored so far in the scholarship on Confucius and Confucian educational thinking and which I unpack in the last section of this chapter. Last is to see the ways in which these ancient Chinese onto-epistemologies, albeit having undergone a radical transformation and cleavage in the modern China, still tacitly order the way living, being, teaching, and learning are said, reasoned, and enacted, in negotiation and confrontation with the globalized Western scientific and learning discourses. As Heidegger (1969) depicts, the past "prevails throughout the tradition in an originary way" (p. 48), originary not in the sense of being original, but in the sense that a lot has remained unsaid in it and can be untapped to shed new light on what has already been said. This historical-archaeological unpacking provides an alternative paradigm to examine China's current education and curriculum at the nexus of and as the (dis)assemblage of past and present, East and West.

Wen 文 Crisscrosses-Patterns Phenomenal Things 象 in the Natural World (ziran 自然)

Wen 文 is a primordial and originary linguistic and natural-cultural notion in the Chinese culture, construing and constructing the multilayered (con) textures of the whole Chinese thought with a significance that only a few notions such as *qi* 氣 and *dao* 道 can compare (Kern, 2001). *Wen* 文 speaks to the nature of Chinese culture, literature, civilization, and writing to the extent that *wen* embraces the following textures and overtones: markings; patterns; stripes, streaks, lines, veins; whorls; bands; writing, graph, expression, composition; ceremony, culture, refinement, education, ornament, elegance, civility; civil as opposed to military; literature (specifically belletristic prose in its distinction from poetry) (see Kern, 2001). The Yijing thought embraces an ordering principle of "transforming-governing the world under the sky with *wen*" (*yiwenhuatianxia* 以文化天下), not by "weapon" (*wu* 武).

In Chapter 3, I scrutinize *wen* as an ordering principle of the Chinese writing characters and literary text by reparsing the two common terms of *wenzi* 文字 (writing and character) and *wenzhang* 文章 (writing and literary text). First, as a nomenclature for the Chinese writing, *wen* gestures the genesis of the Chinese thought by "being the root of the primordial forms of things wherewith words-characters (*zi*) grow up by sucking its milk" (文者物象之本/字者孳乳而浸多也). Second, I pick up the etymological "crisscrossing patterning" texture of *wen* as an analogy to depict the spatial and multilayered crisscrossing form of the Confucian exegetical classics and scriptures. With it, Confucian scripture exegesis entails a rigorous regeneration of each Chinese word-character by tracing back to its originary saying in the past so as to evoke its vitality for the present, which has been preserved by Confucian scholars till the early twentieth century. In this sense, what has been transferred generation after generation is *wen* as "the genealogy of dao 道統" (see, Wu, 2016) in the Chinese culture.

In this chapter, I foreground the etymological "crisscrossing pattern" texture of *wen* as a form to portray the ordering of natural beings, humans included, in the ancient Chinese cosmology. Specifically, "crisscrossing patterning" depicts the juxtaposition of varied natural phenomenal forms like the eight trigram images hung up in the cosmic world into an ever-changing tapestry as an expression or embodiment of the self-revealing "originary Dao" (*yuandao* 原道). That is, it is *wen* that holds together and orders all the phenomenal forms on the spatial–temporal operating table of the cosmos called *ziran* 自然 (the natural world). Here is a delineation of "originary Dao" in the first Chinese literary criticism text of *wenxindiaolong* 文心雕龙 (*The literary mind-heart and the carving of dragons*) by Liu Xie 劉勰 (born around 465 CE):

> The power of *wen* is great indeed: for was it not born together with heaven and earth? Azure and Yellow intermingle their colors, the square and the round differentiate their forms; sun and moon in their recurrent orbs display the symmetrical images of heaven, mountain and river in brilliant pattern work spread forth the ordered shapes of earth; all this the wen of dao.... The mind-heart comes into existence, and words are established; words are established and *wen* gives forth its brilliance—the very way-dao of nature (the natural world).
>
> (Adapted from Saussy's translation, 2001a)

> 文之為德也大矣,與天地並生者,何哉!夫玄黃色雜,方圓體分;日月疊壁,以垂麗天之象;山川煥綺,以鋪理地之形;此蓋道之文也 . . . . 心生而言立,言立而文明,自然之道也.
>
> (文心雕龍/原道)

Here Liu Xie comes to the thesis that the originary and primordial Dao is the Dao of "the natural world as it is" (*ziran* 自然). The Chinese term *ziran* 自然 is often glossed as "nature" in English, just as Saussy does in the above translation, which I think is quite misleading. Distinct from the Western cosmology wherewith "nature" as the physical universe is an object created by God, the Chinese term *ziran* 自然 literally says "self-revealing as it is," resonating with Heidegger's interpretation of *physis* as "the arising of something from out of self, a bringing-forth" (1977, p. 10). *Ziran* gestures the entire cosmic world co-inhabited by a myriad of things (often called ten thousand things 萬物), humans included, which are epistemologically different and yet ontologically equal. This myriad of things all take up "phenomenal forms" (*xiang* 象) that "crisscross each other into a naturally beautiful pattern" called "the wen of Dao" (*dao zhi wen* 道之文).

Such a cosmic viewpoint entails no instrumental subject vs. object style of reasoning that orders humans over and above the environmental world, with the former acting upon the latter as an object or resource. Rather, humans are supposed to attune to, co-respond with, and follow the Dao movement of the physical-natural world, the nuances of which are literally murmuring within such discourses as 順其自然 (literally: following the way as it is) and 與時俱進 (literally: going with the seasonal movement). However, such a Daoist ecological sensibility is no longer easy to discern, partly because language is no longer the "house of Being" (Heidegger, 1978), and the above two terms are now simply glossed over as "following the life course" and "going global" (see, Zhao & Sun, 2017; Zhao & Schmidt, forthcoming).

This statement of *following the way as it is* 順其自然 brings out the nature of the Yijing divination in that it "doesn't deny the natural world for a supernatural realm but 'naturalistically' recognizes and affirms the contingent and transient causal character of the world, revealing an immanent balance, harmony and order with it" (Nelson, 2011, p. 336). Here "harmony" is not a stable state when conflicts are resolved as in the Western thought, but rather, an idealized harmonious society in the Yijing thought is dynamic and will "follow if we human beings comply with the power of the sky and the earth, the brightness of the sun and the moon, the ordering of the four seasons, and the good and bad omens of ghosts and gods" (與天地合其德與日月合其明與四時合其序與鬼神合其吉兇). Thus, the *Way-Dao* of the Yi-thought, as Confucius argues, lies in knowing and feeling the nature of *Yi* and *xiang*, and then following *the heart of sky and earth* without using the seasons, stars, sun, and moon as signs for divination (故君不時不宿不日不月不葡不筮而知吉與兇順於天地之也此胃易道). In such a sense, Nelson (2011) argues:

> Nature might be seen as the locus of the enactment of the ethical rather than an intrinsically alien, indifferent, and value-neutral realm. Ethics is after all *ethos*, a way of dwelling in the world. Ethical disposition or sensibility is an aspect of the way (dao道) in early Chinese thought.
>
> (p. 337)

This understanding of the patterning of the phenomenal forms in the cosmic natural world as the *wen* of Dao not only configures the ancient Chinese cosmology, but also brings out a comprehensive *guan-observing and gan-feeling* as an onto-epistemological principle that orders how humans make sense of and be with the cosmic as well as their cultural world.

Humans Understand the Cosmic World Through Comprehensive "Observation" 觀

Etymologically, the Chinese monograph *guan* 觀 (observation) derives from 萑, a big owl-like bird in oracle bones with sharp eyes burgling out and watching around, and the graph 見 (see) added later to accent a sense of perceptiveness just as sharp-eyed owls can "catch mice in the night and see minute details" (*Zhuangzi: Qiushui*). *Guan* 觀 is less psychological and cognitive than onto-hermeneutic (Cheng, 2011). By onto-hermeneutic, *guan* 觀 suspends a sense of intentional and purposeful seeking toward an encountering, following, and attuning to the Dao movement within the moment (*shi* 時). This onto-hermeneutic sense of *guan-observing* 觀 grounds the Buddhist *guanxin* 觀心 (observing heart), Daoist *guanmiaodao* 觀妙道 (observing the mysterious Dao), and Confucian *guanwu* 觀物 (observing the world) (Chen, 2013). Furthermore, it foregrounds an inherent sense of temporal contingency, marking dynamic *change* as the very nature of the whole Yijing thought and Chinese cosmology. In a word, the Chinese *guan* 觀 nurtures an onto-temporal texture.

This onto-hermeneutic Yijing guan-observing 觀 orders the way people view and make sense of the cosmic and cultural world in ancient China. Through an experiential sense of great, comprehensive, macroscopic, and cosmological *guan-observing*, the world is felt as an adventurous, self-creative yet self-sustainable, and self-ordering divinable cosmos in persistent transformation. Through such long-time empirical looking and feeling, some cosmic bipolar regularities such as the seasonal transitioning out of seemingly chaotic movement of intersected myriad things are discerned, which in turn help to adapt early people's living in response to the naturalized changes as both organic and inorganic. This is what Cheng Chung-Ying means by an "onto-cosmological" or "cosmo-ontological" being (2011). A direct subject–object guan-observing can't be cut out in such case, rather, guan-observing is in motion and helps to *zhao* (照 lighten up) an organic panorama, where the observer, the observed, the act of observing reside and interact in togetherness. Such multi-perspectival guan-observe is claimed to have laid a foundation for the Chinese arts, literature, and philosophy distinct from the Western ontology (see, Ji, 2011; Liu, 2011; Ma, 2007).

Based upon such comprehensive and long-term empirical observation, Fu Xi can draw up "trigrams" (*gua* 卦) to imitate the eight phenomenal forms/images "hung up" (*gua* 挂) in the natural world, a way of reasoning also shown in the homographic forms of *gua* 卦 (trigrams) and *gua* (hang up). This comprehensive macroscopic or cosmological sense of guan-observing 觀 an open world of experience resonates with a principle of *guanxiang shegua* (觀象設卦), literally *guan-observing xiang-images and drawing up gua-trigrams*, retrospectively describing the legendary ruler Fu Xi (or Bao Xi) around the twenty-ninth century BCE:

> In the ancient time when Bao Xi reigns over the world, he observes the *xiang* (象 images/phenomenal forms) in the sky, observes the *fa* (法 pattern/law of things) on the earth, and observes the *wen* (文 patterns/traces) of birds and beasts with regard to fitting in (宜 *yi*) with their localities. He then takes in things close at hand, and things afar, and starts to draw out the eight trigrams (八卦 *bagua*) as a way of understanding the *de* (德 virtues/powers) of spirits, and showing the *qing* (情 textures/states of affairs) of a myriad of things.
>
> (Xici, my translation)

古者包犧氏之王天下也，仰則觀象於天，俯則觀法於地，觀鳥獸之文與地之宜，近取諸身，遠取諸物，於是始作八卦，以通神明之德，以類萬物之情。

Beyond Representation   111

This statement resonates the above-mentioned thesis, namely, the visible patterning of phenomenal forms in the cosmic world (*ziran* 自然) constitutes the *wen* of Dao in that these wen-patterning is further expressed as the specific *xiang* 象 in the sky, *fa* 法 on the earth, *wen* 紋 of birds and animals, *yi* 宜 of the earth-rocks. Fu Xi's "observing the phenomenal forms and making trigrams accordingly" (*guanxiang shegua*) provides a prototype for the later invention of the early Chinese writing (wen 文) by Cang Jie:

> The Yellow Emperor's scribe, Cang Jie, perceiving the tracks left by the claws of birds and animals, understood that their distinct patterns could be used as the basis for differentiating them into classes. So he began to make tallies and writings, producing image and shapes according to the kinds [of the things represented]. Thus the name of writing is *wen*.
> (Saussy's translation, 2001a, p. 67)

Fu Xi draws up eight trigrams to indicate the eight phenomenal forms/images hung up in the cosmic world. Furthermore, he groups them into four mutually generative or complementary pairs, showing the unity of changes in basic bipolar pattern. For example, the sun (日 ri) and the moon (月 yue) constitute the graphic form of *yi* (易), and their trigram images ☲ and ☵ are complementary in the sense of one form being the opposite of the other (understood as yin-yang movement later on). The two characters for the sun and the moon, 日 and 月, also stand for Yin and Yang, which etymologically point to the "shadows and lights that are experienced on a mountain side and river bank" (Cheng, 2011). Thus, they stand for a unity of opposing forces and momentum as people watch how sunlight gives rise to the darkness of night that eventually gives rise to light.

In other words, it is through such an onto-hermeneutical *guan-observing* 觀 and *gan-feeling* 感 over a long time that gradually informs ancient saints' beholding-viewing, seeing, and understanding the natural world, feeling their interlocking and being with the natural world, and partaking in and transforming the natural course of change in their own world of human relations and self-sustenance. As a result, the *gua*-system, as symbols of patterns of change and transformation, was constructed to describe the dynamic changes of myriad things in the cosmos, sharing a basic structure of yin-yang movement, change from opposition and supplementation to mutual transformation. However, such a *guan*-observing and *gan*-feeling as "epistemological foundation and source for understanding change as a system of the transformations and formations" has been paid insufficient attention in traditional accounts on Chinese ancient philosophy (Cheng, 2011, p. 346).

To sum up, these narratives depict a macroscopic observation-mediated experiential onto-being that conjoins ancient human world and the natural world through meta-language notions of *xiang* 象, *fa* 法, *wen* 文, *gua* 卦, *dao* 道, and *ziran* 自然, whose overtones ring in cosmic harmony through

112 *Paradigmatic Unpackings*

seemingly a-cosmic (chaotic) myriad of things. With this comprehensive guan-observing 觀, it is to be noted that the observable *xiang* in the sky, *fa* on the earth, and *wen* of birds and animals, crisscrossing the whole magnitude of heaven and earth, are not viewed as isolated objects, but as an interlocking patterning of natural beings of *ziran* 自然, often glossed as *nature* in English, but literally saying *something that shows up by itself or thing as it is*. The observed rising and falling of the sun and the moon, and the passing and coming of the four seasons are the best expressions of the self-revealing in the natural world. As mapped out above, such natural phenomena (*ziran* 自然) with its certain regularities or patterns (*wen* 文) manifest the movement of the invisible and unnamable Dao 道. Then how is the human cultural world ordered along with the cosmic movement? We now move to explicate a correlative ordering in ancient Chinese onto-epistemology.

A Correlative Cosmic-Cultural Ordering With a Spatial–Temporal "Wind"

In the Yijing thought, an idealized harmonious society will follow if we human beings "comply with the power of the sky and the earth, the brightness of the sun and the moon, the ordering of the four seasons, and the good and bad omens of ghosts and gods." The *Way-Dao* of the Yi-thought, as Confucius argues, lies in human beings' comprehensive observing of the nature of *Yi* and *xiang* and also following *the heart of sky and earth* without using the seasons, stars, sun, and moon as signs for divination. Such a following is not a blind following for sure. Rather, an active co-agency is expected in following the immanent harmonious movement of Dao in the cosmos, society, and self at the moment. Undergirding such a "complying with, comprehensive observing, and following" between the human beings and the cosmic world is what sinologists such as Marcel Granet, Joseph Needham, A.C. Graham, David Hall, and Roger Ames put as a "correlative thinking." That is, Confucianism is embedded within a relational Chinese cosmology that pinpoints a congruence of personal, social, political, and cosmic order and governance.

This correlative ordering can be further unpacked through re-invoking my "wind" aporia, namely, the concentric diagram (Figure 4.1) I draw to show the spatiotemporal as well as cosmic-cultural correspondence among the eight winds (八風), the eight gua-trigram (八卦), the eight spatial directions (八方), the seasonal timings (時節), and pitch tones (八律). Such a correlative ordering by "wind" suspends our common ways of classification and juxtaposition. To borrow Foucault's wording, this correlative ordering like a utopia oddly yet enchantingly heaps all together on an operating table things that are otherwise not appropriately proximate or congruous in our eyes. Specifically, distinct things such as winds, pitch tones, hexagrams, spatial directions, seasonal changes, teaching, and governing are thrust into a heterotopia, which destroys the syntax and meanwhile exposes the limitation

Beyond Representation 113

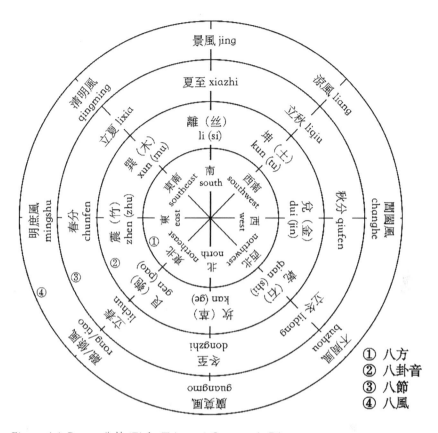

Figure 4.1 Bagua 八卦 (Eight Trigram) Concentric Diagram

of the modern system of thought. This "wind" way of *holding together* things is nowhere to be found in the Western and modern epistemology.

Three points can be explicated regarding the ways in which this "wind" principle co-orders cosmological space-time and human governance. First, the Chinese notion of "wind" here is not just a linguistic signifier denoting the natural-physical air in movement. Rather, "wind" is a phenomenal form in the cosmic world, and its inherent sense of "transforming" makes it a significant onto-epistemological principle in ancient China. It is said that "wind" is used as one trigram image just because it helps to generate and nurture myriad things (*Hanshu-weixiang zhuan*). This *transforming* sense is visible in its defining statement in the earliest Chinese dictionary, namely, "wind blows, and insects get germinated and hatched within eight days," traceable to the text of *Huai Nan Zi* 淮南子,[3] which bears on rich Yijing image-number (*xiang-shu* 象數) mode of reasoning (see Liu, 2002).

Second, "wind" with its dynamic transforming sense structures the co-ordering of cosmic space and seasonal time in ancient China. Specifically, wind permeates into the spatial directions, and the spatial winds intersect with the calendrical seasonal timings. Each calendrical year can be divided into 12 *months* (月), 24 seasonal timings (*jieqi* 節氣), and 72 *hou* (候, 5 days as a *hou*), corresponding to the four seasons and eight sub-seasons (with 45 days a sub-season) that ends with the one following the winter solstice. That is, the first 45 days of the new year that is ushered in by the full moon are ruled by the northeast *tiao* (條) wind, with each subsequent period of 45 days being governed by one directional wind moving clockwise around the compass.

Third, such a spatial–temporal "wind" ordering furthermore rules human governance. Specifically, since it is believed that the human world will thrive in observing/following the heart of sky and earth (the natural law of the cosmic world), human activities are to follow, attune to, and respond to the cosmic seasonal timing and ordering (與四時合其序). Such a congruence between the cosmic and human worlds is vividly demonstrated in the below "wind" text from *Huai Nan Zi: Tian Wen Xun* (淮南子天文訓):

What are the eight winds? Forty-five days after the winter solstice is the arrival of Tiao wind; forty-five days after that is Mingshu wind; forty-five days after that is Qingming wind; forty-five days after that is Jing wind; forty-five days after that is Liang wind; forty-five days after that is Changhe wind; forty-five days after that is Buzhou wind; forty-five days after that is Guangmo wind. During the tiao wind season, issue unimportant dispatches, dismissing, delaying, or restraining. During the ming-shu wind season, first appoint boundaries and repair the fields. During the qing-ming wind season, issue presents of silk and keep all employed. During the jing wind season, give ranks to the nobles and reward the meritorious. During the liang wind season, report on the efficiency of the land and sacrifice at the four suburbs. During the chang-he wind season, receive magistrates and put aside amusements. During the buzhou wind season, repair palaces and dwellings, improve the banks and the city walls. During the guang-mo wind season, close up gates and bridges, and execute punishments.

(Major's translation, 1979)

何謂八風？距日冬至四十五日，條風至；條風至四十五日，明庶風至；明庶風至四十五日，清明風至；清明風至四十五日，景風至；景風至四十五日，涼風至；涼風至四十五日，閶闔風至；閶闔風至四十五日，不周風至；不周風至四十五日，廣莫風至。條風至，則出輕系，去稽留；明庶風至，則正封疆，修田疇；清明風至，則出幣帛，使諸侯；景風至，則爵有位，賞有功；涼風至，則報地德，祀四郊；閶闔風至，則收懸垂，琴瑟不張；不周風至，則修宮室，繕邊城；廣莫風至，則閉關梁，決刑罰。

(淮南子：天文訓)

Baihutong-bafeng says, "From winter solstice to summer solstice, the ordering of wind is set up, and the nature of myriad things are established, each has its own duties and should not interfere with each other" (日冬夏至則八風之序立萬物之性成各有常職不得相幹). Sinologist John S. Major (1979) did a wonderful study on the eight winds' nomenclatures and its relation to the directions. According to him, apart from the fact that the cultural governing in each season is designated to comply with cosmological resonance of the winds blowing in that certain time-space, the wind names are not randomly chosen but carry cultural ways of reasoning. For example, the name for west wind *Changhe* is a cosmic gate to the Purple-Obscurity Palace of the Shang-ti (Lord of Heaven), and the setting down of sun in the west gate symbolizes the waning of the year and the storing up of Yang *qi* together with all the myriad creatures at Yellow Spring in a yin-yang seasonal sequence (Major, 1979).

Such a correlative thinking, Graham (1986) argues, becomes more prominent from the third century BC in cosmological understanding of time, space, yin-yang, *gua* (trigram), and the pentatonic and duodecatonic scales. The correlation between the all-embracing syncretic organic cosmology and human governance reaches its full flowering in the work of Dong Zhongshu 董仲舒 (179–104 BCE) within a few decades of the writing of *Huai Nan Zi* (see, Major, 1979). With such a congruence, sage rulers are expected to govern and transform their subjects through *wen* 文 (letters and culture), not *wu* 武 (weapons). Actually, this correlative thinking between cosmic and human governance defines the entire Confucian educational thought, to be explicated below.

However, it is to be noted that this "correlative thinking" is not Chinese unique. It is just more dominant in the Chinese culture compared to others (Graham, 1986). Even though sinologists tend to use this term "correlative thinking" with such implications as "non/pre-logical" or "non/pre-rational" as against the Western "analytical thinking," Fung (2010) argues that "correlative thinking" can still be understood in terms of analytic concepts.

Confucius' Educational Vision and Wind-Pedagogy as Expressed in *Yijing*

So far, I have unpacked the Yijing thought, specifically a few scaffolding themes, as the primordial-historical conditions of possibility for the entire Chinese thought and knowledge. This unpacking has two intentions. First, it is to show the distinct onto-epistemological conditions and structures of Chinese thought from the Western metaphysics, regarding the configurations of, as well as the ordering between, human beings and language, human beings and the environmental world, and nature and culture. What stands out as being distinct from the Western thought is a Yijing dynamics of change (as the title of *The Book of Change* aptly capitulates) and a Yijing onto-hermeneutic principle of comprehensive *observation*, and a correlative ordering between cosmic movement and the human-cultural governance. Intersecting these principles are the two modes of interpretation of Yijing, namely, a divinatory image-number style of reasoning and a Confucius-initiated meaning–rationale interpretation. As grounding onto-epistemological principles, they form a distinct and originary Chinese system of knowledge and reason in ancient China, which still orders the way education is thought and enacted in today's China. In this light, using the Western epistemological frameworks to encase the Chinese thought would cause an issue of epistemicide and an archaeological-historical mode of inquiry helps to confront such a paradigmatic challenge.

Second and more important, this unpacking explicates the Yijing style of thought as a condition of Confucius' educational vision as expressed in Yijing, which in turn shapes the entire Chinese educational thinking and praxis ever since. As shown above, Confucius plays a key role in re-interpreting the Yijing thought from a "meaning–rationale" perspective, adding a humanistic regard to the divinatory "image-number" mode of interpretation prevalent theretofore. Simply put, Confucius brings out a correlative governing dynamics between the cosmic governance and the cultural regulation through teaching, which is further consolidated in Han dynasty when Confucian thought becomes canonized.

Confucius' educational vision can be gleaned from his commentary on the particular Yijiing *guan*-hexagram. Since the next chapter will read into the *guan*-hexagram text and image, here a brief picture would suffice. Numbered 20 out of the 64 hexagrams, *guan*-hexagram shows an image of "wind blowing over the earth" and depicts an ongoing scenario where the King is performing the highest-ranking ritual ceremony to pay homage to gods and his ancestral forefathers with his subjects watching. The *guan*-hexagram itself has nothing to do with teaching and learning, yet Confucius adds a very brief commentary statement and envisions it into a teaching and learning movement. In so doing, Confucius proposes the themes of "wind-pedagogy," "setting up teaching by observing-following the cosmic Dao movement," and "setting up teaching by observing the local subjects." Then in which ways do the Yijing onto-epistemological principles and themes enable Confucius to envision his educational philosophy, wind-pedagogy, teaching, and learning in his commentary on the particular Yijing *guan*-hexagram? Three points can be made.

First, the Chinese notion of "wind" nurtures an inherent sense of "transforming" and the imagination of ancient Chinese "wind" blows through and across the varying domains of space, time, music, human body, education, and governance. It is this *transforming* "wind" and the hexagram image of "wind blowing over the earth" that Confucius invokes as a fundamental image of his ideal educational vision. Discursively, Confucius adds "the subjects observe from below and get transformed" to the original statement that per se has nothing to do with teaching and learning. In so doing, Confucius foregrounds the *transforming* sense of the Chinese "wind" and mobilizes it as an effect of the teaching and learning engagement, transfiguring *wind-transforming* into *teaching-transforming* (*jiaohua* 教化). Teaching-transforming is indeed the nomenclature for Confucian education for over two millennia until its replacement by "education" (*jiaoyu* 教育) in modern China. Seen this way, the Chinese "wind" is a central principle, a signature language, which grounds Confucius' interlocking of wind-transforming, learning, and teaching, still visible in China's current schooling discourses of "school wind, teaching wind, and learning wind." However, as argued above, confined to a modern grammar and representational signification, people tend to treat them as linguistic metaphors of "school atmosphere, teaching manners, and learning styles," henceforth glossing over the cultural "wind-education" association itself.

Second, the hexagram Confucius relates to teaching and learning is also called *guan* 觀, depicting a ritual-performing scene when "the hands (are) already washed, yet offerings not given, and a sincere outlook therewith," itself not explicitly related to teaching and learning. To envision it into a teaching and learning movement, Confucius ramifies the onto-temporal *guan* 觀 into *daguan* 大觀 (great observing on the top) and *xiaguan* 下觀 (observing from below). Specifically, *daguan* relates to the saintly King who observes, attunes to, and follows "the Dao movement" and sets up teaching accordingly, whereas *xiaguan* speaks to the subjects who watch and follow the saintly King performing the ritual, and in so doing, become transformed and submissive. This multifaceted onto-temporal *guan* 觀, as a grounding principle for Confucius' educational vision, has not won its due attention in scholarship on Confucian educational heritage. The fact that Confucius relates the teaching and learning to the ritual performance brings out a key "body" dimension of education, namely, teaching and learning is embodied to the extent that body configures and enacts education at its root. This "body" dimension is to be further explicated in the next "body" chapter.

Finally, the cosmic-cultural correlation imprints Confucius' educational vision to the extent that "the Confucian state was a large-scale metaphorical school where the ruler–subordinator relationship was reframed to that of the teacher–learner" (Han, 2013, p. 57). This also partly accounts for the fact that education in historical China has been highly bound with state governance, and Confucian scholars constitute the state governing structure in imperial China. Confucius says saintly Kings set up teaching by following, attuning to, and also modeling the Dao movement in the moment for the subjects to imitate, follow, and in so doing become transformed and submissive. This understanding rightly embodies Confucius' humanistic interpretation of the Yi-thought in that in an idealized harmonious society we human beings "comply with the power of the sky and the earth, the brightness of the sun and the moon, the ordering of the four seasons, and the good and bad omens of ghosts and gods." The *Way-Dao* of the Yi-thought, as Confucius argues, lies in human beings' comprehensive observing of the nature of *Yi* and *xiang* and also following *the heart of sky and earth* without using the seasons, stars, sun, and moon as signs for divination.

118 *Paradigmatic Unpackings*

To reiterate, China's current society and schooling feature a prevalent "wind-discourses" such as "party wind, social wind, school wind, teaching and learning wind." However, these wind-discourses are largely silent due to a taken-for-granted treatment of them as dead metaphors. In other words, the close cultural link between the notions of "wind' and "education" has rarely been discerned, let alone problematized and historicized. Suspending the modern conceptual style of reasoning and following the dancing "wind," I was exposed to the Yijing *guan*-hexagram and Confucius' wind-pedagogy and educational vision, which is rarely explored so far in the scholarship on Confucius and Confucian educational thinking.

Current scholarship on Confucius or Confucian educational thinking focus on its content and specific features, rather than the epistemological conditions that make it possible for Confucius to think as he does in the first place. For example, they are mostly based upon a reinterpretation of the texts of *Lunyu* (*The Analects* 論語), *Xueji* (*On Teaching and Learning* 學記), and *Daxue* (*The Great Learning* 大學) as "cultural scripts" (Tan, 2015). *Lunyu* records succinct theme-based dialogues between Confucius and his disciples. *Xueji* systematically discourses on the educational philosophy and practice during the Han Dynasty. *Daxue* emphasizes a transformative character of Confucian education with personal cultivation (person-making) as the root and goal of its learning. Seen this way, my unpacking of the Yijing thought and knowledge and its onto-epistemological principles enriches the current scholarship on Confucian educational culture. It also provides an alternative to cut into China's present knowledge system, its conceptual mode of signification and modern representational language, as well as the educational thinking and praxis.

With such a brief introduction of the onto-epistemological conditions of Confucius' educational vision, we now move on to scrutinize Confucius' commentary on the Yijing *guan*-hexagram in great detail, hoping to get more at Confucius' wind-pedagogy and educational vision and to render visible a holistic Chinese body-thinking as an alternative and complement to the modern mind-based conceptual thinking.

Notes

1. For over 30 years, Liu Dajun, Professor on Yijing studies at Shandong University of China, has been exploring the varied successions and transformations from Old Meaning to New Meaning of the Yijing thought around Han Dynasty. Based upon rigorous textual perusal of (a) the Yi silk texts excavated in 1973 from an early Han tomb found in Mawangdui, Hunan Province; (b) the Han bamboo texts of *Zhouyi* from Anhui in 1977; (c) the Hubei Qin bamboo text *Guizang* in 1993; and (d) the Zhanguo Chu Bamboo texts that Shanghai Museum bought from Hong Kong *wenhu* market in 1994, Liu resolves the historical controversy by affirming that Confucius did study the Yijing seriously and passed it on to his followers. Furthermore, *Xici* is ascertained to be Confucius' commentary and interpretation on Yijing from a newly constructed humanistic and moral regard. Such is an initiation of the New Meaning of Yijing that is further reinstated and

canonized by some of Confucius' followers in Han Wudi period with Confucianism gaining its formal privileged power in Imperial China, which developed into 13 schools of exegesis. Old Meaning, that is., the originary divinatory function of Yijing, including Yinyang, Wuxing, Sishi, etc., visible in the excavated silk texts but absent in the later-present official transcript *Zhouyi*, was also passed down but was accordingly relegated to a secondary status, gradually disappearing from imperial formal learning, and instead spread out sporadically at the grass-root level as unorthodox divinatory skills. *Xiang-shu* starts to become really popular when the *Huangdi Neijing* starts to depict the human body as a small universe with 60 *jiazi (taiyang, taiying lifa)* (see, Liu, 2000, 2001, 2002, 2002, 2010, 2012).

2. Cross-referenced with the Old Meaning fragments in the newly excavated Yi silk texts, Liu finds that *Huai Nan Zi* 淮南子, a text presumably in close relation to *Huai Nan Dao Xun* compiled by King Liu An in Huai Nan as a seminar discussion report among nine invited scholars well-versed in the Yijing and presented to Wu Di in 139 BCE, also contains lots of traces on Old Meaning of Yi. This finding is particularly reassuring to me because my puzzling research statement "wind moves, insects get germinated and transformed in eight days" also comes from *Huai Nan Zi* as its source text, which recurs in *Da Dai Li—Yi Ben Ming* (易本命) (around Dong Han) and *Kongzi Jiayu* (compiled around San Guo, 195–256 CE).

References

Agamben, G. (2009). *The signature of all things: On method*. New York, NY: Zone Books.

Bush, C. (2008). Reading and difference: Image, allegory, and the invention of Chinese. In E. Hayot, H. Saussy, & S. G. Yao (Eds.), *Sinographies: Writing China* (pp. 34–63). Minneapolis, MN: University of Minnesota Press.

Chen, J. (2013). "Guan": Cong Zhouyi dao Fojiao [Guan: From Zhouyi to Buddhism "观": 从周易 到佛教]. *Zhouyi Yanjiu [Zhouyi Study], 119*, 48–55.

Chen, L. (1999). Boshu Yizhuan yu xianqin rujia yixue zhi fenpai [Boshu Yizhuan and pre-qin Confucian yi-study sections. 帛书易传与先秦儒家易学之分派]. *Kongzi Yanjiu [Confucius Study], 4*, 23–31.

Chen, L. (2016). The ideas of "educating" and "learning" in Confucian thought. In X. Di & H. McEwan (Eds.), *Chinese philosophy on teaching and learning: Xueji (學記) in the twenty-first century* (pp. 77–96). Albany, NY: State University of New York Press.

Cheng, C. Y. (2011). Interpreting paradigm of change in Chinese philosophy. *Journal of Chinese Philosophy, 38*(3), 339–367.

Fenollosa, E. (1918/1936). *The Chinese written character as a medium for poetry* (With a foreword and notes by E. Pound). London, UK: Stanley Nott.

Foucault, M. (1973a). *The order of things: An archaeology of the human sciences*. New York, NY: Vintage Books. (Original work published 1966)

Foucault, M. (1973b). *The birth of the clinic: An archaeology of medical perception*. New York, NY: Pantheon Books.

Fung, Y. M. (2010). On the very idea of correlative thinking. *Philosophy Compass, 5*(4), 296–306.

Graham, A. C. (1986). *Yin-yang and the nature of correlative thinking*. Singapore: The Institute of East Asian Philosophies.

Han, S. (2013). Confucian states and learning life: Making scholar-officials and social learning a political contestation. *Comparative Education*, 49(1), 57–71.

He, M. F., & Phillion, J. (2008). *Personal, passionate, participatory inquiry into social justice in education*. Charlotte, NC: Information Age Publishing.

Heidegger, M. (1969). *Identity and difference* (J. Stambaugh, Trans. with an Introduction.). New York, NY, Evanston, IL, and London, UK: Harper & Row Publishers. (Original work published 1957)

Heidegger, M. (1977). *The question concerning technology and other essays* (W. Lovitt, Trans. with an introduction). New York: Harper Torchbooks.

Heidegger, M. (1978). Letter on humanism. In D. F. Krell (Ed.), *Basic writings* (pp. 213–265). London, UK: Routledge.

Ji, Z. Q. (2011). Lun guan zai zhouyi zhexue zhong de jiangou [On the philosophical construction of guan in zhouyi. 论"观"在《周易》哲学中的建构]. *Lan Zhou Xue Kan*, 9, 33–38.

Kern, M. (2001). Ritual, text, and the formation of the canon: Historical transitions of "Wen" in early China. *T'oung Pao*, Second Series, 87, Fasc. 1/3, 43–91.

Liu, C. L. (2011). Waiguan yihua yu neiguan yiming: Zhouyi guangua guankan zhidao de zhexue kaocha [Outer-guan to transform and inner-guan to lighten up: Exploring the philosophical implications of Zhouyi *guan*-hexagram's guan-observing and kan-looking 外观以化与内观以明——《周易·八卦》"观—看"之道的哲学考察]. *Yantai Daxue Xuebao [Journal of Yantai University Philosophy and Social Science]*, 24(1), 5–11.

Liu, D. J. (2000). Guaqi suyuan [Exploring the origin of guaqi"卦气"溯源]. *Zhongguo Shehui Kexue [Chinese Social Science]*, 5, 122–129.

Liu, D. J. (2001). Boshu yizhuan zhong de xiangshu yixue sixiang [image-number way of thinking in silk text *yizhuan* 帛书《易传》中的象数易学思想]. *Zhexue Yanjiu [Philosophy Research]*, 11, 47–53.

Liu, D. J. (2002). Zhouyi guyi kao [Exploring the old meaning of *Zhouyi*《周易》古义考]. *Zhongguo Shehui Kexue [Chinese Social Science]*, 5, 142–151.

Liu, D. J. (2010). Er'shi shiji de yixue yanjiu ji zhongyao tese [Yi study in 20s century and main features: Preface to a hundred yi-study collection. 二十世纪的易学研究及重要特色]. *Zhouyi Yanjiu [Zhouyi Study]*, 99, 3–12.

Liu, D. J. (2012). Huai Nan Zi Yun Yi Kao [Huai Nan Zi Impregnates Yi. 《淮南子》蕴《易》考]. *Zhouyi Yanjiu [Zhouyi Study]*, 114, 3–12.

Ma, J. (2007). Zhouyi Guangua zhi guan yu zhongguo gudai wenxue chuangzuo zhuti lun [Zhouyi *guan*-hexagram's guan and the subjectivity issue in China' traditional literary theory.《周易·观卦》之"观"与中国古代文学创作主体论]. *Tansuo yu Zhengming [Exploration and Argumentation Theory]*, 4, 139–141.

Major, J. S. (1979). Notes on the nomenclature of winds and directions in the early Han. *T'oung Pao*, Second Series, 65, Livr. 1/3, 66–80.

Nelson, E. S. (2011). Introduction: Onto-hermeneutics, ethics and nature in the Yijing. *Journal of Chinese Philosophy*, 38(3), 335–338.

Phillion, J. (1999). Narrative and formalistic approaches to the study of multiculturalism. *Curriculum Inquiry*, 29(1), 129–141.

Saussy, H. (2001a). The prestige of writing: Wen, letter, picture, image, ideography. In H. Saussy (Ed.), *The great walls of discourse and other adventures in cultural China* (pp. 35–74). Cambridge, MA: Harvard University Press.

Saussy, H. (2001b). Outside the parenthesis (Those people were a kind of solution). In H. Saussy (Ed.), *The great walls of discourse and other adventures in cultural China* (pp. 146–182). Cambridge, MA: Harvard University Press.

Tan, C. (2015). Education policy borrowing and cultural scripts for teaching in China. *Comparative Education, 51*(2), 196–211.

Wang, S. R. (2012). *Huigui yuanchuang zhi si* [*Returning to the originary source of thought* 回归原创之思]. Nanjing: Jiangsu People's Publishing House.

Wilhelm, H. R. (1995). *Understanding the I Ching: The Wilhelm Lectures on the Book of Changes (1966 and 1979)*. Princeton, NJ: Princeton University Press.

Wu, K. M. (2011). *Story-thinking: Cultural meditations*. New York, NY: Nova Science Publishers, Inc.

Wu, Z. J. (2016). Person-making through Confucian exegesis. In G. P. Zhao & Z. Y. Deng (Eds.), *Re-envisioning Chinese education: The meaning of person-making in a new age* (pp. 93–115). New York, NY: Routledge.

Zhang, X. L. (2013). *Fujian Tiandixin—Rujia zailin de yunyi yu daolu.* [*Revealing the heart of heaven and earth: On meaning of and path toward authentic Confucianism* 复见天地心——儒家再临的蕴意与道路]. Beijing: Oriental Publishing House.

Zhang, Z. L. (2015). *Zhongguo Gudai Shendao Yanjiu* [*Body-Dao in Ancient China* 中国古代身道研究]. Beijing: SDX Joint Publishing Company.

Zhao, W., & Schmidt, M. (forthcoming). Cultivating "Response-ability" through contemplative practices: Philosophical underpinnings and pedagogical applications in a HK school. In J. Lin, B. Kirby, S. Edwards, & T. Culham (Eds.), *Contemplative pedagogies in K-12, university, and community settings: Transformation from within*. Charlotte, NC: Information Age Publishing.

Zhao, W., & Sun, C. (2017). "Keep off the lawn; grass has life too!": Re-invoking a Daoist ecological sensibility for moral education in China's primary schools. *Educational Philosophy and Theory*. doi:10.1080/00131857.2017.1323623

5 Beyond Conceptual Thinking
Chinese Body-Thinking and Educational Body

This chapter picks up and further explores a historical imprint and destruction of the Chinese "body" by juxtaposing two body events, namely, Confucius' ritual body as performed in the Yijing *guan*-hexagram and the current controversial schooling kneeling-bowing events. Bracketing a naturalized treatment of "body" as a given object of discipline and punishment in educational studies, I historicize the (con)textures and (over)tones of "body" as an exemplar to see how it is constructed to (re)configure the very rubrics of teaching and learning in both events. In so doing, I discern a modern mind–body division–conflation that has made "body" a bone of contention and delimited the Chinese teacher–student ordering to a Confucian hierarchical versus modern democratic relationship. In other words, a binary logic holds sway in modern epistemology and re-conceptualizing the Chinese teacher–student relationship beyond a hierarchy vs. egalitarianism ordering needs to problematize the rule of binary logic itself (a theme to be further scrutinized in the next "difference" chapter). This unpacking further exposes me to an ontological Chinese body-thinking, not bodily thinking, which not only informs the predominant Western(ized) mind-thinking but also reveals the limit of applying Michel Foucault's power-based governmentality to scrutinize the Chinese teacher–student ordering in the first place.

Prologue

In Chapter 4, I followed the Chinese "wind" dancing between cultures and then far back into the ancient Chinese Yijing space. Within that space, human beings and the natural world are experienced as co-dwelling in togetherness (symbiosis) through an ontological mode of observing (guan 觀) and feeling-resonating (gan 感), all moving and pulsating along with a constant cosmic *Dao* movement. Turning myself over to feel and listen to the murmuring wind-languages, I realized two moments of re-turnings on my un-learning way as an effort to stretch, if not explode, my habituated subject–object reasoning mode. My first re-turning is back to the Chinese language with a deep appreciation that an active engagement with the Chinese language entails observing-feeling, and becoming opened up to, its contextures and overtones as a material being, rather than grasping it as a commonplace system of concepts. My second re-turning is back to my bodily reasoning, such as observing and feeling-resonating, which I realize I need to appreciate and evoke further as part of my mode of being to constrain, rather than complement, my abstract conceptual–cognitive thinking and judgment.

With an awakened sensitivity to the Chinese language and a heightened consciousness of bodily reasoning, in this chapter, I move on to *bodily* experience, that is, observe-feel (觀感), the Chinese body and its historical pulsations. Meanwhile, I remain alert to the possible ways such bodily experiencing movement, with its twists and turns, may re-orient my intellectual un-learning way as well as re-shape my mode of being as a learner-inquirer. I use the term *bodily experience* to precaution myself not to conceptualize body as a given object with my subjective mind, but to attend to and co-respond to body as a material being through my own body (observing body with body), although my story will show how deceptively easy it is to slip back into my habituated subject–object reasoning. Please note that I am here picking up a modern mind–body separation as an analytical exigency, yet the categorical mind–body separation is what I aim to problematize in this chapter through re-approaching the Chinese body.

With such an intention, I choose to observe-experience, problematize, and compare two contextualized modes of reasoning on the Chinese body in connection with teaching, learning, and teacher–student dis-ordering as exemplified through two events. In so doing, I also explore the historical tones and textures such commonsensical notions as teaching, learning, and teacher–student relation can nurture. The first example is Confucius' envisioning of the Yijing *guan*-hexagram as *ideal*, in its double sense of *contingent* and *exemplary*, teaching and learning movement that happens like wind blowing over the earth. The second example is present-day public debates on a few recent school kneeling-bowing events that are claimed to have downgraded Chinese education in pain and shame. Those who argue against a reinstatement of such Confucian kneeling-bowing rites in modern China claim that current education should train students into free citizens who are *up-right*, standing both up and right, not slave-like servants with kneels down and genuflected.

I chose Confucius' envisioning with the Yijing *guan*-hexagram for two reasons. First, the Yijing hexagram itself does not explicitly embody a way of reasoning on teaching and learning. It is Confucius who envisions its hexagram image of wind blowing over the earth into an ideal teaching–learning movement, which can be re-viewed as a remote historical prototype for the schooling wind-discourses in contemporary China. Second, Confucius situates his envisioning within a bodily ritual-performing scenario where the King is performing the ritual with his subjects watching. Then how does Confucius' situational reasoning movement start, develop, justify, and constrain itself, and with what principles? What roles does this ritual body play in enacting and justifying his envisioning on teaching and learning? How is it possible for Confucius to observe-feel the ritual body with his body? Lastly, how is it possible for me to observe-feel such a ritual body?

I chose the present-day public debate on a few kneeling-bowing cases because the kneeling body, though still commonly viewed as a form of the Confucian ritual body, is overwhelmingly claimed to have downgraded contemporary Chinese education in pain and shame. Curious about what possible ways of reasoning ground such a claim, I examine the public arguments and feel how the ritual body is re-invoked and re-appropriated by them in supporting and justifying their reasoning on teaching, learning, and teacher–student (dis)ordering. Besides, to what extent do the current public observe-feel the kneeling body through their body? Again, how can I observe-feel such a kneeling body?

Both examples engage a broad yet contextualized form of a ritual body, that is, a body performing rituals in a Confucian sense, yet effectuating sharply distinct reasoning styles. One is envisioned as embodying a saintly teaching and learning, while the other is denigrated as symbolizing a downgrading shame and pain to current China's education reform. Then what can be the historical principles or patterns of thought that have made possible such sharply distinct ways of reasoning? Reading ritual body back into its various historical strata, this chapter aims to solve this discrepancy by showing the complex textures and contextures of the Chinese body as a material being and meanwhile problematizing our taken-for-granted conceptualizations of body, teaching, learning, and teacher–student dis-ordering.

Three Methodological Justifications With Precautions

As I accented in Preface and Introduction, I pick up the Chinese "wind" and "body" not as given concepts but as theoretical constructs, as paradigmatic examples of a style of reasoning, and as strategic signposts to help me cut into, de-construct, and re-envision the ordering of, among other themes, language/reason, the educational body, and the teacher–student difference in China from a cross-cultural and historical-archaeological perspective. Furthermore, I mobilize both "wind" and "body" as an example in Agamben's (2009) sense, with not metaphorical but analogical logic, to make intelligible "a broader problematic context that it both constitutes and makes intelligible" (p. 17). This making-intelligible endeavor entails deactivating Chinese wind and body from their commonsensical uses, suspending them as semantic, linguistic signifiers to designate different things, and presenting the rules of their analogical use as singular cases. The rules cannot be applied or stated a priori but have to be shown and made visible through presenting their singularity as expressed in the aporia-like events.

This said, I would like to explain what I mean by contextualizing, problematizing, and comparing these two examples as two historical modes of reasoning, and how I will unfold my bodily analyses with them. This helps to (a) address a concern of empirical relation and an analytical conundrum in reading historical texts back to its contexts; and (b) raise an awareness of historicity to the extent that arguments about body, teaching, and learning are only contingently valid grounded upon certain historical contexts; and (c) gesture a precaution against treating body as an objective given, or a given object, from a cognitive mind.

These two historical modes of reasoning span a timeline of over 2500 years, and juxtaposing them with each other raises a concern of empirical relations. However, along with Michel Serres, I argue such tempo-spatial juxtaposition can be fully justified if we de-construct, as we should, a notion of linear time wherein things happen along a causal relation. According to Serres (1990/1995), things that seem far removed can operate in similar neighborhoods without being reduced to an illusion of the same. Furthermore, time can be thought through nonlinear folds on a handkerchief rather than simply through a one-dimensional line. To further bracket a causal relation, I am not picking up the Confucian example as an original prototype (though it may be) and the current kneeling-bowing events as its transmogrified form. Rather, my purpose is (a) to juxtapose them in a way for them to dialogue with, inform, and respond to each other; and (b) to problematize and relativize the figuration and configuration of the Chinese body for new openings in understanding teaching, learning, and teacher–student ordering and dis-ordering. To borrow Wu Kuang-Ming's statement as a flipside to the Confucius statement *warming the old to know the new*, I also *warm the new-present to know the old-past* (cited in Goulding, 2008, p. 19).

My intention of reading historical texts back into its contexts raises, or rather, falls into a conundrum. How is it possible for a modern mentality to read historical texts (body in this case) back into their contexts and come up with an understanding, as it was understood? Isn't a historical reading a constructed replica of modernity?

While I am fully cognizant of such a conundrum, I explore a possibility for loosening up, if not fully getting out of, this conundrum by attending to a mode of "evocative dialoguing" (Duarte, 2012) in two senses. First, I don't seek to understand a given meaning commonly assumed to subside in the text but to dialogue evocatively or encounter with its textures, tones, and movement as a way of reasoning. With such an attitude, I don't aim to understand what the narrative means but to undergo with the narrative as a reasoning movement (Wu K., 1997), and explore how it is possible to reason as it does.

Second, seen this way, my questioning moves contingently, dependent upon the way one question may provoke the next. Albeit starting with an unavoidable conceptual way of reasoning, my questioning moves in a way to bring out what can be further questioned, which in turn helps me to turn around and realize the limits of my earlier questions. To be specific, I, unconsciously though, start my questioning on body from a perspective of a physical body separate from a mental mind, then position such mind–body separation as a springboard toward further showing their boundary by rendering something visible that is not reducible to such a binary, and finally use this excessive body-form to show the limits of my body-as-physical-body entry point. Through questioning the movement of my questioning, I aim to problematize, un-learn, and implode a mind/cognition and body/emotion binary separation for new possibilities.

Apart from these two concerns, a word is needed here on my intention of contextualizing these two modes of reasoning. The word *contextualizing* conveys two of my precautions against (a) making universal-abstract, that is; decontextualized, claims about the body, teaching, learning, and teacher–student ordering; and b) picking up other historical judgment as founding principles to support my argument. In other words, a sense of cultural historicity needs to be acknowledged with notions like body, teaching, and learning. I gained such a realization through my own intercultural body experience already shared in Introduction. Here is a brief revisit though. The Chinese culture seems to have a clear "norm" of what counts as a beautiful, up-right, or "right" body or body-form. For example, the first thing to learn when you start schooling is how to hold a pencil "right" because "a person's handwriting belies his/her manner" (*wenruqiren* 文如其人) and one needs to "stand up-straight like a pine tree and sit still like a clock" (站如松坐如鐘). However, my daughter's schooling in the United States plus my own observations helped me realize the cultural not universal boundary of what counts as a "normative" body.

Such a personal realization cautions me against picking up contextualized body claims as grounding principle to support my argument. For example, in comparative cultural studies, the Chinese body is commonly viewed as a "psychosomatic self" (Ames, 1993), coupled with the claim that the Chinese language, as well as its ways of reasoning, are largely bodily as against the abstract–cognitive reasoning prevalent in the Western thought (Sun, 1991; Wu K., 1997). These viewpoints may be very well justified in describing these certain historical events that the researchers have drawn upon. However, if I re-invoke these descriptive terms as founding principles to build my argument, then they tend to become prescriptive categories fossilizing the Chinese body, its language, and ways of reasoning into some fixed entities not susceptible to historical changes. I mean it is not that these viewpoints themselves smell of essentialism, but that the ways they are operationalized beyond their contexts give them an essential flavor. In the latter case, I become a cognitive thinking mind approaching language, body, and language as an object, neglecting a contingent movement between us as co-beings.

With these methodological understanding, I caution myself against building abstract arguments upon over-generalized claims. Instead, I read the Chinese (ritual) body back to two historical texts and contexts to observe-feel how it is reasoned, enacted, and experienced (or rather, reasons, enacts and experiences) in navigating teaching, learning, and teacher–student disordering. The active use of "reasons, enacts, and experiences" alerts me to body's agentive-ness as a material being and draws my attention to possibly encountering the ritual body with my own body, as a reverberation of the Daoist thesis of *observing body with body*.

To transition from the previous chapter on the Yijing *guan*-hexagram, I structurally start this body chapter with the Confucian ritual body, move onto the current kneeling body, and ends with a dialogue evoked between these two forms of body. Such intra-cultural dialogue is to be further placed in a cross-cultural encounter with the recent somatic and affective turn in the Western thought and its possible significance to educational rethinking.

Experiencing the Yijing Guan-Observing Body Through Confucius' Vision

As I mentioned in the previous chapter, the Yijing *guan*-hexagram ䷓, with a trigram of *wind-xun* placed above a trigram of *earth-kun*, shows an image of wind blowing over the earth. This hexagram ䷓ depicts an ongoing scenario where the King is performing the highest-ranking ritual ceremony to pay homage to gods and his ancestral forefathers with his subjects watching. Nourishing a double sense of performing and beholding, this Chinese character *guan* 觀 can be tentatively glossed as *observing*. What is noteworthy is that the eight-character theme statement for this *guan*-hexagram zooms in on one particular scene at which point *hands washed/yet not offering/there is a real reverent outlook with the head(s) up* (盥而不薦有孚顒若).

Confucius views this carved-out hand-washing scene as most worthy of observation in such ritual ceremonies, and he would not even watch the following sacrifice-offering part (*Analects: Baqiao*). He further envisions this contextual ritual-performing and beholding as one exemplar for teaching and learning that happens between saintly kings and his subjects like wind blowing over the earth. Confucius' dovetailing of this hexagram image with teaching and learning is intellectually intriguing since the source text of the *guan*-hexagram apparently indicates no intersection with teaching and learning. Yet, Confucius adds a very brief commentary statement and envisions it into a teaching and learning movement, meanwhile proposing the themes of "wind-pedagogy," "setting up teaching by observing-following the cosmic Dao movement" and "setting up teaching by observing the local subjects." Then how is it possible for Confucius to envision such an ideal teaching and learning movement through this Yijing *guan* scenario and its image ䷓ composed of yin-yang lines? What roles can body play in enacting, embodying, and expressing Confucius' reasoning on teaching and learning? I mean how Confucius' reasoning movement starts, develops, justifies, or strains itself such that an ideal teaching–learning example is envisioned then and there.

To answer these questions, let's first take a close look at Confucius' commentary on this *guan*-hexagram and its image, and hermeneutically feel its textual and imagistic murmuring. Such a textual plus imagistic perusal is

128   *Paradigmatic Unpackings*

important and necessary for two reasons. First, it is Confucius' hermeneutic interpretation of this *guan*-hexagram text 盥而不薦有孚顒若 and its six-lined image ䷓ that depicts the multilayered textures of *guan*-observing movement. Henceforth, Confucius' commentary provides some traces that allow us to glimpse into how the hexagram evokes his envisioning movement.

Second, without following a modern subject–verb–object syntax, the juxtaposition of these monographic characters and the image begs a syntactic, grammatical, and graphic exploration, which meanwhile turns back on and reveals the limits of such subject–verb–object ordering. Thus, hermeneutically interpreting the text-image is not to seek out Confucius' original intention, but to feel and encounter his movement of reasoning by hearing its textual tone and overtone echoing its contextual ritual performance and the hexagram image ䷓. Paying heed to each monographic character, I translate the text as below:

> 大觀在上順而巽中正以觀天下 盥而不薦有孚顒若下觀而化也 觀天之神道而四時不忒聖人以神道設教而天下服矣　風行地上觀先王以省方觀民設教
>
> Great guan-observe on the top . . . (the King is) situated in the *center-right* 中正 positioning to guan-observe the whole world under the sky/ hands washed yet not offering/ there is a sincere reverent outlook with head(s) up/below guan-observe and (get) transformed 化/ guan-observe the magical Dao of heaven/ and the four seasons move unchanged/ saintly kings set up teaching accordingly/ and the whole world under the sky become submissive 服/wind blows over the earth/ancient kings accordingly visited different regions, observed local peoples, and set up teaching.

To examine Confucius' reasoning movement, let's first look at how the hexagram image ䷓ visually places this ritual-performing King in a contingent, not permanent, center-right positioning. Confucius' commentary says "(the King is) situated in a center-right 中正 positioning to *guan*-observe the whole world under the sky." This center-right positioning judgment comes from a visual observation of the hexagram image ䷓. A bit background on the Yijing number-image way of reasoning needs to be revisited here. With a hexagram image, a broken-yin line is numbered *six*, whereas the solid-yang line is numbered *nine*. From bottom up, the lines in this *guan*-observing image ䷓ are numbered *beginning-six* 初六, *six-two* 六二, *six-three* 六三, *six-four* 六四, *nine-five* 九五 and *upper-nine* 上九. A broken-yin line would be in a right positioning when placed in the even-numbered lines counting from bottom up, while a solid-yang line in the odd-numbered lines. Otherwise, they are in a not-*right* positioning. In such image-number reasoning, the yang line assumes its most honorable positioning in the fifth line bottom up, that is, the honor of nine-five 九

五之尊 to which only Kings are entitled. This *nine-five honor* becomes a metonym for Chinese Kings and Emperors. In this *guan*-image ䷓, the fifth line exhibits as a yang line and henceforth this ritual-performing King is situated in a center-right positioning.

Then what does it mean for a King to be placed in a center-right positioning? Is he empowered to do something that he elsewhere can't? Confucius says 中正以觀天下, which I initially put as *(the King is) situated in the center-right* 中正 *(positioning) to guan-observe the whole world under the sky*. Here the English gloss *to* for the Chinese connecting word 以 gestures a sense more of an effectuated result than of a so-as-to purpose. In other words, the King is positioned in the center-right place, not just with an intentional purpose or a mission to *guan*-observe the world under the sky. Rather, he gets into a position, gesturing both a vantage point and an ability, where he *can* guan-observe the world under the sky, *observing* here no longer merely denoting a sense of beholding and watching, but also bringing out its etymological senses of being perceptive to, and being able to see, minute things. The right-positioned King is now perceptive to *the mysterious Dao movement* in a way he can feel the latter pulsating with *the four seasons moving unchanged*.

To a modern mentality, such expressions like observing, perceiving, and seeing belie a cognitive subject–object mode of reasoning in the sense of inner representation of the outside world. However, the Yijing *guan*-observing, as shown in the previous chapter, is ontological in that it is more of being exposed to, resonating with (*gan*-feeling 感), following, attuning to, and comporting with the Dao movement at the moment 時. This ontological sense can be felt through another English gloss for the Chinese *guan* 觀, *contemplation* in Aristotle's, not modern, sense. Not reduced to a cognitive activity like self-reflection or meditation, Duarte (2012) interprets Aristotle's contemplation as "represent(ing) those rare moments when the soul is aware of its connection to the life force which animates all living beings" (p. 3). Duarte says:

> I have offered a (re)-description of contemplation, one which focuses on the capacity of the human being to be with Being, that is, to place oneself in the location (*templum*, a significant place for observation) to observe, 'see' (*contemplare*) the co-existence of oneself with the permanence of Existence. Contemplation, described under these conditions, is thus read with an emphasis on the parts *con* (with) and *temp* (time). The temporal quality of Being suggests that permanence is not a static phenomenon.
>
> (p. 3)

Similarly, the Yijing King contingently placed in a right-center position gains a capacity to observe and feel for this moment a co-existential harmonious movement between him, his fellows, the four seasons, and Dao. To

130 *Paradigmatic Unpackings*

note, within such a Yijing cosmos, humans and the natural world symbiotically co-dwell attuning to and following the Dao movement. In other words, the Yijing *guan*-observing and *gan*-feeling can't be reduced to a modern subject–object cognitive activity wherewith human subjects impose upon and avail of the objective natural world.

Now let's relate this hexagram image back to its contextual inter-corporeal ritual-performing scenario and Confucius' envisioning and portraying of it as an ideal teaching and learning movement that happens like wind blowing over the earth. Since the King is situated in a right-center positioning, then how is it depicted and enacted bodily with the bodily subjects? How can such contextualized bodily engagement be connected to and envisioned as an ideal teaching–learning movement? Furthermore, how can such an envisioning match the hexagram image of wind blowing over the earth?

These questions bring us back to the original hexagram theme statement 盥而不薦有孚顒若, which I word-for-word translate as (washing already done) (but) (not yet) (the offering)/ (there is) (a believing-reverent) (head-up) (outlook). The first part describes two actions in process, that is, washing and offering, whereas the second part portrays a form of bodily comportment, that is, looking head-up and reverent. Without a grammatical subject, these statements don't explicitly specify who is or are looking up with a reverent outlook. The Chinese character 有 can be glossed as both *there is* and *have*, thus opening up two possibilities. With *have*, the statement can be read as "(the King) washed his hands already but didn't offer the sacrifice animals, and (the King) has a reverent outlook with his head raised up." In this case, the description is zoomed in on the King performing the ritual ceremony. With *there is*, the same statement can be read as "the washing was already done, but the offering was not, and there is a reverent outlook with head up." The single-form *head* is still a description of the King. So far, no connection to teaching, learning, and teaching–student movement is easily visible in this original hexagram theme statement.

However, right after this original statement, Confucius adds a commentary sentence 下觀而化, namely, (the subjects) below guan-observe (the King performing the ritual) and (become) transformed. Now the single-form *head-up* becomes a plural *heads-up* in that the subjects also raise their heads as a bodily expression of being transformed by the King's head-up reverent outlook. At this moment, Confucius' description zooms out from the King's body to a broader co-responsive bodily enactment between the King and the subjects, which in turn indicates, if not explicates, Confucius' first connection to a teaching–learning movement.

Still, the first connection needs further support. To us modern people, a corporeal description of *reverent head-up outlook* even in this highest-ranking ritual ceremony can hardly account for Confucius' judgment that the King is in the right positioning, nor can a co-responsive *head-up* movement fully justify Confucius' reasoning that the subjects get transformed and become submissive. Something is missing in this ideal teaching and learning loop. What is it that has enabled the King to assume the right positioning and furthermore to transform the subjects like wind blowing over the earth? For this to happen, the corporeal reverent-looking head-up should not be just a physical body-look but should be a body-form, *necessarily* pointing toward something significant yet non-corporeal about the King that entitles him to take the right position and empowers him to transform his subjects. Then, what can this *something significant* be to Confucius?

The answer can be felt through a re-looking at the notion 顒 in 有孚顒若. The preliminary Chinese dictionary *Erya* 爾雅 interprets 顒顒 as *an exemplary King's virtue* (君之德也), extended from its literal referent of a big head. Intriguingly, the fact that big/great head functions as a metonym for the King's virtue is not explicated, but only mentioned in a fleeting note in the official commentaries I have consulted. Such a fleeting note is provocative to my modern mentality as it turns me around and helps me realize that my earlier assertive questioning, namely, the bodily head-up should point toward something significant non-bodily, has been encapsulated within a habituated mind–body analytic conundrum. Drawn to such a metonymic relation between big head and kingly virtue, I realize corporeal body and non-corporeal dispositions are hardly separable in the Confucian reasoning. To push further, the Confucian body is more than a mere physical body. This is one specific example of what I mean by evocatively dialoguing with the Confucian narrative as a reasoning movement. Instead of understanding what it says, I undergo with its movement.

Such a metonymic relation between head and kingly virtue complies with Confucius' accent on rule by virtue as expressed in the statement "exemplary person's virtue is (like) wind whereas petty person's virtue is like (grass) and when the wind blows grass bends" (see *Lunyu:Yanyuan*). For Confucius, only a virtuous King can take a right-center positioning (正) similar to that of the North Star such that the entire world under the sky would submissively follow (服) him (see *Lunyu: Weizheng*). In this sense, the image of wind blowing over the earth is analogically used to describe the ideal teaching and learning between the King and his subjects. It is here that the transforming tone of the Chinese notion *wind* 風 is foregrounded. Just as wind blows and insects get germinated and transformed, subjects are transformed and become submissive by the saintly king's breeze-like virtue but not weapons. This is the Yijing connotation nurtured within the modern term *wenhua* (文化) for *culture*, namely, to transform the world by *wen*, not weapons (wu 武).

To note, this transforming power doesn't merely originate from the King himself because he is the virtuous King; rather, it is with the Dao movement. As Confucius continues his commentary on this *guan*-hexagram, (the right-positioned King) *guan*-observes the magical Dao of heaven, (feels it resonance with) the four seasons moving unchanged, sets up teaching accordingly, and the whole world under the sky become submissive (觀天之神道而四時不忒聖人以神道設教而天下服矣). In other words, the

King vicariously relays such transforming Dao power onto his subjects. As *Shuowenjiezi* says, the Yijing notion *hua* (transform 化) is not to transform (people), but that people are transformed (by Dao).

Now it is clear that the King's reverent head-up embodies his kingly virtue that entitles him to a right-center positioning. Being in such a right positioning further enables the King to observe-feel a co-existence with the Dao movement and set up a Daoist teaching that can transform his subjects like wind blowing the earth. Confucius depicts a co-responsive or imitating head-up as a corporeal embodiment of such teaching and learning effectuated. Then, why is such imitative co-responsive bodily enactment important in this ritual-performing and beholding? What implications does it have for Confucian teaching, learning, and their effectuations?

Interestingly, such an imitating theme between this bodily teaching and learning is actually nurtured within the etymological roots of the ancient Chinese characters for jiao-teaching 敎 and xue-learning 學. The two graphic forms of jiao-teaching 敎 and xue-learning 學 both contain a graph 子 for a kid and a graph 又 indicating a hand holding a bamboo branch (an early form of bamboo-made writing brush). However, the graph for xue-learning 敩 has an added part 冂 that indicates a sense of being blind and unenlightened.

It is said that before the Qin Dynasty (221 BCE–207 BCE) these two notions 敎+敩 are both called *xue/xiao-learning* in that teaching and learning equally take up the two sides of a coin. It is after the Qin Dynasty that the notion 敩 becomes 學 from which derives its modern and simplified graphic form of 学. That explains why *Shuowenjiezi*, compiled around 100 CE, only has an entry for 敩 but not 學. *Shangshu-duiming* (尚書兌命), the earliest records of Chinese historical governing, says:

> *Xue/xiao xue* half and half. The first *xue/xiao* is xiao-teaching in that teaching others benefits oneself in a way equal to what learning does. Teaching others is called *xuezhe—the person who teaches* (now a common gloss for *scholar*). Teaching is to awaken others through doing, while learning is to self-awaken through imitating (what teachers do). Thus in past times, both teaching and learning are called xue-learning.
>
> (Duan, *Shuowenjiezizu*)

> 兌命曰。學學半。其此之謂乎。按兌命上學字謂教。言教人乃益己之學半。教人謂之學者。學所以自覺。下之效也。教人所以覺人。上之施也。故古統謂之學也。

The description that teaching is to awaken others through doing, while learning is to self-awaken through imitating (what teachers do) echoes the teaching–learning movement that Confucius envisions of the ritual-performing King and his subjects. The King performs the ritual ceremony with a reverent head-up outlook, while the subjects imitate what the King does with a co-responsive heads-up reverent outlook. Such a bodily element of teaching and learning also echoes what Confucius says about himself that is indirectly recorded in *Shiji* 史記: I would rather walk my life than talk my life (我欲托之空言不如載之行事之深切著明也). Maybe the Chinese term *to model your body for others* (以身作則) can also find its echo here.

Such bodily co-responsive imitation in ritual performance also indicates a harmonious affect 和 effectuated between the King's teaching and his subjects' learning, which Confucius envisions as the "most beautiful in the Way of the Former Kings, and manifest in all things great and small" (*Lunyu:Xue'er*). Such a harmonizing affect does not unify teachers and students into a stable relationship, but keeps them in a mutual dwelling yet in separateness.

Now the loop for ideal teaching and learning that happens between the King and his subjects through this ritual observation is closed. Nothing is more appropriate to summarize such a reasoning loop than Confucius' nexus weaving together his notions of *ren* (仁 humane-virtuous heart), *li* (禮 ritual performing), and *he* (和 harmonizing affect). He says, "If a person is not humane (virtuous) in the first place, how can he perform the rites appropriately and how can he enjoy performing the appropriate rituals?" (*Lunyun:Baqiao*). To him, active ritual-performing best embodies a humane (virtuous) subjective being and is to achieve a harmonious intra/inter- personal understanding. This harmonious affect can't be achieved for the sake of harmony itself; it is only made possible as an emergent felt with the inner humane disposition as its source and appropriate ritual performance as its embodied and ordered expression. With such a concern, he would still perform the complicated kneeling-bowing rite even though most people at his time prefer the easy standing-greeting rite (*Lunyu:Zihan*).

Again, such a description of inner virtuous heart and outer bodily comportment, albeit sounding like a binary separation, gestures a holistic understanding of the Confucian ritual body as a "psychosomatic self." This Confucian *ren* 仁, just as Ames (1993) rightly argues, "as a homophone of person (*ren* 人) denoting achieved personhood, is the whole human process: body and mind" (p. 164). Furthermore, Confucian *ren* and *li* are both psychosomatic dispositions in that they differ qualitatively in degree (not in kind) within an ordering of a whole being with *ren* being non-formalized while *li* being formalized and refined structure with bodily comportment. The fullest realization of the human being is as an active and creative participant in experiencing the processing shaping of a harmonious (esthetic, moral, physical, psychical) order with a person and among humans. This harmonizing interpersonal relationship is to be achieved through the actors' productive and active embodiment and expression, as well as the receptive experience of their heart through bodily performances toward each other (Ames, 1993; Hall & Ames, 1987; Qian, 2004, 2005; Hevia, 2005).

So far, I have explored Confucius' envisioning of the ritual performance as an ideal teaching–learning movement that happens by an image of wind blowing over the earth. I have also shown that the corporeal body is a significant and necessary parameter for his teaching and learning movement. Specifically, the body becomes a conceptual boundary that Confucian teaching and learning move within, respond to, or make sense of because it cannot be argued away or around. The body becomes the tool, the form, the possibility, and the function of teaching and learning. To push it further, the body is the matrix of teaching and learning. In so doing, I bracket the givenness of body, mobilize it as a theoretical construct, a paradigmatic exemplar to make intelligible "a broader problematic context that it both constitutes and makes intelligible" (Agamben, 2009, p. 17). This making-intelligible endeavor entails deactivating the Chinese body from their commonsensical uses, suspending it as semantic, linguistic signifier to designate a thing, and presenting the rules of its analogical use as a singular case. Again, the rules cannot be applied or stated a priori, but have to be shown and made visible through presenting their singularity as expressed in the above aporetic body event.

Then how can we understand the necessity of body and its role of body-as-necessity, that, the body as a required matrix in Confucian teaching and learning, being and living writ large?

The necessity of body in ancient Chinese thinking can be felt in two dimensions. First, with an appreciation of the notion *body* gesturing toward a holistic mode of being, I am opened to the nuanced texture nurtured within the Chinese term for body 身體 that says *body experiences*. In other words, body experiences and experiences happen bodily, regarding bodily movement as a mode of being with and in the world, wherein no separation of mind and body, intellect and emotion are applicable. The body is lived experience. Second, bodily experiences are to attune to and comply with each other's body as well as the natural world along with the cosmic Dao movement. In other words, the body is exposed to the worldly environment, rather than an instrument for consciousness to make an inner representation of the outside world.

Seen this way, it is understandable that Confucius attaches great importance to self/body-cultivation to become a jade-like exemplary person (*junzi* 君子) through learning. Learning as body/self-cultivation is to beautify one's body. As Confucian thinker Xunzi says,

> An exemplary person's learning (is supposed to) enter into his ear, reach his heart, permeate through the limbs and embody itself fully in a person's every single movement and posture, spanning a whole body of 7 feet, while petty person's learning enters into his ear and exits from his mouth, spanning only four inches.
>
> (*Quanxue*)

君子之學也，入乎耳，箸乎心，布乎四體，形乎動靜；小人之學也，入乎耳，出乎口。口、耳之間則四寸耳，曷足以美七尺之軀哉？

（荀子：勸學）

According to the *Great Learning*, such self/body-cultivation functions as a root and paves its way for a person to regulate a family, and then to govern a nation, and then to level the whole world under the sky.

Experiencing China's Current Educational Body

In Confucius' envisioning of the *guan*-hexagram ritual body, the straight heads-up is reasoned as a form of beautified body, visually embodying a saintly teaching and learning movement between the King and his subjects. Confucian learning through beautifying body is still visible in contemporary Chinese schooling. For example, sitting up with a right writing posture can be seen as its tacit ramification in modern times. However, I did not realize such a culturally unique "normative" learning body until after my *cross-cultural* learning experiences.

While these tacit "normative" body-forms are hard to perceive without a cross-cultural perspective, the fact that the Confucian ritual body-form has become a most controversial topic in contemporary Chinese schooling is also puzzling cross-culturally, especially when China is constructing a nationalism of Confucianism at the same time. Confucian kneeling-bowing ritual, used to be a highest-ranking ritual body, is now receiving nationwide diatribe in that it has downgraded contemporary Chinese education in pain and shame. Intrigued by such public reasoning, I wonder how the Confucian kneeling body is enacted, re-invoked, and mobilized by the public in their debates on teaching, learning, and teacher–student dis-ordering. Does the Daoist statement of *observing body with body* still work at the present, and if yes, to what extent? Before moving onto the kneeling-bowing events, I provide a brief background on the historical life of the claimed Confucian kneeling-bowing rite.

Background on the Confucian Kneeling-Bowing Rite

In ancient China with no chairs or tables, people all kneel-sit on the floor mattress with their hands laid on laps. When receiving honorable guests who also kneel-sit on the floor, people simply conveniently straighten them up into a kneeling posture and lay their hands on the floor. Such a posture, when developed into head touching down to the ground, becomes a highest respect-showing performance, formalized as a court ritual in Han Dynasty (202 BCE–220 CE) when Confucian ideas and thoughts are canonized as the ruling ideology (see, Yan, 1999).

In the imperial Qing Dynasty (1616–1911), the kneeling-bowing rite develops into nine stratified sub-formats and reaches its heyday in ordering the then hierarchical society. Its canonical status starts to be challenged through the few historical, cross-cultural events where the 1783 McCartney Mission Group and the 1873 Foreign Mission Groups refused to perform the full kneeling-bowing guest rites to the then Qing Emperors (see Hevia, 2005; Wang C., 2004). New Cultural Movement radicals like Tan Citong and Liang Qichao blame such traditional kneeling-bowing rites as imperial rulers' mechanism to enslave and constrain mass subjects' mind-heart. With that, the subjects can only develop a slave-like blind loyalty and filial piety at the cost of their independent personality and sense of democracy. Therefore, they hold that revolution should first of all start with the debasement of the superior and the cancelation of kneeling-bowing ritual practices (Wang C., 2004). Finally, the kneeling-bowing rite was constitutionally banned and replaced with the standing-bowing rite in daily and social life by the 1912 Sun Yat-sen administration.

In 1949, when Chairman Mao claimed sonorously in the Tiananmen Square that "Chinese people finally stood up," standing up mainly symbolizes a gained independence of the Chinese people from the imperial colonialism and feudal lords. Meanwhile, it also implies that Chinese people's knees can't be genuflected again because kneeling down has already become a suppression–submission symbol of a feudal society, which should have been sent to tombs for good. After that, kneeling-bowing disappears from the public view and only remains with some Chinese families as an important festival rite for kids to show gratitude to their parents or grandparents. Movies, TV plays, and museums, like the Last Emperor produced by Bernardo Bertolucci in 1986, become the last few remaining venues for visually refreshing this historical memory about the imperial China.

However, in recent few years, along with a rising Confucian nationalism, kneeling-bowing is creeping back to the contemporary Chinese schools, along with Confucian primers like *San Zi Jing* 三字經. It is a social consensus that the national morality level is degrading, and students/children are expected to become more respectful to their teachers and parents. Still, whenever hundreds or thousands of students are called upon to kneel-bow to their teachers and parents as an expression of gratitude, willingly or unwillingly, it immediately incurs heated debates nationwide with a loud outcry that such kneeling-bowing events have downgraded China's current (morality) education in pain and shame. Then what modes of reasoning ground such claims and with what kind of historical principles? With this question, I move on to observe-feel the kneeling-bowing events in the next section.

Experiencing the Current School Kneeling Body

Here is a playback of the few controversial kneeling-bowing events that happened in recent China's schools. Right before the 2007 Teacher's Day and in his lecture at the Inner Mongolia high school, Li Yang, an English teacher famous for promoting his Crazy English pedagogy at Chinese schools, called upon over 3,500 students to kneel-bow toward the few teachers on the stage to show their gratitude (Wang Y., 2007). On June 6th, 2010, over 900 high school seniors in Wuhan City were asked to kneel-bow toward their teachers to show gratitude in their Commencement Ceremony. The school leader said they would develop this kneeling-bowing rite into a school commencement culture.[1] On May 4th, 2011, the well-known Guangdong Experimental Middle School held a Passage Rite for the eighth graders where they were called to kneel down to receive a Family Letter from their parents in the school sports field. This youth Passage Rite was claimed to commemorate the 1919 May 4th Spirit, that is, Science, Freedom, Democracy, and Progress. The principal said this nice Passage Rite idea, actually from a student, would be continued in the future because they believe this kneeling-bowing rite, as a highest Confucian ritual format, would remain profoundly impressive to the students in their whole life.[2]

Every kneeling-bowing event incurs heated debates nationwide with an outcry that it has downgraded contemporary Chinese education in shame and pain. The pain-shame debate plays out in an incessant discursive battle mediated through numerous online media reports and personal weblogs, entangling a whole ensemble of social and cultural issues related to (Confucian) tradition and (Western) modernity, and Chinese teacher–student dis-ordering through embodied (ritual) education. Examining these debating discourses, I mainly explore (a) how the public reasons the kneeling body in relation to Chinese teaching, learning, and teacher–student dis-ordering; and (b) what historical and cultural theses are re-invoked by the public to ground their reasoning and how they are mobilized as grounding theses.

Foucault's governmentality reasoned as "the conduct of conduct" effectuated through "the contact between the technologies of domination of others and those of the self" (1988, p. 19) enables me to do the below analysis. Its focus on how governing is carried out rather than on who does the governing shifts my focus from institutional (say, schools) pragmatics of enforcing the kneeling-bowing practices or teachers' psychological will to govern students to unpacking the various cultural principles that have legitimized the various kneeling-bowing ways of reasoning. It sets the teacher–student ordering into a broader social and historical context and conceives the pragmatic objectives and psychological will (if there is) as effects of historical power relation dynamics, embodied through the subjects' conducting of conduct in the Foucauldian sense.

With Foucault's governmentality theory (1998), I discern a sharp binary mode of reasoning beneath the outcry. This binary reasoning views the kneeling-bowing performance as a highest Confucian ritual (to be welcomed back to contemporary China, and hereafter highest-ritual reasoning) versus servile feudal dross (to be sent to tombs for good, and hereafter feudal-dross reasoning), dismissing a barely audible ethical sensibility voiced by some performers (which I will pick up in the next section). The highest-ritual reasoning, not a popular viewpoint and mainly drawing upon some traditional cultural principles, argues (a) since tradition says that "it is parents who give children the bodies but teachers who cultivate (illuminate) the bodies," it is surely appropriate for students to kneel-bow toward their parents and teachers to show respect and gratitude, and (b) that the reinstatement of this kneeling-bowing rite in China's contemporary schooling symbolizes a "Chinese Renaissance" (Wang Y., 2007), would produce virtuous students and revive China's boasted old civilization of "respecting teachers and prioritizing education."[3]

The feudal-dross reasoning is overwhelmingly popular with its supporting arguments mainly drawn from the 1919 May 4th New Cultural Movement thought, a cultural milestone highlighting the introduction of modern Western notions such as Science, Freedom, Democracy, and Progress into the modern China. This reasoning argues that (a) the kneeling-bowing act, as a most humiliating demeanor signaling an absolute servile submission to power domination, humiliates whoever performs it and should be sent to tombs for good; (b) its reappearance in schooling has downgraded China's current education in pain and shame as it distorts the students' soul and personality, thus turning them into abject servants, rather than the sought-after independent, free, and modern citizens; and (c) its reappearance in the current democratic, modern, and rational China marks a humiliation to the Chinese people who finally and just recently stood up as Chairman Mao claimed in 1949[4] (Zhang, 2007; Wang X., 2011).

Then what specific cultural principles are drawn upon to support their distinct reasoning? The highest-ritual reasoning, grounded upon some broadly claimed traditional Confucian cultural principles, defines a Chinese teacher–student ordering as what is now commonly labeled and understood as hierarchical. Teachers, dubbed as *laoshi* (old master 老師) in Chinese, enjoy a superior and authoritative status demanding highest respect from students. One such traditional principle is that teachers historically and ideally enjoy a very high social status ordered right after heaven, earth, emperors, and parents such that *teachers for one day should be treated by their students as fatherly fathers for a whole life* (一日為師終身為父). For example, till the 1940s, there are still many intellectual or prestigious families what hang high on their sitting-rooms wall an inscribed motto tablet of 天地君親師 (heaven–earth–emperors–parents–teachers).

A second such principle is that a teacher's role is to illuminate and cultivate a student body in an authoritative and strict way (师道尊严), and a lack of strictness symbolizes the laziness of a teacher (教不嚴師之惰). Such a cultural sense is widely known among kids who recite the Confucian primer *San Zi Jing*. Drawing upon these cultural principles, the highest-ritual supporters conclude that it is surely appropriate for students to kneel-bow to their parents and teachers to show respect and gratitude, and the reinstatement of this kneeling-bowing rite (not only) in China's schooling would produce virtuous students. In other words, students should be virtuous and respectful, and teachers/parents should be authoritative and respectable.

The feudal-dross reasoning, on the other hand, is grounded upon the dominant theses representing a democratic and progressive spirit in the eyes of its supporters. The first principle comes from Lu Xun, a cultural movement forerunner who adamantly challenges the Chinese hierarchical ordering between parent/teacher and child/student. In his *How Do We Make Parents for the Present*, Lu Xun (1919) makes a statement "there is no gratitude between parents and children." According to him, the Chinese hierarchical parent–child way of thinking entails parents' total psychosomatic domination of children. That is, parents' giving bodies to children entails parents' owning children's body (and self) and children's paying the gratitude-debt for a whole lifetime. This mode of thinking, Lu Xun further argues, works against the natural law such as Darwinism and eugenics and has caused Chinese society to retrogress. He wishes that "the then fathers would shoulder the dark inheritance burden and liberate their children to bright places for living a happy life as rational humans" (as cited in Wang X., 2011). Grounded by such a style of reasoning, teachers (parents) and students (children) should be first of all egalitarian so that children can become free citizens.

The second thesis comes from Hu Shi, another cultural movement forefather, who appealed to the then youth "to fight for your freedom and integrity is to fight for freedom and integrity for your nation." Free and equal society can't be built by a group of servile subjects. This thesis is re-invoked and mobilized as an admonition to be given to every current educational worker who should regard it as their obligation to clear away the servile factors in the students, help students establish ideals of democracy and equality, and train students to become modern citizens with independent integrity (Wang X., 2011). Such reasoning views the kneeling-bowing as a 100% servile demeanor distorting the students' soul and personality into abject servants, rather than the sought-after independent, free, and modern citizens.

The third thesis picks up a popular book title *(Teachers) Can't Teach with Kneels Down* by Wu Fei (2004), a well-known high school teacher in current China, who argues that "teachers can't teach with kneels down if they want their students to become a standing-up person" because "kneeling down is a symbol of servile submission to power dominance and a constraint of free and independent thinking." Therefore, he retorts, "If teachers can't think independently, what kind of people his students would be?" (Quoted in Chou yu ni mo, 2010). Visible in his reasoning is an expressed conflation between physical genuflections with mental submission, an epitomic of the inherited May 4th New Cultural Movement thinking.

Interestingly, no matter whether it is to be welcomed back to contemporary Chinese society or to be sent to tombs for good, underpinning this prevailing binary reasoning are three shared presumptions on the Chinese body and teacher–student ordering. First, a Chinese body after it is borne by parents can and is to be cultivated or beautified through teaching and learning, as expressed in statements like *it is parents who give children the bodies but teachers who cultivate (illuminate) the bodies*. In other words, the body is not treated as a fixed entity or a container for a Western sense of self, rather, it functions as an object that can be beautified, formed, re-formed, and transformed through learning. The thesis that learning helps to cultivate one's body is homologous to Confucian envisioning on learning as being body-beautifying.

Second, such visibly beautified-or-not body or its movement correspondingly symbolizes some invisible quality of a person, no matter whether the kneeling-bowing can produce a virtuous exemplary person in a Confucian sense or a servile subject in a modern democratic sense. Furthermore, such a bodily posture of kneeling-bowing, that is, knees' up–down distance is symbolically superimposed upon and gets associated with a cultural and national honorable or shameful self. These presumptions bring out not only an ancient Chinese body-self ambiguity, but also a separation–conflation between a physical body and a cultural, social, and political individual/collective self. In other words, such a conflation already subsumes a separation between a physical body and a mental/cultural self. Such bodily turned to a socialized/politicized entanglement of body and self has become the core of contention in the kneeling-bowing events. It can be viewed as one expression of an epistemic entanglement between bodily reasoning and mental thinking writ large in current China.

Finally, teacher–student ordering is reasoned along a culturally imposed should-be axis, whether in a vocabulary of hierarchical Confucian or egalitarian, democratic teacher–student ordering. By that, I mean their various historical theses are collected by the contenders as a source of examples for the truth to espouse their contention, and further re-invoked to adjudicate their argumentation, while rejecting the other argumentation as wrong. Both sides of the contenders deploy a typical causal reasoning that because it was thought this way, it should still be thought this way. As a consequence, historical knowledge camps are further consolidated against each other along a moral judgment of right and wrong, and making such discursive judgment neglects the material contextualized struggles performed between the living bodies. In a word, body no longer experiences but is manipulated as a sign or metaphorical device.

So far, I have found that the endless debates on the kneeling-bowing events are heavily confined to a binary logic, ordering the teacher–student governing along a hierarchical versus egalitarian pendulum. In such reasoning, the kneeling-bowing rite and the body are treated as a decontextualized cultural symbolic object. While such analysis is informative and revealing, it is limited for two reasons. First, treating the public debating discourses as ways of reasoning, I find myself again captivated by a subject–object conceptual thinking. I have examined these discourses as an objective object from a conceptual mind, have judged others' discourses on the kneeling body, and observed the kneeling body, with my mind (see, Zhao, 2013, 2015). How ironic! Did I miss a wholesome, if not a whole, point? Second, I have neglected the kneeling body as well as its performers just like the public. How the kneeling body materially enacts the teacher–student ordering is glossed over. Then how do the performers themselves observe-feel the kneeling body? And how can I observe-feel the kneeling body with my body, not my mind? The next section encounters these two questions and to do so, a paradigm shift from mental judging to somatic feeling is required.

Paradigm Shift: From Judging to Feeling the Kneeling Body

Then how can I enact, more than envision, such a paradigm shift, from judging to feeling the kneeling body, or to put differently, from a discursive reasoning to a practical mode of being? Chinese thinking is commonly claimed to be bodily or concrete thinking as against Western mind or abstract thinking (Wu K., 1997; Ames, 1993). I guess I am quite familiar with, and accordingly, assume that I "know" such discursive claims, however, at the same time, I find myself naturally bound up with a conceptual thinking, as the above analysis already shows. In other words, I notice a nuanced gap between my knowing and my being.

With such a gap, I doubt a Daoist endeavor of observing-feeling body with body can be fulfilled through drawing upon historical texts to abstractly reason out an understanding on being-body. Instead, I need to turn my subjective mind judgment over to a space or position wherein my own body participates in a contingent, not necessary, inter-corporeal movement. By contingent, I mean whether, and if yes, how the inter-corporeal practically moves about can't be foreseen by a rational judging mind.

With such an appreciation, I move on to observe-feel how the performers bodily co-respond to the kneeling body with my body, how the kneeling body navigates an inter-corporeal being with between the performers. Within such a concrete situation, how experiencing moves bodily, or how the body experiences through bodily movement? This questioning first brings me back to the kneeling body, its performers and receivers, and a voiced sense of ethical and transformative inter-corporeal understanding (empathy), which the public debaters have neglected and which my previous discourse analysis has also passed over. Here is a media description of the Guangzhou Middle School Passage Rite:

> Most parents were deeply *moved to tears* by this kneeling ceremony. One father looked very serious all the time, but *tears rolled down the moment* when her daughter dropped her kneels in front of him. With tears, he said he found his daughter had already grown up and he felt deeply *moved* but also *felt guilty* as he did not care enough for her daughter at other times. The daughter said with tears in eyes that she was very *surprised* to hear such words from his father and although

most classmates hesitated a bit about kneeling down at first, afterward they felt *touched*.

(Xin Kuai Bao, May 5th, 2011, all italics mine)

Honestly, when I first examined this narrative, I noticed in a fleeting note the touchy feeling discourse yet felt nothing. When I am reading it again with an evoked bodily reasoning, I am drawn to the emotive bodily terms such as *feel moved/touched to tears* and *feel guilty and surprised*. Furthermore, I realize that such an empathetic feeling-touching emotion was not anticipated or rationally planned. It happened at the moment when the emotional heart was plucked, and an emotional resonance was felt, as the interviewed serious-looking father burst into tears at the moment his daughter kneels down in front of him. At such moments when hard reason gave its way to soft emotion, the father expressed his felt guilt toward his daughter that he didn't care for her enough at other times. Such an emotional hearty feeling reciprocally invites the surprised-touched felt of the daughter. Then and there, an inter-corporeal empathy is heartily felt for the moment between the father and the daughter with both of them in tears. Within such an understanding, a discursive hierarchical relation between parents and children dissolves into a mutual responsiveness between two bodies that are simultaneously moving and being moved, moving in a double sense of motion and affect.

Well, turning myself over again to the media narrative, I feel like I understand the above empathetic resonation between the father and the daughter. It is true that I cannot directly experience the father–daughter's bodily movement. Still, I can feel it vicariously through my own bodily resonation experience with my parents, as expressed in the Chinese term 感同身受 (to feel as if my own body experienced the same thing). As shown in their etymological roots, both characters of 感 and 應 have a *heart* 心 radical as a passage for empathetic resonation. Such bodily empathetic feeling or resonating 感應 brings out one significant parameter of body-thinking or experiencing, or thinking with bodily movement. As Wu K. (1997) rightly claims, "Thinking about the body is not body thinking. Body thinking is thinking in terms of the body, in the perspective of the body, thinking body-wise" (p. 8).

Since body experiences through the heart, then just as Pascal aptly puts, the heart has a reason that mind does not. To be specific, body-heart reasoning is contextual, concrete, and bodily, rather than abstract and universal removed from specific contexts. Seen this way, inter-corporeal resonation happens practically rather than discursively. By that, I mean inter-corporeal inter-subjective co-being is enacted in a practical context, rather than discursively constructed with decontextualized representational principles and thus imposed onto the context. Seen this way, normalized hierarchical representations on what teachers and students should be bracketed, or rather *forgotten*, for the moment toward a bodily movement and enactment constructing a practical, affective, and emotional teacher–student inter-subjective co-dwelling. I will come back to this sense of forgetting in the next chapter when I experience the principal's kneeling event.

In the above father–daughter kneeling case, a common sense discursive ordering would be that the father enjoys more power over the daughter in the sense that the father actively speaks whereas the daughter listens passively. However, from the bodily perspective, it is the father that succumbs his body to the daughter's body in the sense of being evoked, called forth by the daughter's bodily movement. The daughter's body takes up an active role, while the father's body listens and dwells along. Once an empathetic feeling is evoked, it invites further bodily co-responding and co-attuning as a practical co-dwelling. The individual rationality and the common sense hierarchical ordering are effaced and submerged. Instead, a milieu is created within which mutual acceptance as well as genuine realization of another's presence in all its difference is heartily felt.

According to Wu Kuang-Ming, such bodily thinking, commonplace in Chinese people's daily life since ancient times, is a Chinese cultural peculiarity distinct from the Western formal or abstract thinking traceable to Plato. Interestingly, as my example shows, current Chinese people are indispensably bound up with a predominant formal abstract thinking before we know it. Bodily thinking may still function implicitly as well in current China. However, a conscious effort is called for to bring it back to an explicit recognition and to get out of the deceptively easy formal reasoning. Furthermore, how can these two modes of thinking, namely, a classical bodily thinking and a current conceptual thinking, encounter each other in ordering the way current Chinese people say and reason in their daily life needs rigorous exploration beyond this project.

On the Western side, in the past four decades, a somatic or affective turn is effectuated with psychoanalytic feminist critiques and critical phenomenological thinking. Along with such a re-turning, emotion or emotional empathy (what it means for one to feel the complexity of affect experienced by another) is to be reinstated in educational thinking (O'Loughlin, 1997, 1998). In the next section, I briefly dialogue the possible Chinese body experience with the somatic-affective turn in the Western educational thinking. Before that, let's first briefly compare how the body is reasoned in these two examples in Table 5.1.

Juxtaposing these two modes of reasoning on the body, we can see an epistemic shift from an accent on ontological body experience in the Confucian case toward an epistemological judgment of body as a cultural and discursive sign in the current kneeling body event (see, Zhao, 2015). If in the former case, body enacts and experiences as a necessity for teaching and learning, in the latter case, the body becomes a discursive device to be mobilized by the public in their discursive quarrel. In other words, a mode of observing body with body gave its way toward a counterpart of observing body with the mind.

Table 5.1 Confucian Ritual Body Versus Current Schooling Body

	Confucian reasoning on ritual body in relation to teaching/learning	Current public reasoning on kneeling body in relation to teacher–student ordering
Body	Body as a tacit matrix of a human being Body experiences	Body as a cultural sign or metaphor Body is experienced symbolically
Mind–body ambivalence	Metonymic relation between "big head" and "kingly virtue" Reason and emotion dwells within a bodily person	Bodily outlook (up-right and kneel-down) symbolize social differentiation Mind–body separation yet in conflation
Body–teaching/ learning	Body is a necessary matrix for imitative teaching and learning. Learning is to beautify one's body.	Body becomes an object to be inscribed, regulated, and disciplined. Normative—should-be
Body episteme	Observe body with body Ontological body through guan-observing and gan-feeling Reason and emotion co-dwell	Observe body with mind Epistemological judging based upon discursive representations Reason or emotion
身體 Body experiences	和 Inter-corporeal harmonious affect	Empathic inter-corporeal understanding remains as one parameter of body experiencing.

Still, a significant parameter of bodily experiencing is visible in the current kneeling case in that the kneeling body engenders a wholehearted engagement between some performers, as shown through the father–daughter example. In this case, the body is turned back into a body that experiences, enacts, and engages other bodies, wherein an emotional resonation is felt, imploding the wielding power of intellect or a cognitive mind. Here heart reasons in a way mind can't. In other words, a bodily paradigm calls for a wholehearted engagement with the body not the minds, or the bodily actors not a discursive representation of who the subject should be.

Such a corporeal reinstatement might provide a paradigm shift for researching China's current (physical) education that loosens up a grip on the body as an object toward a liberating subject. It also challenges the way researchers approach what they research, say, body to the extent that "we must watch out for questions that arise from the viewpoint of thinking, from a formal perspective, that is, from the angle of linkage of ideas" (Wu K., 1997, p. 11).

Then what can be the implications of such a paradigm shift in examining teaching, learning, and teacher–student engagement? The Western body or somatic turn in the Western academia might offer some insights, as to be shown in the next section.

Dialoguing With the Western Somatic Turn in Ordering Inter-Subjective Relationship

Alfred North Whitehead once claimed Western philosophy to be "a series of footnotes to Plato" in that it operates a "Platonic scheme of the ontic versus the universal, the universal versus existence" (Wu K., 1997, appendix 2). A progeny of such Platonic scheme is a Cartesian separation of mind from body with the former rational consciousness presiding over and utilizing the latter fallacious body as an instrument. Accordingly, airplane-like rational thinking that resides within an Enlightenment mind-self subject becomes formal, abstract and universal, "reading off the universal structure of the historical existence, the ground of being" (Wu K., 1997, appendix 2), including the physical body as a material being.

Marjorie O'Loughlin (1998) gives an apt overview of the body vicissitudes in the history of Western philosophical and cultural thinking. According to her, although always present in the major philosophical tradition, the body is inevitably conceptualized as separate from mind or intelligence. Within a modern world of knowledge privileging a rational mind, bodily pathetic and affective fallacies have been largely submerged not only in science, but also within the study of humanity and culture. In ethics, bodily affect or the emotion has been relegated as at most "an emollient addition to the hard cognitions of rationality in action" (p. 287).

However, in the past few decades, a somatic or affective turn has occurred, mainly as a critique and rectification of the rational Enlightenment subject in the Western academia. Such a somatic turn was largely initiated by Merleau-Ponty's body-self (1962) and further developed through psychoanalytic feminism's articulations of gendered subjectivities. Merleau-Ponty claims that, in O'Loughlin's words, "bodies are lived experience and inter-subjective encounter occurs when body-subjects, *not minds*, have understood each other" (1998, p. 289, italics original).

Afterward, Foucault conducted exemplary research on the ways body and embodied subjectivities can be variously disciplined and regulated as a problematization or replacement of the rational Enlightenment subject. As an effect, the notion "body" has been foregrounded to its present prominence, encompassing the idea of materiality as an embodiment and playing a significant role in constructing subjectivity and inter-subjective relation. As O'Loughlin rightly states, this somatic turn releases subjectivity from the confinement of a rational consciousness and relates it with bodily affect or emotion. After that, a conception of subjects becomes grounded in everyday activities.

With such an understanding of the somatic turn, O'Loughlin (1997, 1998) calls for a reinstatement of emotion in educational thinking and philosophizing. Through analyzing Australian civics education discourses, she shows that binaries of reason and emotion, knowing and feeling still order current conceptualizations of learner/knower, knowledge, and knowing within an Enlightenment mode of reasoning, wherein bodily affect or emotion is submerged. To be specific, the concept of the learner/knower still rests with a cognitive self with knowledge mainly focused on knowing how and knowing that. The idea of genuine knowledge is still a manifestation of rationality, transcending particulars and perspectives. The concept of learners and knowledge still deal with discursive consciousness at the expense of practical consciousness. By the former, she refers to those thoughts or cognition rendered possible through the systems of presentation, while the latter takes into account each's material well-being or socially situated body-self in inter-subjective interaction.

All these conceptual thinking modes fail to recognize the roles body and emotions may play in structuring who we are and what we do, and a reinstatement of body or emotion in looking at educational inter-subjective relation helps to rectify such decontextualized exercise of intellect. Finally, O'Loughlin argues only when we somaticize our education, renew our appreciation of bodily experiences in all its dimensions, and learn to engagingly put ourselves in the shoes of another to feel the complex affect which other body-self experiences, can the educational difference be overcome in a real sense. If the body turns in the Western thinking endeavors to bring the airplane-like formal abstract reasoning back to its material ground, the Chinese mode of body experiencing seems to be moving in an opposite direction. Commonplace in ancient Chinese society, body experiencing is now being largely submerged by a conceptual judging and reasoning. Mind, not body, has become a habituated mode of life.

Then how is it possible to recognize and then get out of such a habituated mode of being and reasoning? As is shown in this chapter and my whole project, an intercultural and historical detour and access provide a practical strategy. Indispensable to such a strategy is an explosion of the binary logic that orders subject and object, mind and body, intellect and emotion, and more important, the researcher and the researched. Now we move onto the next chapter to further problematize this binary logic that orders the Chinese teacher–student relationship.

Notes

1. 重庆 900 名高中生毕业典礼跪拜谢老师 Chongqing Morning News, June 6, 2010. Retrieved on April 28, 2018, from http://news.163.com/10/0606/09/68G2957U00014AEE.html
2. 广东一中学组织全体学生给父母下跪 Xin Kuai Bao. May 5, 2011. Retrieved on August 18, 2017, from http://news.qq.com/a/20110505/000562.htm.
3. See, e.g., 近千学生集体下跪是耻辱是美德？Chou Yu Ni Mo. June 7, 2010. Retrieved on April 28, 2018, from http://blog.sina.com.cn/s/blog_44491d9d0100iaey.html
4. Qin Ge. October 5, 2007. 三次"下跪"，现代中国教育的最大耻辱！Retrieved on August 18, 2017, from http://blog.sina.com.cn/s/blog_4a56f20d01000bu4.html

References

Agamben, G. (2009). *The signature of all things: On method*. New York: Zone Books.
Ames, R. T. (1993). The meaning of body in classical Chinese thought. In T. P. Kasulis, R. Ames, & W. Dissanayake (Eds.), *Self as body in Asian theory and practice* (pp. 39–54). Albany, NY: State University of New York Press.
Chou Yu Ni Mo. (2010, June 7). Jinqian xuesheng jiti xiagui shi chiru shi meide? [Is it shame or virtue for thousand students to kneel down? 近千学生集体下跪是耻辱是美德？] Retrieved on April 28, 2018, from http://blog.sina.com.cn/s/blog_44491d9d0100iaey.html
Duarte, E. M. (2012). *Being and learning: A poetic phenomenology of education*. New York, NY: Sense Publishers.
Foucault, M. (1988). Technologies of the self. In L. H. Martin, H. Gutman, & P. H. Hutton (Eds.), *Technologies of the self: A seminar with Michel Foucault* (pp. 16–49). Amherst, MA: University of Massachusetts Press.
Goulding, J. (Ed.). (2008). *China-west interculture: Toward the philosophy of world integration (Essays on Wu Kuang-ming's thinking)*. New York, NY: Global Scholarly Publications.
Hall, D. L., & Ames, R. T. (1987). *Thinking through Confucius*. Albany, NY: State University of New York Press.
Hevia, J. L. (2005). *Cherishing men from afar: Qing guest ritual and the Macartney Embassy of 1793*. Durham, NC and London, UK: Duke University Press Books.
Lu, X. (1919). Women xianzai zenyang zuo fuqin [How do we make parents for the present? 我们现在怎样做父亲] *Xin Qing Nian*, 6(6). Retrieved August 18, 2017, from www.southcn.com/news/community/shzt/youth/forerunner/200404280880.htm
Merleau-Ponty, M. (1962). *Phenomenology of perception* (C. Smith, Trans.). London, UK and New York, NY: Routledge. (Original work published in 1945)
O'Loughlin, M. (1997). Reinstating emotion in educational thinking. Retrieved August 18, 2017, from http://ojs.ed.uiuc.edu/index.php/pes/article/view/2225
O'Loughlin, M. (1998). Overcoming the problems of "difference" in education: Empathy as "intercorporeality". *Studies in Philosophy and Education*, 17, 283–293.
Qian, M. (2004). *Wenhua yu jiaoyu (Culture and education)*. Beijing: Guangxi Normal University Press. (Original work published in 1974)

Qian, M. (2005). *Lunyu Xinshi [New interpretations on Analects]*. Shenghuo, Dushu, Xinzhi: San Lian Shu Dian.

Qin, G. (2007, October 5). Sanci "xiagui", xiandai zhongguo jiaoyu de zuida chiru [Three "kneeling" events are the greatest humiliation to modern China's education 三次"下跪"，现代中国教育的最大耻辱！] Retrieved August 18, 2017, from http://blog.sina.com.cn/s/blog_4a56f20d01000bu4.html

Serres, M. (1990/1995). *Conversation on science, culture, and time (with Bruno Latour)* (R. Lapidus, Trans.). Ann Arbor, MI: University of Michigan Press.

Sun, L. K. (1991). Contemporary Chinese culture: Structure and emotionality. *The Australian Journal of Chinese Affairs*, 26, 1–41.

Wang, C. S. (2004). A critical reflection on the thought of "despising knowledge" in Chinese basic education. *Beijing University Education Review*, 8(4), 5–23.

Wang, X. J. (May 5, 2011). Guifumu de qingnianli yu wusijingsheng gegeburu [Kneeling-to-parents passage rite goes against the May fourth spirit 跪父母的青年礼与五四精神格格不入]. Retrieved on April 28, 2018, from http://news.ifeng.com/opinion/gundong/detail_2011_05/07/6232765_0.shtml

Wang, Y. (2007, September 10). Dui laoshi xing "guibaili", shi zhongguo de wenyifuxing! [Performing the kneeling-bowing rite to teachers symbolizes the Chinese Renaissance—supporting Li Yang's Kneeling-bowing rite 对老师行"跪拜礼"，是中国的文艺复兴！—支持疯狂英语李阳设计的"拜师礼"]. Retrieved August 18, 2017, from http://blog.sina.com.cn/s/blog_49c77aad01000eoh.html

Wu, F. (2004). *Bu guizhe jiaoshu* [Teachers can't teach with knees down 不跪着教书]. Shanghai: Huadong Normal University Press.

Wu, K. M. (1997). *On Chinese body thinking: A cultural hermeneutic*. Leiden, The Netherlands and New York, NY: Brill Academic Publishing.

Xin, Kuai Bao. (May 5, 2011). Guangdong zhongxue zuzhi xuesheng gei fumu xiagui [Guangdong middle school organizes all students to kneel to parents 广东一中学组织全体学生给父母下跪]. Retrieved April 28, 2018, from https://news.qq.com/a/20110505/000562.htm

Yan, C. F. (1999). On ancient kneeling-bowing rite [Gudai Guibaili Zhishu 古代跪拜礼摭述]. *Jiangxi Guangbo Dianshi Daxue Xuebao*, 4, 50–51.

Zhang, J. (2007, September 29). Xiagui pinxian, zhongguo jiaoyu yijing zouxiang tuifei [Kneeling down often has led Chinese education to an end 下跪频现，中国教育已经走向颓废]. Retrieved on April 28, 2018, from http://blog.blog.tianya.cn/blogger/post_show.asp?BlogID=775914&PostID=11229293

Zhao, W. L. (2013). Reinstating bodily kneeling-bowing Rites (跪拜禮) sets education in pain and shame in modern China: Voluntary servitude as a new form of governing. *Revue Internationale de Sociologie de L'education*, 31(1), 65–80.

Zhao, W. L. (2015). Voluntary servitude as a new form of governing: Reinstating kneeling bowing rites as educational pain and shame in modern Chinese education. In T. Popkewitz (Ed.), *The "reason" of schooling: Historicizing curriculum studies, pedagogy and teacher education* (pp. 82–96). New York, NY: Routledge.

6 Beyond Identity vs. Difference Division
A Daoist Teacher–Student (Re)Ordering

With the examples of "wind" and "body," this project addresses the big concern of epistemicide in comparative and cross-cultural studies. In doing so, it hopes to map out China's educational sensibilities as they are and in the English wor(l)d with and beyond the Western categories, concepts, and frameworks. In other words, the issue of "difference" and how to explicate cultural "differences" strike out as a central concern for the whole book. For example, a rethinking of the comparative method entails a strategy of picking up "difference at its limit" as an entry point (Chapter 2). An archaeological-historical mode of inquiry is proposed so as to rethink the issue of epistemicide beyond a geographical boundary of East and West (Chapter 1 and 2). An ontological language–discourse perspective is also to map out the distinct Chinese Yijing thought as conditions of possibility for the entire Chinese thought and system of reason (Chapter 3 and 4). The Chinese body-thinking is another example of difference that compares the ordering and structuring of "body" in traditional and modern Westernized China (Chapter 5).

In this chapter, I push further the theme of "difference" by confronting the binary mode of reasoning itself, often claimed as the specter and yoke of the modern Western epistemology. The analysis unfolds in two parts. First, I show such a binary reasoning largely structures China's current teacher education reform, ordering its teacher–student relationship along a hierarchical vs. egalitarian power pendulum. To do so, I pick up Foucault's division of "knowing self" and "caring of self" as an entry point and paraphrase it into the two categories of "modern conceptual knowledge" and "the Confucian care of self-others."

Second, I intend to flatten out this abyssal binary logic as a governing rule of the modern epistemology by turning to the Chinese Daoist yin-yang wisdom for new openings. Drawing upon another aporetic kneeling event in recent China, I explicate the underpinning principle of identity and power beneath the mainstream reasoning of (teacher–student) difference, and argue "difference" can only regenerate itself from a different starting point, a different epistemological framework beyond using identity and power as its grounding principle. Specifically, I unpack the Chinese Daoist yin-yang wisdom as such a different starting point to help us re-envision the issue of difference, the ordering of difference and identity, and the binary logic in general. In so doing, this chapter re-envisions the teacher–student ordering, and education more broadly, beyond a separation of mind and body, care of self-others and knowledge, domination and resistance, subject and object, teaching and learning, and most of all, hierarchy and egalitarianism (i.e., difference and identity).

Foucault's *Caring Self* and *Knowing Self* as a Cross-Cultural Entry Point

In Chapter 5, through an evocative dialogue with Confucius' commentary on the Yijing *guan*-hexagram, I was exposed to the *body* rubrics, that is, being embodied–somatic–affective, of the Confucian teacher–student ordering. Such an opening experience has two interesting outcomes. On the one hand, it shows the limit of applying Foucault's governing theory to gauge the Chinese teacher–student ordering along a power dimension, which presumes and reproduces the fixed identities of teachers and students. On the other hand, it draws my attention to Foucault's unpacking of the historical contestations between a care of self and a knowing self as two disparate modes of reasoning in the Western history of episteme. According to Foucault (1997, 2011), the former prevails over the latter during the Greco-Roman era for eight centuries. Nevertheless, ever since some un-definable moment during the Christianity period, this self-care becomes subsumed to self-knowledge, which in turn assumes a form of seeking knowledge-truth during the Enlightenment movement and finally secures its unwieldy power in the Western culture and beyond.

Varied forms of scientific research and human inquiry have since been inevitably obliged to revolve around this single theme of seeking new knowledge-truth. This obligation of truth, Foucault (1997) said in one of his last interviews in 1984, has enveloped all of the Western cultures to such an extent that

> Nothing so far has shown that it is possible to define a strategy outside of this concern. It is within the field of the obligation to truth that it is possible to move about in one way or another, sometimes against effects of domination which may be linked to structures of truth or institutions entrusted with truth.
>
> (p. 295)

Accordingly, Foucault claims the following question as *the* question for the whole Western culture: How did it come about that all of the Western cultures began to revolve around this obligation of truth which has taken a lot of different forms (p. 295)? Meanwhile, Foucault (2011) could not help wondering: If the Greco-Roman care of self continues to govern the way people think and act all the way down the Western history, then where would the Western thinking possibly go?

I find Foucault's questioning and wondering particularly enticing to the present China. If his division between self-care and self-knowledge as two modes of reasoning makes sense, then current China is witnessing an unparalleled interesting contestation between these two modes of reasoning, which I would like to paraphrase as Confucian care of self-others and modern conceptual-metaphysical knowing. In this chapter, I limit my examination to how these two modes of reasoning govern the Chinese teacher–student (dis)ordering.

On the one hand, a Confucian discourse of care of self-others apparently has never lost its dominant place in the Chinese history of thought. For example, Confucian learning is to beautify one's body toward becoming a virtuous *junzi* (exemplary person 君子) through a lifelong stone-carving-like process. The current Chinese government promotes a rule of virtue along with the rule of law toward building a harmonizing/harmonious society. Its education agenda for 2010–2020 aims to be human based with a priority placed on *virtue* (de 德) education. On the other hand, as the previous chapter shows, today's Chinese teacher–student ordering is popularly confined to an argument built upon a binary division of hierarchy versus egalitarianism along a power pendulum, neglecting a contextualized affective co-dwelling in-between. Furthermore, global discourses such as the twenty-first-century skills/competencies/literacies, learning outcome, student-centered, learner autonomy, knowledge-based, task-based, and lifelong learner are becoming dominant concepts at policy and praxis levels in shaping the way teacher education reform is said and enacted in China (as is to be shown below). I analytically describe such decontextualized conceptual and knowledge-based reasoning as a modern mode of mind-thinking, as differentiated from an affective-ethic mode of body-thinking/experiencing; albeit in reality, these two are unavoidably entangled with each other.

In such a cross-cultural context, I intend to further explore, in the next section on China's teacher education reform, how a Confucian care of self-others is confronting a modern conceptual knowing/knowledge in (dis)ordering China's teacher–student relation. In other words, how are this Chinese *body* and the Western(ized) *mind* reasoned as a binary ordering in constructing the Chinese teacher–student difference? That is, in which ways does a binary logic constructs and reproduces the teacher–student difference or dis-ordering along a hierarchical vs. egalitarian power pendulum?

China's Teacher Education Discourse Metamorphosis From 1984 to 2016

Care of Self-Others Towards Professional Knowledge

China's educational blueprint for 2010–2020 features to be human based with its priority placed on virtue/moral education (*deyu* 德育). Interestingly, with its latest 2012 teacher education policy, virtue-education is placed before a student-based pedagogy (Middle School Teachers' Professional Standards). After issuing 12 policies to guide its teacher virtue-morality construction since 1984, in 2010 the Chinese government launched a 5-year National Training Plan for Primary/Secondary School Teachers,

152 *Paradigmatic Unpackings*

short-termed as National Training Plan, with a total budget of 0.55 billion RMB from its Ministry of Finance (Ministry of Education). In 2012, the Ministry of Education stipulated a standard curriculum for this National Training Plan, covering 67 subject-based and teacher role-based curricula[1] (see Chapter 1 for a more detailed account).

It is true that China's teacher education reform is picking up global discourses such as student-centered, learner autonomy, knowledge-based, task-based, and lifelong learner. Still, this re-invoked Confucian virtue-thesis strikes out as a cultural sensibility. Picking up Foucault's division of care of self and knowing self as two modes of reasoning, I ponder what kind of *discursive features* work as the possible embodiment of such distinct modes of reasoning. To probe into this question, I juxtapose China's teacher education policy documents and pinpoint in particular its discursive metamorphosis on teacher–student ordering in Table 6.1.

Table 6.1 China's Teacher Education Policy Documents on Teacher–Student Ordering

1984 中小學教師職業道德要求 1984 Middle-Primary School Teachers' Code of Ethics	…循循善誘，誨人不倦，不歧視、諷刺、體罰學生，建立民主、平等、親密的師生關係 … gradual step-by-step inductive guiding and pointing, being never tired of learning and never bored with teaching, not mock, satire, disparage, beat students, construct democratic, equal and close teacher-student relationship
1991 中小學教師職業道德規範 1991 Middle-Primary School Teachers' Code of Ethics	…循循善誘，誨人不倦， 保護學生身心健康 … gradual step-by-step inductive guiding and pointing, being never tired of learning and never bored with teaching
1997 中小學教師職業道德規範修訂 1997 Middle-Primary School Teachers' Code of Ethics First Revision	… 耐心教導 … patient teaching and guiding
2008 中小學教師職業道德規範二次修訂 2008 Middle-Primary School Teachers' Code of Ethics Second Revision	… 对学生严慈相济，做学生良师益友 … be both strict with and caring for students and become a mentor and friend of their students
2012 中學教師專業標準（試行） 2012 Middle School Teachers' Professional Standards	關愛中學生，重視中學生身心健康發展，保護中學生生命安全。/ 尊重中學生獨立人格，維護中學生合法權益，平等對待每一位中學生。不諷刺、挖苦、歧視中學生，不體罰或變相體罰中學生/尊重個體差異，主動了解和滿足中學生的不同需要/信任中學生，積極創造條件，促進中學生的自主發展。/強調中學教師應注重學生的個別需要和自主發展 Love students, pay attention to their healthy mind-body development, protect their life safety, respect their independent personality/integrity, protect their legal rights, equally treat each student, respect individual differences, understand and satisfy their varied needs, promote their autonomous development.

Beyond Identity vs. Difference Division 153

Reading carefully into the above discourses renders visible two interrelated features. First, the classical Chinese ontological speaking language is becoming a modern spoken discourse entangled within a seeking of knowledge/truth. That is, the cultural notion *de* 德 as a care of self and others has already metamorphosed into a modern concept of *de* 德 as a form of professional knowledge, that is, *a body mode of experiencing has metamorphosed into a mind mode of knowing*. To echo what Foucault says, seeking knowledge or truth has also become the predominant delimiting thinking box in current China. Second, teacher–student difference is mostly thought in a metaphysical-binary form in that teachers are teachers and students are students, presuming two distinct subjectivities. Underneath is a presupposition of who teachers/students should be and what their ordering is. Let's look at these two features one by one.

Speaking Language Toward Spoken Discourse

I distinguish a speaking language from a spoken discourse to hopefully show that a speaking language is a material being in itself pregnant with meaning, whereas a spoken discourse is made of common sense concepts with their meanings abstractly represented. Below I list two examples to demonstrate their nuanced differences.

The first example is the Chinese term for *teacher education*, which has metamorphosed from *shifanjiaoyu* 師範教育 to *jiaoshijiaoyu* 教師教育. Chinese normal schools or teachers' college are usually called *shifan* 師範, a term shortlisted from the often-heard motto statement 學高為師身正為範, literally saying *intellectually higher makes a teacher and an up-straight/right body (self) makes a role model*. In the Chinese culture, this *bodily straight* indicates, or rather, is synonymous to a virtuous self in two aspects. On the one hand, as the previous body chapter shows, the Chinese *body* imbricates a holistic domain of heart, mind, and body in their modern senses. On the other hand, the term *de* (virtue 德) in pre-Han times was often used as a cognate for *zhi* (straight 直), a notion now often assembled with *zheng* (up-right 正), both nourishing the senses of *de* 德. That is to say, a physical shape of *being straight/up-right* equals or is homologous to a moral/spiritual mindset of *being honest and virtuous*.

Furthermore, the Chinese notion *fan* 範 has a cultural sense that teachers are role models for students to imitate, a sense that echoes the imitating overtone expressed within the classical Chinese homophonic graphs *xiao/xue* 教/斆 for *teaching* and *learning*. This sense of "model" (*fan* 範), still partially audible at a discursive level in the policy title, *Secondary and Primary Teachers Codes of Ethics* (1984, 1991, 1997, 2008), gets totally lost to "standard" (*biaozhun* 標準) with its 2012 title, *Middle School Teachers' Professional Standards*. That is, a relational modeling-imitating teacher–student ordering gives its way to some measurable standards that teachers are supposed to meet to become qualified teachers. In other words, the identity of teachers moves away from some relational teacher–student inter-subjectivity toward an individual subjectivity. In this sense, I want to say *shifan* 師範 (teaching model) speaks of some cultural textures, whereas *biaozhun* 標準 (standards) becomes a spoken discourse, representing some abstract and conceptual meaning.

The second example is the re-invoked classical Confucian statement 循循善誘誨人不倦 (step-by-step soul induced and never tired of teaching/learning) in the 1984 and 1991 texts, which is replaced by a modern concept of 耐心教導 (patient teaching and guiding) in the 1997 text and disappears in the 2008 and 2012 documents. This re-invoked eight-character classical statement 循循善誘誨人不倦, rich in cultural meaning, is the most well-known statement to modern Chinese in describing an ideal image of good teaching/teacher. The first four-character term 循循善誘 is what Yan Yuan, Confucius' most favorite disciple, describes Confucius' teaching as an image of "gradual step-by-step soul induced guiding and pointing" (see *Lunyu:Zihan*), whereas the second four-character term 誨人不倦 is how Confucius depicts his attitude as "being never tired of learning and never bored with teaching" (see *Lunyu:Shu'er*).

Seen this way, reading into this Confucian statement feels like delving into the historical sea of meaning in that a whole array of images about the teaching and learning stories between Confucius and Yan Yuan would be revived. Although its modern replacement term 耐心教導 still conveys a sense of patient teaching and guiding, it is severed from its historical and cultural contexts that embed it and becomes a drab and sapless signifier of conceptual meaning. The former, aptly put as 代聖人言 (speaking in the place of sages), provides a bridge connecting the present with the past into a flowing river of *wen* 文 (culture and language) and brings out some of the shining patterns, textures and crisscrossing that Chinese language/culture impregnates (see, Wu, 2014, 2016). Such is what I mean by a speaking language, and it is hardly translatable or reducible to modern grammar without losing its historical and cultural contexts and overtones.

Such untranslatability or irreducibility of a speaking language to modern grammar can be seen as a flipside to mirror the problem that modern spoken discourse has. That is, it has become an enclosed meaning-making linguistic system following a typical modern grammar of Subject + V + Object. For example, the 2012 teachers' professional standard text in the above table can be put like this:

> Love students, pay attention to their healthy mind–body development, protect their life safety, respect their independent personality/integrity, protect their legal rights, equally treat each student, respect individual differences, understand and satisfy their varied needs, promote their autonomous development.
> 關愛中學生，重視中學生身心健康發展，保護中學生生命安全。/尊重中學生獨立人格，維護中學生合法權益，平等對待每一位中學生。尊重個體差異，主動了解和滿足中學生的不同需要/信任中學生，積極創造條件，促進中學生的自主發展。

Without a need of any cultural or historical background, this narrative is fully understandable to the outside world. Each concept signifies a certain knowledge, and its meaning is fully caught as long as we understand/know the concepts. In this sense, these discourses are abstract symbols signifying an enclosed meaning-making system.

Chinese Teacher–Student Difference Entangled Within a Binary Mode of Reasoning

Now let's look at how a binary logic still dominantly orders the Chinese teacher–student difference as shown in the above documents. Interestingly, the 1984 text expects teachers to build a *democratic, equal, and close relationship with students* (建立民主、平等、親密的師生關係) and the 2008 revision text expects teachers to have a lifelong learning attitude and *be both strict with and caring for students and become a mentor and friend of their students* (对学生严慈相济，做学生良师益友). These two statements strike out to me as they strive for a togetherness between teachers and students, even though according to Heidegger this togetherness still indicates a mediating, unifying, and harmonizing togetherness rather than a belonging-together with an accent on the active belonging and letting belong (as is shown in the next section). In other words, even with a togetherness, the teacher–student difference is still thought from the point of A and/or B, that is, (who are) teachers and (who are) students.

Nevertheless, the remainder texts listed above mostly use a sentence structure of teachers + verb + student, which presumes more an individual subjectivity of teachers and students than a mediated or unified togetherness. For example, teachers (should) love, understand, manage, protect, respect or equally treat students, meet/satisfy students' needs, and promote students' autonomous development. Seen this way, the noun teacher becomes an empty signifier or container, and we can fill it up with varied roles like manager, protector or responsibilities like promoting students' development or satisfying students' needs. A mode of questioning is who are or should be teachers/students, or what are the essential qualities of teachers/students.

In other words, the nouns of teachers and students presume a conceptually definitive, fixed, and objective meaning. In this case, the teacher–student difference is defined either through teacher or student without entering into a domain of belonging-together. Such a teacher–student ordering can be viewed as A vs. B in that A and B are metaphysical categories signifying individual subjects imbued with a list of imposed characteristics. Its relationship is built upon a dualistic ordering, whether it is teacher centered or students based, with a result of reaffirming the priority of one over the other. Such dualistic thinking underpins what counts as metaphysical conceptualizing.

To push one step further, even though these categories like care, love, protect smell of a care of self and others, they are thought within a knowledge-truth framework of what is care, love, and protection. Henceforth, teachers should not mock, satire, disparage, beat students (不諷刺、挖苦、歧視中學生，不體罰或變相體罰中學生) because these acts are not a knowledge-truth of care, love and/or protection. Again, this negative relation of A and not-A reaffirms the existence of dualism, the underpinning of metaphysical thinking.

On the other hand, as long as the subjectivity of teachers and/or students is maintained as it is, the teacher–student ordering can hardly escape the A vs. B form indicating a power confrontation between teachers and students. In other words, our representational thinking is just too ready to insert the difference ahead of time between teachers and students. That is why China's teacher education reform has been confined to an argument on the priority of a teacher-centered pedagogy or a student-based pedagogy, of virtue-education or knowledge-education, of teachers being students' manager or guide or friend, etc. However, what begs further questioning, that is, the active belonging-together or letting teachers and student belong together as they already do in real life, gets glossed over. To borrow Foucault (1997), "One escaped from a domination of truth not by playing a game that was different from the game of truth but by playing the same game differently or playing another game, another hand, with other trump cards" (p. 295).

Then how is it possible to loosen up, if not break apart, the domination of truth, the dominant binary mode of reasoning that structures the Chinese teacher–student difference along an identity politics and power pendulum? Let's now move to another aporia-like kneeling event for new openings.

Aporia Kneeling Event as an Opening: Rethinking Difference and Binary Reasoning With Daoist Wisdom

This kneeling event is an aporia in the sense that it is not students who are called to kneel down and show respect for teachers and parents. Rather, it is a middle school principal who drops his knees in front of over 1,000 students and teachers as his last pedagogical resort. It immediately incurs nationwide outcry because it overturns the principle of identity and power that grounds the reasoning of (teacher–student) difference in the first place. Then, when the normative subjectivities of teachers and students are bracketed and even flipped upside down, can difference still be upheld through a power(less) pendulum? Or when difference is pushed to its limit and even past its boundary, how can it regenerate itself and in what possible form? With the below aporia event, I would argue that "difference" can only regenerate itself from a different starting point, a different epistemological framework beyond using identity and power as its grounding principle, say, the Daoist wisdom.

Now let's look at the radical kneeling event. On a morning of 2006, a principal drops his knees in front of over 1,000 students and teachers in a Chinese middle school. Here is an account which was given by ninth-grade students present at this event. One morning after routine collective exercises when students and teachers were lined up on the sports field, Principal Zhou suddenly went before the students in Class 145, put his palms together, dropped to the ground and shouted: "Please! Stop fooling around and focus on your study!" The over 1,000 teachers and students present were shocked into sudden silence. School leaders hurried to get Principal Zhou up, but he refused. Only when Class 145 regained their reason and said "Principal, we won't fool around any longer and please, please get up" did Principal Zhou slowly come to his feet. Students were moved upon realizing what had happened, some bursting into tears. After this event, the school became the best example of teaching and learning in the district.[2]

Principal Zhou's gesture of kneeling immediately provoked public outcry and controversy at the national level, as it goes against the cultural norm that Chinese teachers historically enjoy a most respectable status right after heaven, earth, emperors, and parents. As the previous body chapter shows, Confucian culture says it is usually students who should kneel toward parents and teachers to show their gratitude. Even so, the majority people in current China criticize such Confucian ritual as some feudal dross that should be sent to tomb forever. How can a school principal drop his knees in front of students?!

Within such a context, Principal Zhou experienced overwhelming criticism, including for a "sick personality."[3] Recognized as an act sharply "opposite to what is normal Way-Dao," his kneeling triggered a wave of deploring China's "deformed" pedagogical practices that trample Confucian tradition respecting teachers and honoring education.[4] Occasionally it won him praise as a principal with great wisdom and courage since most would not be willing to sacrifice dignity.[5] It stirred up adamant disbelief among most toward what they perceived as an impossible, useless pedagogical mission.

To this questioning disbelief, Principal Zhou replied calmly:

> Everyone, principal or common teacher, has genuine dispositioning of heart. My spontaneous kneeling that day was a true expression of, and induced by, my heart filled up with my students, which squeezed out all concerns of dignity and personality. I don't feel ashamed at all. . . . In historical China it is usually juniors/students who kneel down before seniors/teachers, so my students would surely feel awkward and dislike my kneeling. . . . Contemporary Chinese would feel uncomfortable about me kneeling down before students, but at that time I had no thought but a genuine concern and affection in my heart for this poorly-disciplined Class 145. . . . This was my last kneeling though, and I wouldn't kneel again nor is there any further need. Otherwise, there would be more media coverage and outside intervention with school management. . . . If I kneel down again, it will become an affected show to others.
>
> (Hainan Jingji Bao, 2007)

Reasoning through the current tradition of education, teachers, parents, and the public made Principal Zhou a subject of humiliation and an example of the threat to Chinese education in general. Even those who gave praise reasoned through this tradition inasmuch as they recognized his kneeling gesture as negative, a sacrifice. Yet if we go with Principal Zhou's experience, he felt no loss of dignity and the students of Class 145 experienced a suspension of their own thought/action and were moved toward transforming in some way. Reasoning through the tradition of education cannot explain either the principal's or the students' experiences and relegates them outside pedagogy to utter *inexplicability*. What seems to have achieved the desired end of pedagogical reasoning remains in it as an unintelligible aporia.

However, this unintelligible aporia gets clarified if we hear the murmuring in the Dao De Jing Chapter 40 statement "what is *opposite and returning to root* keeps Dao in movement; what is weak sustains Dao in functioning" 反者道之動弱者道之用, especially the two sense impregnated within the Chinese monograph fan 反, that is, *being opposite* and *returning to root* as separate and belonging together (Chen, 1987, p. 223). This evokes an ambiguous double movement. Placing this ambiguity beside what is unintelligible and un-experienced in Principal Zhou's kneeling gesture, I open to realize this double movement. My realizing comes in two moments. In the first, I notice that Principal Zhou did not intentionally drop to the ground. He was at a complete loss for what to do. His previous efforts and those of other school leaders along the lines of traditional education failed to affect Class 145. His being at a loss grew in intensity to the point that he could not help suddenly dropping to the ground, not knowing what to do or what would happen afterward.[6]

In addition, Principal Zhou did not negate a traditional pedagogical approach. He merely acknowledged that it was not working. In kneeling he held to this approach as suspended, and at the same time disposed himself toward the students by opening to what appeared as undisciplined and unacceptable in them. His intention was not a matter of willing or doing, such as enacting pedagogical wisdom or expecting learning outcomes. He exposed himself to dwelling in emptiness welcoming his own and students' impropriety. He opened to the presence of what educators, following pedagogical tradition, could not grasp.

This is a movement on nothing, from teacher and student acting in opposition (the plane of doing and willing) to being opposite and returning to root (the plane of modes of being) dwelling empty of pedagogical reason, opening to welcome what is weak or impropriety and unteachability. The presence of what is weak, unteachable student and principal without dignity sustains this movement. In the second moment, I realize that the teacher–student relation is not a binary opposition. The current tradition of education differentiates and orders teacher and student along with a binary reasoning in which harmony is the relation of governing authority and submission.

But Principal Zhou's gesture suddenly, inexplicably inverted this harmony-relation. "The Principal would not get up until students unanimously pleaded for him to do so."[7] What appeared in traditional reasoning as Principal Zhou's self-negation and abandonment of teacher dignity invited students to suspend their being agents of mischief and give themselves over, pleading with Principal Zhou. Going with students' testimony, theirs was not a willed submission to pedagogical norms. It was being "in a dreamlike trance" from which they had to regain.

Further, they were not simply passive. Self-suspending intellection, students disposed themselves toward Principal Zhou in his heart. Reciprocally, in self-suspension of traditional dignity and teacher identity Principal Zhou disposed of himself, welcoming students. What held between them was not a relation, whether of norms or lawful ordering and regulation. It was nothing, and yet each's gesture conditioned the presence of the other in affection and heart. Now I realize how affection and heart are not teachable as characteristics or qualities. Instead, principal and students were shared in an experience of *the affectionate heart*. Neither an act of sacrifice nor submission, an affectionate heart is something like being devoted.

Even though there was a disparity in their respective circumstances, experiencing affectionate heart renders ambiguous the traditional differentiation of teacher and student. It was no longer important as a pedagogical mark since teachers reside where Dao dwells, it is not a matter of nobility or humbleness, youth or oldness; students need not know less than teachers, and teachers need not be more sagely than students (see, Han Yu, 802).

This movement, as not a relation binding in an oppositional order, released principal and students from obligatory conduct (governing and servitude) into a mode of being: harmonizing, separate belonging-together. In the pedagogical reasoning of tradition, harmony is the predetermined propriety of teaching–learning manner and conduct. In the kneeling event harmonizing happened as an experience of devotion in unteachability and unlearnability that came into being, while suspending, and in this way keeping hold of, its Confucian tradition.

With such a new understanding, I am now open to some new murmurings, that is, a mutual transforming and returning within the *Dao* movement as expressed in Chapter 25 of Dao De Jing that is quoted above, which can be experienced through the principal kneeling event. Please note here yin and yang are two symbolic modes of being that can be used to describe broader things such as *to know the white-being, one has to remain in the black-being*. First is expressed in the statement "moving everywhere gestures toward permeating into the far and permeating into the far gestures a returning to a starting point." Similarly, Principal Zhou's efforts with traditional pedagogical reasoning move "into the far" in pursuing it to its furthest point, reaches its limit, exposes its inability to teach students. This limit was not an impasse, as teachers experienced in their pedagogy with Class 145.

In the limit Dao was passing, moving formlessly and constantly moving into an actual gesture of returning to root, welcoming the unteachable and improper, sustaining Dao to its starting point. This echoes through Dao De Jing text as, for instance, returning to blackness from whiteness (Chapter 28) and the emptiness of a wheel, vase, and house from their having functions (Chapter 11). I also notice Dao movement occurring in a fundamental absence or nothing, "prior to the appearance of heaven and earth." In the passage, nothing manifests the very medium of movement at all. I also observe that nothing is without place or proper presence, yet movement vague yet irreducible and formless is somehow present. This presence of nothing permits an analogy of students' experiencing suspension of reason and Principal Zhou's experiencing self-suspension of dignity, being one's own lack. The presence of moving formless in nothing exists as both (yin) negative and (yang) positive. In this way, Dao entails a contingent co-being: at the same time darkness and lighting, far and nearing, permeating and returning.

In a similar line, the Dao De Jing statement of "what is opposite activates Dao in movement and what is week sustains Dao in movement" also sound a tone of yin-yang movement in that being opposite and being weak could be analogically treated as a yin in bipolar relation to a yang of being normal and being strong. With such a yin-yang movement, the identities of teachers and students are exploded, and nothing functions as a foundation. Relating this to the Chinese teacher–student difference and ordering, this yin-yang movement overturns the principle of identity and power that grounds the reasoning of teacher–student relationship in the first place. It brackets the normative subjectivities of teachers and students and collapses a power differentiation between them. It doesn't mean that there are no longer differences between teachers and students. Rather, differences whether epistemological or practical no longer matters as teachers and students become ontologically equal to each other in their co-dwelling.

Then, what significance and implications can such a bipolar yin-yang movement have for rethinking difference itself and in relation to identity as a binary ordering in education and beyond? With this question, I below further explicate and dialogue the Daoist yin-yang movement with Heidegger's rethinking of the ordering between identity and difference as an effort to constrain the Western metaphysical thinking on knowledge and system of reason at large.

Daoist Yin-Yang Movement and Heidegger's Reordering of Identity and Difference

Dao De Jing 道德經 is a classical Chinese Daoist text with succinct statements, and Dao is a primordial notion in Chinese thought with varied nuances of meaning along the historical strata. For example, *Yijing* says,

"One yin and one yang constitute Dao" (一陰一陽之謂道) (Xici). Chapter 25 of Dao De Jing depicts Dao as:

> Something vague yet irreducible was there/prior to the appearance of heaven and earth/soundlessly quiet and moving formlessly/totally independent and constantly moving by itself/reaching everywhere yet immune to danger/It may be considered the mother of the universe/I do not know its name/I exigently call it Dao/If forced to give it a name, I shall call it Great. Being great gestures toward moving everywhere. Moving everywhere gestures toward permeating into the far. Permeating into the far gestures a returning to a starting point.
>
> (see Chan, 1963, p. 152)

With these two statements, I would treat Dao not as a concept, but as a *yin-yang* movement, a style of reasoning that can be analogically picked up to suspend the Western-dominant binary reasoning toward a bipolar movement. Just as the Yijing image-number mode of interpretation portrays (see Chapter 4 and 5 for more details), the *yin-yang* lines are symbolically adopted to show the juxtaposition, constellation, opposition, supplementation, transformation, and translation within and between things, with human beings included as one such thing. Thus, *yin* and *yang* don't refer to a certain substance or ontology, but rather embody signs, signals, or elements that can be symbolically placed within any-thing and between any-things (Zhao & Ford, 2017). Etymologically, *yin* and *yang* are shadows and lights on a mountain side and river bank, forming a pair of "opposing forces and momentum as we watch how sunlight gives rise to the darkness of night that eventually gives rise to daylight" (Cheng, 2011, p. 343).

A Daoist yin-yang movement then foregrounds the dynamic, mutual informing, grounding, confronting, transforming, and re-turning movement as a movement, bracketing the fixed identities of things and a binary power pendulum. This yin-yang movement can be dialogued with Heidegger's rethinking of the ordering between identity and difference in two ways. First, the Daoist movement as movement resonates with Heidegger's thinking of relation as relation in re-envisioning the notion of identity. Second, the dialectical yin-yang ordering echoes Heidegger's interpretation of ontological difference between Being and beings. Below is a more detailed unpacking of these two points.

In *Identity and Difference* (1969), Heidegger maintains the nature of identity appears as unity in the history of Western thought. Re-invoking Parmenides' statement *Thought and Being are the same* into *Being belongs, together with thought, into the Same*, he translates A = A into A is (transitively) A, bringing out a new sense of belonging together. This belonging-together, Heidegger argues, indicates two modes of reasoning on the constellation of man (thinking) and Being. If the accent is on the unifying *together*, then the essential qualities of thinking (man) and Being are to be asked, and the relation is defined either through man or Being without entering into *the domain of the belonging-together*. If the element of *belonging* within belonging-together is emphasized, then thinking (man) and Being are held apart and at the same time held together, not fitted together, in the belonging-together. In this way, the relation is examined as the relation (see, pp. 23–32).

Heidegger uses the notion of "the event of appropriation" (p. 14) to re-configure the latter dynamic *belonging*-together of Being and thought. Within this event of appropriation, man and Being reach toward each other and achieve their active nature by "losing those qualities with which metaphysics has endowed them" (p. 37). Man can enter into such an event of appropriation through a "leap (Satz)" (p. 12) out of metaphysics, not by a "series of reasoned conclusions." That is, it is not that humans as anthropocentric subjects seize upon Being willfully, rather, humans relax and move forward by stepping back, opening to the call of Being and thus co-dwelling poetically. Such a leap in general becomes possible when language is (re)-treated as the primal dimension, or as what Heidegger aptly put as the "house of Being," within which "man's essence is first able to correspond at all to Being and its claim, and, in corresponding, to belong to Being. This primal corresponding, expressly carried out, is called thinking" (1977, p. 40, italics original).

Heidegger mentions that "the event of appropriation" is not a happening or occurrence, and also is no more translatable than the Chinese *Dao* (p. 36). To Heidegger, it requires a leap to spring out of the metaphysical thinking. To me, the Dao De Jing Chapter 40 statement 反者道之動弱者道之用 (what is opposite activates Dao in its movement, and what is weak sustains Dao in its movement) can also provide a leap or abrupt entry into the domain of event of appropriation. To echo Heidegger's attitude that such leap is possible in general with the primal language, I argue it becomes possible with the Chinese notion 反 in this Dao De Jing statement, which impregnates a double sense of *being opposite* and *returning*. A further understanding of the mutual appropriating movement between Being and beings helps to clarify this point.

To Heidegger, there exists an ontological difference between Being and beings, ontological in the sense that it is not something that we can make, but something that can encounter us. Gadamer (2007) clarifies for us this ontological difference in the below quote:

> [Heidegger says] "But no, this differentiation was certainly not something made *by me*." This was in 1924, long before the "turn". Those who know the later Heidegger know that the difference [*das Unterschied*] he [Heidegger] spoke of then was not something that we have made, but rather we are placed into this difference [*Unterschied*], in other words, into this *Differenz* [difference] [Sic].
>
> (p. 360)

Heidegger claims the constitution of metaphysics is defined by *difference*, that is, this ontological difference between Being and beings. However, since metaphysics has been thinking Being as the foundation or cause of beings, such ontological difference has remained un-thought in the Western history. Still, Heidegger argues this oblivion belongs intrinsically to difference. Why so? In his article *the Turning* (1977), Heidegger points to the necessity of this oblivion:

> But when this entrapping-with-oblivion does come expressly to pass, then oblivion as such turns in and abides. Thus rescued through this abiding from falling away out of remembrance, it is no longer oblivion. With such in-turning, the oblivion relating to Being's safe keeping is no longer the oblivion of Being; but rather, turning in thus, it turns about into the safe keeping of Being. When the danger is the danger, with the turning about of oblivion, the safe keeping of Being comes to pass; world comes to pass. That world comes to pass as world, that the thing things, this is the distant advent of the coming to presence of Being itself.
>
> (p. 43)

"This coming to presence of Being itself," the "necessity of the oblivion of Being" as "the safe keeping of Being," or simply put, the movement between Being and beings can be further clarified through some Dao De Jing statement in two ways.

First, it is the turning-in of the oblivion of Being that sustains the safe keeping of Being. Just as Dao De Jing says, "to understand the white, one has to remain in the black" 知其白守其黑 (Chapter 28). Here *white* and *black* are two symbolic modes of being like yang and yin that can be used to describe and correlate broader things. In this case, unconcealment is being-white whereas concealment is being-black. Being in the black is a necessary condition for being-white to come to its presence, or rather, being-black is subsistent in being-white as the former turns in and about into the latter's safe keeping.

Second, Heidegger's statement, "Being becomes present in the manner of transition to things," rather than going over to things, can be analogically identified with the constellation between Chinese *dao* 道 and *ziran* 自然 (literally put as *myriad things as they are*). Dao De Jing Chapter 25 says 道法自然 (Dao permeates into myriad things). It is not that Dao as some metaphysical top-down rule governing all the things from above, rather, Dao transits, becomes present in the manner of transition to things, yet remaining concealed. Similarly, the Dao De Jing statement "road to Dao is flat and straight whereas man prefers zigzagging detours" 大道甚夷而民好径 (Chapter 53) shows that "Dao is not far from humans" 道不远人 (*Zhongyong*), and we humans already reside sufficiently with Dao in reality. Similarly, Heidegger says we are in reality already within the mutual appropriating between Being and thought (p. 33), a self-vibrating realm wherein man and Being actively belong and let belong together. It is just that mainstream metaphysical thinking has blinded us to such a dwelling.

Through the above juxtaposition, we can see some resonance between Heidegger's rethinking of identity and difference and the Chinese Dao as a yin-yang movement. Just as yin and yang, Being and beings move away from fixed conceptual-objective identities toward a temporal, contingent, and dynamic mode of existence. Being and beings are placed in a horizontal plane such that Being no longer functions as the cause or foundation for beings, nor are beings what is caused. Being and beings appropriate and are mutually dependent upon and constitutive of each other, with one renders possible and visible the other, and with Being unconcealed in concealment.

However, if Heidegger's main critique is on the metaphysical ordering between man/beings and Being, my focus is particularly on the binary mode of reasoning. Seen as a dualistic relation in itself, a nuanced distinction can be drawn between this non-metaphysical Being-being belonging-together and a bipolar yin-yang movement. That is, if both forms share a mutually appropriating and belonging, then the bipolar yin-yang movement nourishes a more explicit sense of mutual transforming and returning as a further flattening out of a dualist mode of reasoning. Furthermore, yin and yang here are not fixed entities, but modes of being that can correlate into other things. In this sense, bipolar yin-yang thinking is also named "correlative thinking" (A. C. Graham, 1986) (see Chapter 4 for a more detailed account of this correlative mode of thinking).

Re-Imagining Difference Beyond a Binary Division: Some Implications

This chapter provides a different way to engage in the issue of difference, its entanglement with a binary mode of reasoning, namely, the ordering of difference and identity. Specifically, I explicate the underpinning principle of identity and power beneath the mainstream reasoning of (teacher–student) difference, and argue "difference" can only regenerate itself from a different starting point, a different epistemological framework beyond using identity and power as its grounding principle. In so doing, it relates to and also supplements the way difference is challenged and rethought in recent Western academia.

In the Western academia, difference is becoming a dominant discourse that submerges the principle of identity, the backbone of Western metaphysics, and marks a new way of thinking (Scott, 1989), through the works of critical thinkers like Foucault, Deleuze, and Derrida. Following Foucault, Deleuze claims that difference has never been thought in itself in the Western history of philosophy except as an attribute, an effect subordinate to the four ordering fetters of representation, the Image of thought, that is, the Identical, the Similar, the Opposed, and the Analogous. Deleuze (1969/1990) recognizes the Epicurean thesis that "nature as the production of the diverse can only be an infinite sum that does not totalize its own elements" (p. 267) and argues for a re-conceptualizing of difference as difference in and of itself, independent of the representation of the Same. In his way of thinking, difference as an independent concept in and of itself becomes a source of potentiality alongside, but not reducible to, the general conceptualization of identity. In his view, difference, as the true beginning of philosophy, is pre-individual and sub-representative (Deleuze, 1968/1994).

Deleuze's thinking is provocative in that it moves Foucault one step further in critiquing the Western epistemology, its representational way of reasoning that treats identity (the Same) as the grounding principle for difference. However, even though Deleuze turns around such an ordering to the extent that difference becomes the ontogenetic groundless principle for identity, it follows the same rule of the game. That is, a binary reasoning between identity and difference holds sway as a specter of the modern conceptual way of reasoning that orders man and world, words and things, and subjects and objects. Similarly, it orders, affirms, reproduces, and delimits the way China's teacher–student difference is reasoned and enacted to a power pendulum. In other words, *whether it is teacher-centered pedagogy or student-based learning, as long as teachers and students are treated as A versus B in the sense that identities of teachers and students are presumed and stuck with, teacher–student difference would not possibly go beyond an ordering of hierarchy and/or egalitarian.*

Furthermore, entangled within a power pendulum, the issue of difference becomes political and the binary ordering of difference and identity engenders social and cultural injustice. Sousa Santos (2007) names such a binary mode of reasoning as "abyssal thinking," which he claims to be a specter and yoke of the modern Western mode of thinking. Specifically, "abyssal thinking" constitutes a system of visible and invisible distinctions, with the latter grounding the former. It presumes a radical line between "this (visible) side" and "that (invisible) side" such that the invisible "vanishes as reality, becomes nonexistent, and is indeed produced as nonexistent" (p. 45), nonexistent in any relevant or comprehensive way of being. That is, whatever analytically comes out as nonexistent is radically excluded ontologically. This abyssal thinking, partly accountable by the Western logocentric metaphysics, conflates an analytical categorization of the visible and the invisible with an ontological inclusion-exclusion, leading to an "impossibility of the co-presence of the two sides of the [division] line" (ibid.), say, identity and difference, self and others, presence and absence.

This chapter brings in the Daoist yin-yang movement as an alternative way to flatten this binary reasoning toward a bipolar movement, making it possible for identity and difference, self and others, presence and absence to co-dwell along the movement and beyond the division line. Nevertheless, it is one thing to claim and totally another thing to enact such a yin-yang thinking. Here *enact* may be misleading as such thinking is not subject to an anthropocentric subject, doesn't follow a certain route, nor does it guarantee an expected destination. It is more of an encounter, an un-learning, an opening and attuning to. Heidegger says, "What matters are whether one can co-enact [his] path of thinking and that "the only significant thing is 'to be on the way'" (Petzet, 1993, p. 176, as cited in Ma, 2008, p. 44). With such a vision, I move on to the last chapter of my dissertation to briefly revisit my intellectual *journey* as a Daoist onto-un-learning-thinking *way*, with *way* gesturing a journey, a method, and a Dao movement. I revisit my journey in a way to theorize it as an exemplar of post-foundational *study*, the emerging gesture as an alternative to the learning logic predominant in the current globalized neoliberal society.

Notes

1. More information on this National Training Plan can be found on China's Ministry of Education website: http://old.moe.gov.cn//publicfiles/business/htmlfiles/moe/s6811/201209/141516.html
2. 海南中學校長千余師生前下跪，求學生學習 Hainan Jingji Bao, September 24, 2007. Retrieved on April 24, 2018, from http://edu.qq.com/a/20070924/000107_1.htm
3. 校長為何下跪求學生學習？ Xinxi Shibao, September 25, 2007. Retrieved on August 18, 2017, from http://edu.people.com.cn/BIG5/6309148.html
4. 下跪：沉重而失敗的教育方式 Xia Yucai, September 25, 2007. Retrieved on April 28, 2018, from http://www.neworiental.org/news/news/200709/1135269.html
5. 大智大勇的周常德校長 Yuanye Tianjian web blog, September 24, 2007. Retrieved on April 28, 2018, from http://blog.sina.com.cn/s/blog_3f9a560701000ad9.html
6. 海南下跪校长：下跪是真情流露，以后不再跪 Guangzhou Daily News, October 5, 2007. Retrieved on April 28, 2018, from http://learning.sohu.com/20071011/n252595336.shtml
7. 海南中學校長千余師生前下跪，求學生學習. Hainan Jingji Bao, September 24, 2007. Retrieved on April 24, 2018, from http://edu.qq.com/a/20070924/000107_1.htm

References

Chan, W-T. (1963). *A source book in Chinese philosophy*. Princeton, NJ: Princeton University Press.

Chen, G. (1987). *Notes and comments on Laozi* [Laozi zhushi ji pingjie]. Beijing: Zhonghua Shuju.

Cheng, C. Y. (2011). Interpreting paradigm of change in Chinese philosophy. *Journal of Chinese Philosophy*, 38(3), 339–367.

Deleuze, G. (1969/1990). *The logic of sense* (M. Lester and C. Stivale, Trans., & C. V. Boundas, Ed.). New York, NY: Columbia University Press. (Original work published 1969)

Deleuze, G. (1968/1994). *Difference and repetition* (P. Patton, Trans.). New York, NY: Columbia University Press. (Original work published 1968)

Foucault, M. (1997). The ethics of the concern of the self as a practice of freedom. In P. Rabinow (Eds.), *Ethics: Subjectivity and truth* (*The essential works of Michel*

Foucault 1954–1988) (R. Hurley et al., Trans., pp. 281–302). New York, NY: The New Press.

Foucault, M. (2011). *The government of self and others: Lectures at the College de France, 1982–1983* (A. I. Davidson, Ed., & G. Burchell, Trans.). New York, NY: Picador.

Graham, A. C. (1986). *Yin-yang and the nature of correlative thinking*. Singapore: The Institute of East Asian Philosophies.

Gadamer, H-G. (2007). *The Gadamer reader: A bouquet of the later writings* (R. E. Palmer, Ed.). Evanston, IL: Northwestern University Press.

Guangzhou Daily News. (2007, October 5). Hainan xiagui xiaozhang: xiagui shi zhenqing liulu, yihou buzai gui 海南下跪校长：下跪是真情流露，以后不再跪. Retrieved on April 28, 2018, from http://learning.sohu.com/20071011/n252595336.shtml

Hainan Jingji Bao. (2007, September 24). Hainan zhongxue xiaozhang qianyu shisheng qian xiagui, qiu xuesheng xuexi 海南中學校長千余師生前下跪，求學生學習. Retrieved on August 18, 2017, from http://news.qq.com/a/20070924/001830.htm

Han, Y. (802). Shishuo. Retrieved April 27, 2018, from http://fanti.dugushici.com/ancient_proses/70568

Heidegger, M. (1957/1969). *Identity and difference* (J. Stambaugh, Trans. with an Introduction.). New York, NY, Evanston, IL, and London, UK: Harper & Row Publishers. (Original work published 1957)

Heidegger, M. (1977). The turning. In M. Heidegger (Ed.), *The question concerning technology and other essays* (W. Lovitt, Trans. with an introduction, pp. 36–49). New York, NY: Harper Torchbooks.

Ma, L. (2008). *Heidegger on East-West dialogue: Anticipating the event*. New York, NY: Routledge.

Scott, C. E. (1989). *The language of difference*. New York, NY: Prometheus Books.

Sousa Santos, B. (2007). Beyond abyssal thinking: From global lines to ecologies of knowledges. *Review*, *XXX*(1), 45–89.

Petzet, H. W. (1983/1993). *Encounters and dialogues with Martin Heidegger 1929–1976* (P. Emad and K. Maly, Trans.). Chicago, IL: University of Chicago Press. (Original work published 1983)

Wu, Z. J. (2014). "Speak in the place of the sages": Rethinking the sources of pedagogic meanings. *Journal of Curriculum Studies*, *46*(3), 320–331.

Wu, Z. J. (2016). Person-making through Confucian exegesis. In G. P. Zhao & Z. Y. Deng (Eds.), *Re-envisioning Chinese education: The meaning of person-making in a new age* (pp. 93–115). New York, NY: Routledge.

Xia, Y. C. (2007, September 25). Xiagui, chenzhong er shibai de jiaoyu fangshi 下跪，沉重 而失敗的教育方式. Retrieved on April 28, 2018, from http://www.neworiental.org/news/news/200709/1135269.html

Xinxi Shibao. (2007, September 25). Xiaozhang weihe xiagui qiu xuesheng xuexi 校長為何下跪求學生學習? Retrieved on April 28, 2018, from http://edu.people.com.cn/BIG5/6309148.html

Yuanye Tianjian Weblog. (2007, September 24). Dazhidayong de Zhou Changde Xiaozhang 大智大勇的周常德校長. Retrieved on April 28, 2018, from http://blog.sina.com.cn/s/blog_3f9a560701000ad9.html

Zhao, W., & Ford, D. R. (2017). Re-imagining affect with study: Implications from a Daoist wind-story and yin–yang movement. *Studies in Philosophy and Education*, 1–13.

China Ministry of Education Policies Retrieved from www.gov.cn

China Mid-Term 2010–2020 Plan [China Mid-Long Educational Reform and Development]
MOE News Brief 2015 N.49 [National Training Plan Achievement in its 5-year Implementation]
MOE 2010 National Training Notice [MOE and MOF Notice on Implementing the National Teacher Training Plan]
National Training Curriculum Standard (2012)
National Training Curriculum Implementation Guideline (2012)
Shide-Training Curriculum (2012)
Teacher Morality Codes [教師職業道德規範] (2008)
Teacher Professional Norms [教師職業標準] (2012)
1984 中小學教師職業道德要求 Middle-Primary School Teachers' Code of Ethics
1991 中小學教師職業道德規範 Middle-Primary School Teachers' Code of Ethics
1997 中小學教師職業道德規範修訂 Middle-Primary School Teachers' Code of Ethics First Revision
2008 中小學教師職業道德規範二次修訂 Middle-Primary School Teachers' Code of Ethics Second Revision
2012 中學教師專業標準（試行）2012 Middle School Teachers' Professional Standards

Part III

Revisiting My Research-Learning Journey as a Post-foundational Case Study

7 Daoist Onto-un-learning Way and Post-foundational Study

This chapter revisits my learning and un-learning research trajectory, which I call a Daoist onto-un-learning way, as a post-foundational case *study*, and explicates the possible contributions this book has to the studies of difference and context in and beyond the field of comparative and international education for the twenty-first century. *Study* is a newly emerging Western concept, envisioned as an alternative or oppositional rationale to the predominant *learning* logic in educational thinking global-wise. I bring in the notion of *study* for three reasons. First, I would like to differentiate my own Daoist onto-un-learning from a mainstream psychology-based notion of *learning*, the latter often bespeaking an outcome-based learning process. That is, although I use the first person to story-tell my own learning-research experiences and trajectory, my intention is not just to unfold it as my personal psychological growth process, but to proffer it as an example and a new form of *learning*, akin to *study*, with significant implications for re-problematizing and cutting into schooling in current China and beyond. Second, I hope to situate and dialogue my Daoist onto-un-learning way with the emerging Western *study* scholarship for mutual informing. In so doing, I situate the Daoist thinking into an international and cross-cultural landscape to caution against a cultural relativist stand. Finally, I move one step further to envision *learning* and *study* into a Daoist yin-yang movement wherewith *learning* and *study*, analogous to the yin-yang elements, always happen together, mutually informing, confronting, and transforming each other. This last step is to further suspend and implode the binary division as a surreptitious ordering principle that often creeps back and essentializes the absent, the different, and the secret into an identity politics in the (post)-modern and (post)-structural thinking in general, from which we are yet to emerge.

Revisiting My Daoist Onto-Un-Learning *Way* as a Post-Foundational *Study*

As I pointed out in Preface, this book has two dimensions that parallel at one point and intersect at another. Besides historicizing the issues of language, knowledge, body, and difference to cut into the present China, it also recounts and envisions my Daoist onto-un-learning way as a post-foundational case *study*. The term "post-foundational" gestures a sense of going beyond such modern principles of representation, given body, identity politics, and binary reasoning that order the way knowledge, reason, education, and curriculum are thought and enacted today. The notion "Daoist onto-un-learning" comes directly from the Dao De Jing statement that "a follower of learning gains each day, whereas a follower of Dao loses each day." By learning, I mean the gaining and accumulation of knowledge and skills toward a certain goal, whereas by losing, I mean the unexpected yet transformative suspense, bracketing, and overcoming of the above-mentioned principles and other naturalized presumptions and positions my subjectivity is built upon. In losing, I am open to new horizons of thinking possibilities. In this sense, my entire research-learning *way* can be theorized as an exemplary case of post-foundational *study*, a study that doesn't start with an a priori theory and method, nor does it reproduce the founding presuppositions and principles, but is *on its way* of wandering and wondering, with *way* intersecting a *journey*, a *method*, and a *Dao movement*, each element worthy of some further elaborations.

Study is a newly emerging Western concept, proffered as an alternative or oppositional mode of educational engagement and logic to push back against the dominant neoliberal *learning* logic in current educational thinking and praxis global-wise (see, e.g., Ford, 2016, 2017; Harney & Moten, 2013; Lewis, 2013; Rocha, 2015). For example, Tyson E. Lewis (2013) proposes a rigorous theory of *study* based upon Georgio Agamben's (1999) interpretation of the distinctions between Aristotle's notions of generic potential and effective potential. Generic potential is already commonly thought in education as to be realized and fulfilled, as expressed in this statement, "education is to elicit or realize students' potential to its maximum." In realizing, generic potential is partially destroyed. However, effective potential, rarely explored so far in relation to education, is a kind of potential that remains immanent to itself insofar as it is not actualized. It is the potentiality of freedom of thinking. Seen this way, generic potential and effective potential order by different rules in that the former operates along a "what is" (learning) logic whereas the latter along a "what can be" logic, the latter Lewis develops into a *study* rationale.

With a *learning* logic, education is collapsed into socialization and qualification (Biesta, 2006; Autio, 2017) that make students into subjects who can fit into the already-existing order of things. Thus, learning is to learn the so-called twenty-first-century skills, competencies, or literacies phrased as indispensable and necessary skill sets that students would need to succeed in their life and career. The goal of education is thus limited to social efficiency, making students into certain kinds of human capital without nurturing their idiosyncratic subjectivities. Many educational theories, whether in the name of constructivist, progressivist, and critical, are subsumed to this *learning* logic, henceforth depriving students of some educational event, an opportunity to be themselves as human beings and learn *otherwise*. Simply put, *learning* involves the acquisition of predetermined knowledge that can be measured and quantified, whereas *studying* as a weak educational logic shuns predetermined goals and cannot be easily measured and quantified.

I bring in the notion of *study* to further suspend and implode the binary division as a surreptitious ordering principle that often creeps back and essentializes the absent, the different, and the secret into an identity politics in the (post-)modern and (post-)structural thinking. For example, the fact that Western scholars encase *study* as an alternative or oppositional logic to *learning* runs a risk of analytically and ontologically dividing them as two separate *things*. As a yin-yang movement, *learning* and *study* are no longer divided, nor does one element preclude the happening of the other along the way. Instead, they support, ground, confront, transform, re-turn within a dynamic bipolar yin-yang movement to the extent that "what is opposite to the normal re-activates Dao in its movement and what is weak sustains Dao in its function." In such a movement, *study* could be analogically viewed as a yin-element and *learning* a yang-element. In the current neoliberal society, learning takes up such a dominant position that it marginalizes study to the point that the yin-yang movement is stagnate. However, *study* could happen and regenerate its power at certain disruptive moments, like what I describe as aporia moments, when the Dao movement is reactivated and maintained toward a new re-turning and dynamic.

With this clarification, I now unpack my Daoist-onto-un-learning way as an exemplary case of post-foundational *study*, a study that is *on its way* of wandering and wondering, with *way* intersecting a *journey*, a *method*, and a *Dao movement*, each element worthy of some further elaborations as below. In particular, I pay attention to the learning-study movement and the taking-place of *study* as singular and transformative event along the way. In unfolding my way, I explicate the possible features of a post-foundational *study*, how it is possible to discern and portray the foundation-less *study* moments, and what implications this project has for rethinking schooling in current China at the next of East and West, past and present in a post-foundational way. Post-foundational in the sense of not getting bogged down to or reproducing the East–West boundaries, whether cultural or geographical; not reproducing the modern epistemology of representation and signification; not taking body as a given; and not reproducing the binary reasoning that orders identity and difference, teacher and student, subject and object, knowledge and reason. Rather, a post-foundational study scrutinizes the very foundation we start with and stand upon, cuts into our taken-for-granted knowledge and reason, and opens to new horizons of thinking.

A Daoist Onto-Un-Learning Journey That I Have Walked Out

Post-foundational *study*, treated as being antagonistic to the *learning* logic, first of all demands a radical denial of not just particular ends but ends in general and in toto (see, Zhao, 2017; Zhao & Ford, 2017; Lewis, 2013). *Study* is to "move beyond any pragmatic notion of capabilities oriented toward particular projects with definitive success conditions as an educational ideal" (Lewis, 2013, p. 52). A studier, accordingly, is one whose subjectivity is no longer definable by any metrics of mastery or accomplishment. Put simply, *study* is to describe those educational experiences not reducible to a linear actualization of a predetermined learning goal. It is more about the means or the meandering wonder and wander about, with no clear destination in mind, a matter of *being and encountering on the way* so as to enact one's path of thinking.

This is the first feature of my Daoist onto-un-learning journey. Like *study*, my journey doesn't have a planned itinerary or an anticipated destination. It is simply *being on its way*, a way set off upon my *encountering* the culturally unique "wind-education" discourses in China's current schooling. Yet, this *being on its way* does not march down a forward path toward progress but alternatively wanders sideways in the labyrinth, sometimes following this dancing "wind" and sometimes dancing along with it, both amazed and paralyzed by the wonderful yet aporetic concepts and ideas encountered along the way. It is by *encountering* that transformative *study* moments happen. This doesn't mean that my mind was totally empty when I embarked on this journey. Rather, I have an overall guiding direction, namely, how it is possible to constrain the epistemicide concern in cross-cultural educational studies, and how to discern and render intelligible some (Chinese) cultural-historical sensibilities in the English wor(l)d without getting bogged down to some indispensable yet insufficient Western theoretical frameworks and categories. It is just that as *study* happens at eventful moments along the way and through encountering, the overall agenda retreats.

My Daoist encountering entails a cross-cultural detour and access strategy, which facilitates the happening of *encountering* something I otherwise take for granted. Looking back, my intellectual journey engages both detouring into the intellectual and cultural other to access the Chinese educational reasoning, and the historical other to access the present self. This detouring strategy helps one to distance from his or her own naturalized cultural and political position and thus provides an alternative perspective to discern what is otherwise tacit and commonsensical. This new perspective enables one to get out of an otherwise normalized self-other division to look at the Other and the self in comparative studies and to use self as a framework to gauge the other as being different. It helps to contextualize one's positions and norms, and brings to the fore the core issue of context in comparative and difference studies. Detouring into the cultural and historical other is to help better understand the cultural and present self in two senses.

First, the often exotic and different other helps the self to see its own thinking limit. For example, the exotic Chinese animal classification enables Foucault to see the limit of the Western mode of reasoning. To flip it around for me, the question becomes how it is possible to first *discern* the cultural uniqueness of such Chinese sensibilities, which are otherwise tacit to me as native Chinese, and then render them intelligible cross-culturally as they are. Foucault and Heidegger's critique of modern language as an enclosed meaning-making system alerts me to the logic of signification and representation that also configures the modern and Westernized Chinese language. To explore the ordering of the Chinese language then needs a historical unpacking. That is, I approach and appropriate Foucault and Heidegger's thinking not as some universal theories that can be applied to the Chinese context. Rather, I treat their thinking as a movement, a method, and ponder how their thinking styles shed new light upon, and help me to enact, my own thinking. In a word, detouring into the other is to better see the self.

Second, the cultural-historical other and the cultural-present self are not to be put into a binary division with one as the *not* of the other, or one as the origin of the other. An issue of epistemicide, or epistemological crisis, will follow otherwise, whether in the form of applying the Western theoretical frameworks to gauge the non-Western cultural contexts, or of romanticizing the past into a cultural relativist stand. On my journey, I move between East and West, past and present into a flowing river to see how they converge and diverge, mutually suspending and re-informing each other.

For example, I bring in Paraskeva's (2016) critique of epistemicide as a coloniality matrix of knowledge, power, and being on the international landscape, and his call for the necessity to bring to the foreground (an)other forms of knowledge in its genealogy. Yet, I move one step further to bracket a geographical boundary between East and West, North and South, and propose a historical-archaeological mode of inquiry as a paradigm to unpack other forms of Chinese knowledge in its historicity. Furthermore, I draw upon Michel Serres' "handkerchief folds" analogy to disrupt a linear past–present–future timeline, and juxtapose the past and present into historical strata that crisscross and intersect each other. This style of reasoning makes it possible for me to historicize the ancient Chinese Yijing thought not as an origin, but as an originary (re)source, of the entire Chinese thought, knowledge, and reason, originary in the sense that it is not reducible to what has been thought. It always nourishes something that has not been thought, which in turn sets free traditional thinking. In so doing, I move away from the trap and trope of describing the Chinese language by the Western categories of "representation" or "non-representation." Instead, I relate the Chinese language/writing back in its own historical-ethnographic and among the conceptions it echoes or answers as expressed in *Yijing*.

Detouring into the other and past is to better cut into the self and present by re-turning to an alternative thought, system of reason, or a style of reasoning that has not fallen into the trap of modernity and thus can be picked up as an alternative paradigm to cut into the present. It can be said that my respective encountering of the Chinese "wind" and "body" each follows such a going back, re-turning, or retrospective way. Parsing the manifest "wind-discourses" brings me back to the Chinese classical book of *Yijing* with a mode of reasoning woven with *image* and *number*, opens me to an onto-hermeneutic *co-dwelling* between man and the natural world, as an alternative to the modern conceptual thinking and to an ordering of man as a master of the natural world, which is an object. Deploying the manifest Chinese body discourses brings me back to the Yijing *guan*-hexagram, which Confucius invokes and envisions into an ideal and exemplary teaching–learning movement between teachers and students that happens like wind blowing the earth. It helps me realize that classical Chinese thinking is holistically and holistically embodied, that is, body-thinking, and Confucian learning is to beautify one's body through lifelong stone-like cutting and grinding, as an alternative to a modern mind–body dualism, a mind or conceptual thinking, and a treatment of educational body as a given, a conceptual sign.

This being said, this study is post-foundational as it renders visible and problematizes the possible foundations, norms, and principles presumed and often reproduced in comparative and educational studies. These principles include but are not confined to the politics of sameness and identity, the given notion of context, and the conceptual mind-thinking. The politics of sameness is presumed when we reason difference as an effect of identity. The notion of context is often delimited to a geographical location, and its historical, epistemological, and cultural dimensions have not been rigorously explored. That is, in which ways are knowledge contextualized in the first place? How is it possible to juxtapose varied contextualized systems of reason on a comparing operating table? How is it possible to rethink the role and rubrics of body in ordering who we are and how we learn and study?

A Daoist Onto-Un-Learning Method That I Have Worked Out

Ford (2016) believes that a taking-place or encountering of study is a singular event and the singularity needs to be "learned, unlearned, and relearned" (p. 92). Whereas a learner tends to collect signs and things to reproduce them as evidence of their realized potentiality, a studier often collect them to get lost, wander, and thus experience the freedom of being and thinking. The signs and things that I collect in this project are the Chinese notions of "wind" and "body" not as given conceptual signifier or material object. Rather, I mobilize them as singular examples in Agamben's sense, as theoretical constructs, as paradigmatic examples of a style of reasoning, and as strategic signposts to help me cut into, de-construct, and re-envision the ordering of, among other themes, language/reason, the educational body, and the teacher–student difference in China from a cross-cultural and historical-archaeological perspective. In other words, the rule of paradigmatic use of "wind" and "body" cannot be applied or stated (a priori) but can only be shown in the exhibition alone of the paradigmatic case that constitutes a rule, and the paradigm is never already given but is generated and produced by showing and exposing.

As a studier, I have learned, unlearned, and relearned two interrelated strategies to show, expose, and explicate the problematics of "wind" and "body" as shown in the previous chapters. First is an *evocative dialogue* with language and body itself, which I unpack as below. Second is a move away from a conceptual thinking toward what Heidegger (1977) terms as a *meditative thinking*, which I further unpack in the next section.

Here is a retrospective story on the movement of my evocative dialoguing on the body, retrospective in the sense that it has led me to somewhere I could not anticipate in the beginning. I picked up the term "evocative questioning" (Duarte, 2012) as a signature to treat the historical discourses as a mode and movement of reasoning, and to watch out for the possible dialogic movement that can be evoked or called forth between us as co-beings. I started my questioning with a habituated modern mentality presuming a body and mind separation. However, I did not realize such a positioning until evocatively dialoguing with the two contextualized examples, namely, Confucius' commentary on the Yijing *guan*-hexagram and the controversial kneeling events in current China, brings out something not reducible to, and henceforth can't be answered through, such a mind–body binary.

In the Confucian case, when I was called forth to a metonymic relation between "a big head" and "kingly virtue," namely, a big head in ancient China is homologous to being virtuous, I realized my questioning *what non-bodily qualities could a big head signify* already presumes a binary separation between an outer physical body and an inner disposition. Furthermore, when I was exposed to a necessity of body in enacting teaching and learning as a limit/foundational point, I realized that the Confucian body is never merely a physical body, nor is it ordered through a mind–body separation. Rather, it is a necessary matrix for being and living, as well as teaching and learning. If I can say that I have come to such a realization through a discursive evocative dialoguing with the Confucian narrative movement, then the current kneeling body example helps me realize the limits of such a discursive reasoning, and opens me up toward a practical reasoning-experiencing, namely, how it is possible to observe body (and body experience) with body?

With the current kneeling body example, I examine the public debating discourses to notice a binary logic, reasoning the same kneeling-bowing performance as highest Confucian ritual format versus feudal dross. Furthermore, both sides draw upon historical principles to adjudicate their righting and wronging claims. In such a reasoning, the body becomes a cultural symbol tossed back and forth by the public in their discursive quarrel, detached from the bodied actors. Such reasoning also molds the bodied actors into a free citizen or enslaved servant, a mode of subject constructed through a system of discursive representation, not related to any particular person. However, turning back to the bodily kneeling-bowing performers, and in particular, drawn to a visible inter-corporeal dwelling and resonating between some body actors, I realize inter-body interaction engages a practical experiencing. That is, body experiences; experiences happen in bodily terms through bodily engagement, the nuances of which are nurtured right within the Chinese term for body, 身體, resonating with a Daoist theme of *observing body with body*.

It is there I realized that I always examine the Confucian ritual body and the current kneeling body from a discursive perspective, rather than a practical perspective. Concomitant with such a discursive perspective was a nuanced gap between knowing and being. Even though I thought I knew common claims like "Chinese thinking is embodied," I found myself naturally bound up with a conceptual thinking mode. Even though I consciously endeavor to constrain such conceptual thinking, it is still deceptively easy to fall back within. To practically observe body with body calls for a paradigm shift from mental judgment toward a somatic experience, or to put it differently, from a mode of knowing toward a mode of being.

Such an exposure helps me realize a nuanced gap between my knowing and my being, as well as the difficulty involved in un-learning a mind-conceptual mode of reasoning toward engaging (wholeheartedly) a body-experiential mode of being.

In an international landscape, with the emerging Western scholarship on new materialism by Karen Barad and Gilles Deleuze, scholars have started to explore the entanglement of body and learning in classrooms around the concept of "embodied cognition" (see, de Freitas & Sinclair, 2014). However, while "body" becomes a very popular discourse across the globe, are we indeed talking about the same senses and overtones of body? For example, what counts as body and its limits and boundaries? How is it constructed contextually? Are we observing body with body or mind? Are we idealizing or materializing body? These questions all beg further explorations both conceptually and practically toward a more productive dialogue cross-culturally and cross-disciplinarily. This book situates itself within this emerging scholarship and provides a distinct and contextualized picture of what counts as a Chinese body and how it configures and reconfigures in relation to education historically and cross-culturally.

In so doing, the book once again alerts us to the theme of "context" that is constantly used and yet largely presumed in comparative studies, ethnographies, and historical studies as a geographical notion. As such, context is often a set dimension of identity and representation. How context can be mobilized as a concept, a theoretical construct, which orders the way people think and act and the languages they speak has not been scrutinized philosophically and historically. This book foregrounds the role of language and discourse as an ingredient of context that informs our understanding of culture, knowledge, and cultural differences.

A Daoist Onto-Un-Learning Movement That I Have Experienced

As argued in Chapter 6, the modern Western mode of thinking features a yoke of binary logic which Sousa Santos (2007) calls "abyssal thinking." It constitutes a system of visible and invisible distinctions, with the latter grounding the former. As a principle, it conflates an analytical categorization of the visible and the invisible with an ontological inclusion-exclusion and orders the way identity and difference, presence and absence, subject and object, self and other, teacher and student are thought in modern epistemology. Looking back at my own intellectual way, I notice the specter of metaphysical "abyssal thinking," that is, binary mode of reasoning, has taken four overlapping forms: a subject–object binary reasoning with an anthropocentric subject; a presumed fixed meaning and entity beneath a pro-noun; a treatment of language as a closed meaning-making discourse; and a calculative truth/knowledge-seeking reasoning. Below is a clarification of these four forms.

Within this binary mode of reasoning, human beings are presumed as a subject, or a rational mind to be specific, who treats all the other things as objects and examines what they approach, no matter whether it is discourse, or body, or social equity and difference, as an object represented through language. To borrow Foucault's wording, we are entrapped within the trope of philology, namely, "assuming the a priori existence of grammatical arrangements in a language for what can be expressed in it" (1966/1973, p. 298). Seen this way, it is the human subjectivity and modern grammar that hold sway and delimit the ways other material things unfold and interact with human subjects. Just as Heidegger argues in *What is a Thing* (1967), physical things which used to be subjects that can light up have become (linguistic) objects of the human subjective mind.

To add on top of this, human beings have also become subjected and subjugated to such an idea-bound conceptual-representative mode of thinking, wherein language becomes an enclosed system divorced from the material things. Such a subject–object way of reasoning is also visible and actually shapes most educational research wherein the researcher works as a doctor, diagnosing what is investigated and reporting what is found. How the researcher moves along with or is moved by what is investigated is, if not deliberately, neglected. Narrative or story-telling studies can be an exception to this, but still largely confined to the identity issue whether it is caught within a struggle or a reconstruction (Wang H., 2004; He, 2000) or a way of pedagogy (Li, 2005). How is it possible for an educational research to be explicitly turned over into a new form of learning, say, study, is rarely demonstrated.

My project demonstrates the happening of a Daoist onto-un-learning as a case *study*, which is turned over into a new form of learning and un-learning.

On my way, I realize what I un-learn is actually the specter of metaphysical thinking and gesture toward a non-metaphysical, non-foundational or what Heidegger (1977) put as "meditative thinking." A non-metaphysical meditative thinking, as Heidegger argues, is to relegate an anthropocentric subject to a mode of being, to give up a willful mind toward an attitude of being willing to succumb to the calling of being, to explode a subject–object logic toward an event of appropriation as a self-vibrating domain wherein man/beings and Being mutually appropriate toward each other. A Daoist learning and un-learning thinking as a movement further flattens out such a binary reasoning with a mutual transforming and re-turning into a Dao movement.

However, such a non-metaphysical thinking is not replicable, nor can it be planned, anticipated, and/or willed. Looking back at my own experience, it is more of an encountering, a movement, a confronting, and a negotiation between myself and language, body, and teacher–student difference. What I have learned is to stop and enjoy my journey, my way and my Dao, as well as its unpredictability, rather than head all the way toward some imagined end or goal which often turn out to be futile. Meanwhile I need to watch out not to slip back into the trope of metaphysical thinking. What Foucault says rings back: Education can hardly transform a society but can indeed transform a person's mode of reasoning.

What is transformed is not only a person's mode of reasoning but also a person's mode of being or subjectivity. On my Daoist way, I play a double role of an inquirer-researcher and a learner, or rather, a studier. As a researcher, I treat language, body, and teacher–student difference as my object of examination. I explore how they are said, reasoned, enacted, legitimized, and/or contested in current China's educational reform from a cross-cultural perspective. As a learner/studier, I watch out for the turning and re-turning moments of my own thinking and my own mode of being, and savor the new meaning and value of teaching and learning, and much more.

For example, my unplanned Daoist journey confronts me with aporetic limits again and again, whereupon I find my anthropocentric being no longer in power and my knowledge coming to an end. Following the dancing wind, I find myself paralyzed by its Chinese definition as *wind blows and insects get germinated and hatched in eight days* because words stop in their tracks and modern grammar simply collapses. However, a Daoist onto-un-learning journey welcomes such aporetic limits, plays with them seriously, and if lucky enough, turns them about toward un-trodden paths opening to extraordinary views. That is, an aporia is a moment of being opposite to the otherwise normalized way (*yang*) and re-activates the movement of Dao toward a returning to the root (*yin*). Foucault's below statement in *The Order of Things* can be seen as a vivid description of my Daoist-onto-un-learning journey in its unfolding:

> Modern criticism does not proceed from the observation that there is language towards the discovery of what that language means, but from

the deployment of manifest discourse towards a revelation of language in its crude being. . . . Hence the *need* to work one's way back from opinions, philosophies, and perhaps even from sciences, to the words that made them possible, and, beyond that, to a thought whose essential life has not yet been caught in the network of grammar.

(1973, p. 298, my italics)

Seen this way, my Daoist onto-un-learning way becomes an un-thinking way in that *doing learning gains and doing Dao loses each day* (Dao De Jing, Chapter 48). Muddling up a distinction between learning and being, I explore the possibility of learning as a form of *study*, a way of being, a working and walking out of a path/way (Dao), a re-turning to bypaths, and a sustained self-turning. Or as Plato puts it, *education is not an art of putting sight into the eye that can already see, but one of turning the eye toward the proper gaze of Being* (as cited in Duarte, 2012).

Post-foundational Educational Studies Beyond Representation, Body, and Identity Politics

I unfold my Daoist-onto-un-learning way as above to show that I am building a style of thought outside of the conventions of sorting out literature reviews, defining concepts, and applying borrowed methods. That is, a dividing line between theory, method, and practice is obscured in its pavement toward a space where they intersect and play with each other seriously. To be specific, I work out my own method with particular "wind" and "body" examples from both classical and contemporary Chinese discourses and practices as a demonstration and enactment of my own *transformative* learning and un-learning way. My Daoist onto-un-learning is not merely my own personal psychological growth process. Rather, I want to proffer an example, in Agamben's sense of singular and unique and sensible only in its own unfolding, and a new form of *learning*, which has implications for re-problematizing and cutting into schooling in current China and beyond.

This new form of learning can be called a *post-foundational study*. Now it is time to explicate the possible features of a post-foundational study, how it is possible to discern and portray the foundation-less educational moments, and what implications this project has for rethinking teaching, learning, and teacher–student movement in current China at the next of East and West, past and present.

Put simply, a post-foundational study problematizes the grounding principles of modern epistemology, including the representational language, a given educational body, and an identity-based difference. This book provides an archaeological-historical mode of inquiry and an ontological language–discourse perspective to disrupt the above principles of modernity and as a paradigm to rethink educational thinking and praxis in current China with and beyond Western categories and frameworks, namely, a developmental comparative logic and a globalized Western discourses as epistemic rules. An archaeological-historical mode of inquiry not only suspends the rational value or objective form of knowledge toward a problematization of the positivity of knowledge itself, but also transforms the inquirer's very mode of being or subjectivity. As Agamben (2009) argues, in archaeological inquiry, "it is not possible to gain access in a new way, beyond tradition, to the sources without putting in question the very historical subject who is supposed to gain access to them" (p. 89).

Furthermore, an archaeological-historical perspective reconfigures time, history, and tradition no longer as some static, irreversible and irreducible essences (data), but as happening, events, movement, and moments of arising possibly external to any timeline. The aim of disrupting the fixed and canonized tradition and history is to set back into motion the original inner happenings of the presently silenced "wind-body" rationale by tracing its way back to its self-laid grounds to found itself anew out of them. Henceforth, an archaeological-historical inquiry implodes our otherwise naturalized canonization and compartmentalization of Chinese wisdom into distinct Yijing, Confucianism, Daoism, and Buhhism schools of thought. Instead, I re-treat them as historical and primordial sources of Dao where the varied forms of thinking burgeon from, yet not reduce or condense to, like a river of *wen* 文 that nourishes the latter to happen, coagulate, and move along. To use Agamben's (2009) words, I treat them as an originary thought "where something remains obscure and un-thematized" which "does not conceal its own unsaid and can constantly be taken up and elaborated for new openings" (p. 8).

An archaeological-historical mode of inquiry examines the conditions of possibility of knowledge and reason, rather than the form, content, and value of the latter. With a focus on knowledge's conditions of possibility, this book distinguishes itself from other books on China's education and curriculum mostly focused upon explicating its content, features, knowledge, as well as changes thereof along a what-is question or a history-of-ideas logic. In contrast, this book aims to discover on what basis knowledge and styles of reasoning about China's education and curriculum become possible, and within what space of order are they constructed. It explicates the historical-cultural *a priori* that makes it possible for teaching, learning, and the teacher–student difference in past and present China to be said and enacted as they were and are. In other words, this book doesn't track the historical vicissitudes of China's education and curriculum reform; rather, it gets deeper into the epistemological field, examining the positivity of knowledge as well as the historical-cultural principles as conditions of possibility for today's educational thinking and practice in China on a cross-cultural landscape.

The theoretical and paradigmatic significance of both language and historical-archaeological mode of inquiry is just beginning to be recognized in current comparative cultural studies of education and world order. For example, scholars (see, e.g., Baker, 2009; Popkewitz, 2013, 2015; Popkewitz, Khurshid, & Zhao, 2014; Popkewitz, Diaz, & Kirchgasler, 2017) strive to map out historical-cultural heritages in transnational studies of education, knowledge, and power without centralizing them as boundary fields or reproducing the second-order normativity embedded in the a priori definitions of these terms. Specifically, Popkewitz (2013) examines the broader theoretical/philosophical debates within the international field of historical studies and unpacks its implications for the study of education and forming of the educational problems. Popkewitz (2015) problematize the "reason" of schooling by historicizing the conditions of possibilities of curriculum, pedagogy, teacher education, and the sociology of knowledge in varied cultural (con)contexts. Popkewitz, Khurshid, and Zhao (2014) gives an example on how to see differences in varied cultural contexts without using the Western framework as a reference in comparative educational studies. Put simply, these studies treat the formation of the modern school as and at the interplay with social, cultural, and political events and provide new modes of inquiry for educational studies.

Built upon and into this above scholarship as an intellectual base, this book pushes further the study of how to map out cultural differences in comparative educational studies without reproducing the epistemological crisis or adopting a stagnant cultural relativist position. Specifically, this book brings together different philosophical styles with an ordering through a linguistic tradition and rethinks educational difference and knowledge in a way not to replicate but intellectually play with them. It weaves together interdisciplinary literatures in a manner to enable the reader to rethink the ordering of knowledge and body in China's current schooling as well as the methods through which China's historical educational understanding can be illuminated. In so doing, it builds a way of thinking that was not there before in these books and scholarship.

Regarding the language force, Horlacher (2016) historicizes the German notion of *Bildung* as an educational language–discourse and explores how this notion gets deployed in other linguistic and cultural contexts, say, the Scandinavian countries and the English-speaking world, to impart varied educational aspirations and styles of reasoning. Daniel Tröhler's *Languages of Education* (2011/2013) provides an original narrative on how the rooted religious languages of Protestantism and republicanism, in confrontation or negotiation, have historically, ideologically, and politically structured the schooling in Germany, the United States, and Switzerland. These are wonderful books within a particular tradition of language, but this book provides a different way of thinking about language as a cultural and social phenomenon, yet with philosophical, epistemological, and ontological significance.

This being said, however, in studies on current China's education, not much research has been done from a historical-archaeological and language perspective, except Zongjie Wu (2011, 2014, 2016) who has been in search of an appropriate language to re-talk about China's reason, knowledge, education, and pedagogy to loosen up their imprisonment by a Western Enlightenment rationale. In recent years, he has been examining Confucian cultural and educational heritage through some material and spatial imprints. Wu (2016) argues that the purpose of Confucian person-making was primarily to

> Establish a language instead of knowledge so that learners could speak/act in the place of the sages. This linguistic perspective, hardly explored today, may offer an alternative way of thinking, an intellectual tool to reconstruct visions of person-making pedagogy that resonate with the Western and Eastern pasts.
>
> (p. 98)

With my cross-disciplinary training in linguistics, sociolinguist, critical discourse studies, and curriculum studies, I have combined an ontological language–discourse perspective and historical mode of inquiry to rethink modern China's knowledge, reason, education, and curriculum issues. It assembles the Eastern and Western notions, frameworks, and styles of reasoning in a manner that is unique for me to rethink about current China's knowledge, education, and curriculum at the nexus, and as the (dis)assemblage of East and West, past and present.

In this sense, this book provides a paradigmatic example on how to unpack the cultural-historical sensibilities of China's education on a cross-cultural landscape, with and beyond a Westernized epistemological framework. The Western notions and concepts are indispensable and important in the sense that they provide me with a language and a style of reasoning that as a cultural Other helps me to encounter what I otherwise take for granted as tacit knowledge and system of reason. Yet, I am not applying the Western notions and concepts to delineate the Chinese cultural–educational–historical sensibilities. Rather, I play with, juxtapose, and dialogue them with the ancient Chinese thoughts and styles of reasoning for mutual informing. In this sense, I can say I relate the Western and Chinese thoughts, concepts, and styles of reasoning into a yin-yang movement wherein each representational identity is suspended toward an opening to the Other through a mutually appropriating movement. It is in this relation and movement per se that the issues of knowledge, language, body, and education get unraveled, explored, intersected, transformed, and re-turned as a Daoist post-foundational *studying* way.

Epilogue

Interestingly, academic research is supposed to end with significance and value. Well, what I feel comfortable to say is that my own learning and un-learning story at most provides a method, a particular case, or at least some serious efforts, on how to map out cultural differences in a globalizing and globalized world. Chinese oracle bone inscriptions on four winds depict the homophonic characters of feng (鳳/phoenix) and feng (風/wind) interchangeably. Though not aiming for a possible re-birth of phoenix anew out of its ashes, my Daoist onto-un-learning-thinking experience has transformed my mode of being as a researcher, a learner, and more importantly as a human being. Maybe it is surprising to say this, but I have found my own intellectual journey so far happy and enjoyable. *Learning/study* now takes on a new outlook as embodied in the very murmuring of its Chinese term for learning, 學習.

The first statement in Confucius' *Analects* (*Lunyu* 論語) says, "learning/studying and reviewing it from time to time, isn't it a happy thing?!" (學而時習之不亦說乎). Now it speaks different to me: The Chinese character for "review," 習, actually contains an enactment, a flapping of the wings when a baby eagle learns to fly. In other words, learning/studying is not simply accumulating knowledge, but entails a bodily enactment, a walking out of a way (Dao), our own way.

Inspired by his own cross-cultural shock experiences, Professor Wu Kuang-Ming claims that a Western conceptual mode of thinking helps him to discern and play with the Eastern bodily thinking just like a winnow swimming back to its home river. While I am still unable to savor such a feeling, I do appreciate his other statement that "studying my own cultural classics in its original language is indeed fun and an objective presentation of my own culture is as elusively difficult as explaining my mother tongue, its syntax and usage" (cited in Goulding, 2008, p. 22).

Still, retrospectively, I have enjoyed walking and working out my own Daoist-onto-un-learning way, and by looking back into the past, I am ready to move ahead.

References

Agamben, G. (1999). *Potentialities: Collected essays in philosophy* (Ed. and Trans. D. Heller-Roazen). Stanford, CA: Stanford University Press.
Agamben, G. (2009). *The signature of all things: On method*. New York, NY: Zone Books.
Autio, T. (2017). Reactivating templates for international curriculum consciousness: Reconsidering intellectual legacies and policy practices between Chinese, Anglo-American and European curriculum studies. In K. J. Kennedy & J. C. K. Lee (Eds.), *Theorizing teaching and learning in Asia and Europe* (pp. 38–54). London, UK and New York, NY: Routledge.
Biesta, G. J. J. (2006). *Beyond learning: Democratic education for a human future*. Boulder, CO: Paradigm Publishers.
de Freitas, E., & Sinclair, N. (2014). *Mathematics and the body: Material entanglements in the classroom*. New York, NY: Cambridge University Press.
Duarte, E. M. (2012). *Being and learning: A poetic phenomenology of education*. Boston, MA: Sense Publishers.
Ford, D. (2016). *Communist study: Education for the commons*. Lanham, MD: Lexington Books.
Ford, D. (2017). Studying like a communist: Affect, the party, and the educational limits to capitalism. *Educational Philosophy and Theory*, 49(5), 452–461.

Foucault, M. (1973). *The order of things: An archaeology of the human sciences.* New York, NY: Vintage Books. (Original work published 1966)

Goulding, J. (Ed.). (2008). *China-west interculture: Toward the philosophy of world integration (Essays on Wu Kuang-ming's thinking).* New York, NY: Global Scholarly Publications.

Harney, S., & Moten, F. (2013). *The undercommons: Fugitive planning and black study.* New York, NY: Minor compositions.

He, M. F. (2000). *A river forever flowing: Cross-cultural lives and identities in the multicultural landscape.* Charlotte, NC: Information Age Publishing.

Heidegger, M. (1967). *What is a thing?* (W. B. Barton, Jr. and V. Deutsch Trans. with an analysis by E. T. Gendlin.). Chicago, IL: Henry Regnery Company.

Heidegger, M. (1977). The turning. In M. Heidegger (Ed.), *The question concerning technology and other essays* (W. Lovitt, Trans. with an introduction, pp. 36–49). New York, NY: Harper & Row Publishers.

Lewis, T. E. (2013). *On study: Giorgio Agamben and educational potentiality.* New York, NY: Routledge.

Li, X. (2005). A Tao of narrative: Dynamic splicing of teacher stories. *Curriculum Inquiry, 34*(3), 339–366.

Paraskeva, J. M. (2016). *Curriculum epistemicide: Towards an itinerant curriculum theory.* New York, NY: Routledge.

Popkewitz, T. (Ed.). (2013). *Rethinking the history of education: Transnational perspectives on its questions, methods, and knowledge.* London, UK: Palgrave Macmillan.

Popkewitz, T. A., Diaz, J., & Kirchgasler, C. (Eds.). (2017). *A political sociology of educational knowledge: Studies of exclusions and difference.* New York, NY: Routledge.

Popkewitz, T. P., Khurshid, A., & Zhao, W. (2014). Comparative studies and the reasons of reason: Historicizing differences and "seeing" reforms in multiple modernities. In L. Vega (Ed.), *Empires, post-coloniality and interculturality: New challenges for comparative education* (21–43). Rotterdam, The Netherlands: Sense Publishers.

Popkewitz, T. S. (Ed.). (2015). *The "Reason" of schooling: Historicizing curriculum studies, pedagogy, and teacher education.* New York, NY and London, UK: Routledge.

Rocha, S. D. (2015). *Folk phenomenology: Education, study, and the human person.* Oregon: Pickwick Publications.

Sousa Santos, B. (2007). Beyond abyssal thinking: From global lines to ecologies of knowledges. *Review, XXX*(1), 45–89.

Tröhler, D. (2011/2013). *Languages of education: Protestant legacies, national identities, and global aspirations.* New York, NY: Routledge.

Wang, H. Y. (2004). *The call from the stranger on a journey home: Curriculum in a third space.* New York, NY: Peter Lang Publishing, Inc.

Wu, Z. J. (2016). Person-making through Confucian exegesis. In G. P. Zhao & Z. Y. Deng (Eds.), *Re-envisioning Chinese education: The meaning of person-making in a new age* (pp. 93–115). New York: Routledge.

Zhao, W. (2017). Review of Derek R. Ford, *Communist Study: Education for the Commons.* Lexington Books, 2016. *Studies in Philosophy and Education, 36*(2), 217–223.

Zhao, W., & Ford, D. R. (2017). Re-imagining affect with study: Implications from a Daoist wind-story and yin–yang Movement. *Studies in Philosophy and Education, 1*–13.

Index

a priori 3, 14, 16, 25, 29, 36, 38, 62, 65–6, 80, 83, 100, 124, 134, 172, 176, 179, 182, 183
A vs. B 155–6
abyssal thinking 18, 26, 165, 179
academic aphasia 28, 38
acquiescence 61
Agamben, Giorgo 1, 4, 16, 25, 39, 60, 62–8, 101, 124, 134, 172, 176, 181–2
analogy 78, 107, 160, 175
anthropocentric 162, 166, 179, 180
aporia (Derrida) 1–2, 5, 8, 15, 17, 57, 59, 65, 99, 112, 124, 156, 158, 173, 180
archaeological-historical (mode of) inquiry 16, 25, 51–66, 181–2
archaeology 63–4, 75
Aristotle 13, 85, 129, 172

Bagua (eight trigram) 1, 101–2, 107, 110–1, 113
Baker, Bernadette 52, 66
belonging-together 155–6, 159, 161–2, 164
Bildung 74, 183
binary logic 19, 40, 55–7, 60, 94, 122, 140, 146, 149, 150–1, 155, 177, 179
binary mode of reasoning 137, 149, 155–6, 164–5, 179
bodily experience 123, 134, 146
bodily reasoning 123, 140, 142
bodily thinking, body-thinking 12, 18, 40, 94, 99, 118, 122, 142–3, 149, 151, 176, 185
body-Dao 40
body-self 140, 145–6
Borges 59

care of self-others 14, 150–1
caring of self 149
co-dwelling 122, 143, 151, 160, 162, 176
comparative and cross-cultural studies 93, 149
comparative education 52–3, 83
conceptual-cognitive thinking 123
conceptual-metaphysical knowing 151
conduct of conduct 137
Confucian educational thinking 3, 43, 67, 106, 118
Confucian Heritage Culture(CHC) 9, 67, 101
contextualizing 124, 126
core suyang definitions 36
correlative thinking 112, 115, 164
cosmic-cultural ordering 112
cosmo-ontological 110
critical discourse analysis 4
critical theory 53
cross-cultural comparison 60
cultural-educational sensibilities 35
cultural-historical other 175
cultural-present self 175
curriculum superdiscourses 38

Dao De Jing 19, 40, 59, 81, 93, 158–60, 162–3, 172, 181
Daoist bipolar movement 18
Daoist onto-un-learning 15, 19, 65, 81, 101, 166, 171–85
Daoist yin-yang movement 160–1, 165, 171
decolonial 27, 38
de-construct 13, 56, 124–5, 176
Deleuze, Gilles 4, 73, 82, 164–5, 178
Derrida, Jacques 1–2, 4, 57, 59–60, 82, 84–5, 164

Index

dualistic thinking 155
Duarte, E. M. 129

East-West dialogue 57
educational body 1, 13–4, 17, 94, 122, 124, 135, 176
educational rethinking 127
embodiment 74, 107, 132–3, 146, 152
Enlightenment movement 29, 150
epistemicide 4, 15, 23, 25–96, 116, 149, 174–5
epistemological crisis 15–6, 25, 28, 38–9, 41, 53, 65, 81, 175, 183
eugenic 15–6, 26, 130, 132–3, 139
event of appropriation 162, 180
evocative 125, 150, 171, 177
exemplary person (junzi君子) 134, 150

feudal dross 16, 31–2, 137–9, 157, 177
Foucault, Michel 3–5, 7–8, 14, 16–8, 25, 29, 38, 41, 51, 57, 59–60, 62, 68, 74, 76–84, 90, 92, 100, 112, 122, 137, 145, 149–56, 174–5, 179–80,

gan-feeling 感 111
genealogy 27–8, 40, 62–3, 88, 92, 107, 175
genealogy of Dao(道统) 88, 92, 107
globalized discourses 25, 27, 29, 34–5, 44, 75
governmentality theory 137
grammatology 84
grid of intelligibility 14, 36
guan, guan-observing 觀 99, 106, 109–10, 117, 122, 127, 129
guan-hexagram 2, 8–9, 13, 17–8, 99, 100, 105–6, 116, 118, 122–3, 127–8, 131, 135, 150, 176–7

Heidegger, Martin 4, 16–9, 25, 29, 39–40, 55, 57–9, 61, 67–8, 76, 92–3, 100, 106, 108, 155, 160–4, 175, 177, 179–80
hierarchy vs. egalitarianism ordering 122
horizontal-regional way of thinking 39
house of Being 59, 101, 108, 162

identity and difference 17–8, 26, 57, 60, 160–1, 164–5, 173, 179
ideogram 85–7
image-number (xiang-shu象数) 9, 103–5, 113, 116, 128, 161
inclusion-exclusion 26, 165, 179

inter-subjective 26, 34, 142, 145–6
Itinerant Curriculum Theory (ICT) 27

kneeling-bowing rites 123, 136
knowing self 149–50, 152

Laozi 40, 59
Lewis, Tyson 15, 19
Logogram 87

meaning-making (linguistic) system 4, 38, 55, 87, 9–4, 106, 154–5, 175, 179
meaning-rationale (yi-li義理) 103–5, 116
meditative thinking 177, 180
mental colonialism 28
metaphysical thinking 57, 156, 160, 162, 164, 180
mind-body binary, mind-body dualism 176–7
mind-thinking 12, 18, 40, 122, 151, 176
mode of being 65, 68, 81–3, 106, 123, 134, 141, 146, 159, 178, 180, 182, 185
mode of signification 4–5, 16–7, 29, 35–8, 68, 81, 84, 88, 92–3, 106, 118
modernity 26–7, 29–30, 34, 39, 55, 125, 137, 175, 181

natural phenomena (ziran自然) 107, 112
New Cultural Movement 15, 27, 30–3, 39, 87, 102, 136, 138–9
New Imperialism 28
non-metaphysical Being-being 164

ongoing un-learning 100
onto-epistemological 17, 40, 93, 99, 103, 109, 113, 115–8
onto-hermeneutic 17, 44, 99, 106, 109–10, 111, 115, 176
ontological language-discourse 16, 25, 73–96, 149, 181, 184
ontology 80, 110, 161
ordering: (dis)ordering 17, 124, 151; (re)ordering 25, 51, 149
Orientalism 53

Paraskeva, João M. 4, 15, 25–30, 34–5, 38, 41, 53, 88, 175
Plato 40, 62, 143, 145, 181
Popkewitz, Thomas 16, 52, 55, 66, 183

Index 189

post-colonialism 27, 74
post-deconstructive 84
post-foundational study 15, 19, 65, 81, 166, 171–3, 181
post-modernity 27
post-structuralism 53
power-based pendulum 94

re-envision 13, 17–8, 41, 43, 45, 83, 124, 149, 161, 176
regenerate 102, 149, 156, 164, 173
re-invoke 12, 34, 42–3, 84, 126
representational system 4, 29, 73, 81, 83
representational thinking 156
rethink 17–9, 41, 68, 85, 94, 149, 156, 160, 173, 176, 181, 183–4
re-turning 122–3, 143, 161, 173, 175, 180–1

self-care 150
self-knowledge 150
shi 時(timing) 99, 103, 106, 109
shide 師德 35–6
Shi-xu 76
shu 數 (number) 99, 106
shuowenjiezi 5–6, 89–91, 100, 104, 132
signifier-signified 5, 29, 37–8, 60, 77, 84, 88, 93
Sousa Santos, B. 18, 26–7, 165, 179
spatial temporal 107, 112, 114
style of divination 103
style of reasoning 9, 13, 16, 26, 29–30, 38, 40, 66, 68, 84, 93, 99–100, 103, 106, 108, 116, 118, 124, 139, 161, 175–6, 184
su + yang (素+养) 38
Subject + V + Object 154
subject vs. object style of reasoning 108
suyang curriculum reform 36

teacher-student difference 1, 13–4, 17, 65, 124, 151, 153, 155, 160, 165, 176, 180, 182
teacher-student ordering 18, 51, 65, 94, 122, 125–6, 137–41, 149–56
teachers + verb + student 155
teaching-transforming (jiaohua 教化) 117
teaching-virtue-modeling-transforming 36
togetherness 82, 110, 122, 155
transformative self-critical attitude 43
trap of philology 3, 16, 29, 80, 83, 100
Tröhler, Daniel 74–5, 183
Tyler curriculum rationale 36

virtue (de 德) education 151
virtue/moral education (deyu 德育) 43, 151

wen 文 (crisscrossing pattern) 5, 99, 106
West-Eurocentric 15–6, 26–9
wind-discourses 3–4, 14, 99–100, 118, 123, 176
wind-education 2–4, 14, 17, 77, 99–100, 117, 174
wind-pedagogy 8–9, 17–8, 44, 65, 99, 106, 115–6, 118, 127
wind-transforming 117
Wu Kuang-Ming 12, 40, 125, 143, 185
Wu Zongjie 76, 183

xiang 象 (phenomenal forms) 99, 102–4, 106, 108, 11,
xiang-style of reasoning (象思維) 40

Yijing (The Book of Change) 83
Yijing dynamics of change 115

Zhang Xianglong 39
Zhuangzi 40, 56, 109
Zi (字) 5